HEALTHCARE'S REIMBURSEMENT MAZE

The Ecosystem Regulates Market Access to Medical Innovation in the US

Susan Xu

Contact Info: Info@WyDus.llc

Cover Design by: Longze Zhang
Cover Image Credit: Can Stock Photo Inc. / Seamartini
Editor: Sam Wright
Formatting: Longze Zhang
Author Photo by: Hope He

ISBN 979-8-9882694-5-8
ISBN 979-8-9882694-0-3 (ebook)

To my parents, my sister, and my squad of friends,
for always cheering me on

CONTENTS

CONTENTS

CONTENTS

PREFACE

A JOURNEY OF TEN THOUSAND MILES

The scene at the dusty construction site of Beijing Xiaotangshan Severe Acute Respiratory Syndrome (SARS) Hospital is still vivid and breathtaking, refusing to fade away from my memory after two decades. Thousands of people in various uniforms buzzed around, and all the essential parts for a hospital, from the building's roof, and ventilation system, to the communication network and even medical devices, were being installed simultaneously.

I was left in awe by what unfolded before my eyes. For a moment, I just stood there amidst the hustle and bustle, taking it all in. I noticed the bloodshot eyes of the passersby, the hoarse voices echoing through the air, and the exhausted construction workers finding brief respite as they lay or leaned against the walls for a quick nap. These small details offered a glimpse into the extraordinary efforts that made it possible to construct a hospital for SARS patients in just seven days!

Like its counterpart, COVID-19, SARS is caused by a strain of coronavirus. The 2002-2004 SARS outbreak infected over 8,000 people, mostly in China, and tragically claimed nearly 800 lives worldwide.

My visit to the hospital construction site had a purpose: conducting interviews for a special column I was writing for *International Medical Devices,* a MedTech industry magazine. Working as a journalist and an editor for the magazine was a side gig while I pursued my career as a research scientist at a Beijing research institute, following my graduation with a master's degree in biomedical engineering. Research work often delves deeply into narrow topics, akin to tendering individual trees and witnessing their growth from sprouts. My work at the magazine provided a vantage point to see the larger forest of healthcare and innovation.

Reporting on the SARS outbreak in 2003 and engaging in post-outbreak discussions and reflections ignited my fascination with health policy and revealed its profound impact on society. It was a collective sigh of relief when the SARS outbreak was contained within several major cities in China, sparing rural areas from its reach.

China established a three-tier health system in the 1950s with a network of health service facilities at county, township, and village levels, achieving nearly universal coverage. However, the introduction of privatization and market-based reforms in the 1980s caused the collapse of the rural healthcare financing mechanism, the rural cooperatives under a planned economy. In the next two decades, focusing on economic growth, little attention was paid to the deterioration of the healthcare delivery system and insurance coverage. By 1998, only 5% of the rural population and 38% of urban residents in China had any form of health insurance coverage.

The SARS outbreak served as a wake-up call for government leaders, highlighting the consequence of underinvestment during the 1980s–1990s. Within a few months of the SARS outbreak, Chinese leaders decided on massive public health system investments, including heavy subsidies to expand a new type of rural cooperative medical scheme. More than 96% of China's population now has some health insurance coverage.

On a smaller scale, the growth of a startup company during and after the SARS outbreak illustrates the impact of policy changes. When I interviewed Changying Li, the founder of Yi'An, a medical device company manufacturing medical ventilator and anesthesia equipment, the company was barely two years old with fewer than 200 employees. The startup doubled its production in response to soaring demands during the SARS outbreak. And the company doubled again after the SARS outbreak in response to the government's procurement orders and initiatives to equip rural hospitals with essential medical equipment. Today, Yi'An has established itself in China and globally, with offices in North America and Europe.

In early 2000, public policy was a relatively new topic in China, and top universities had only recently offered Master of Public Administration (MPA) program. Hence, I looked afar. I came to the US in 2006 to pursue my MPA study, embarking on a new journey that aligns with the Chinese saying, "Walk ten thousand miles. Read ten thousand books."

As my graduation date approached in 2008, the US economy slid into the Great Recession. After my interview at the Healthcare Association of New York State (HANYS), Steve Harwell, then the Vice President, Economics, Finance, and Information, pulled me aside and jokingly said, "I am not as smart as you are, but I can learn, so you should be fine." During the interview, Steve dived deep into the graduate studies I shared. One was a paper evaluating the subprime mortgage crisis's impact on hospital financing, and the other was a publication assessing returns on investment in electronic health records. I was pleasantly surprised by the level of detail of his inquiries. Shortly after the interview, I started at HANYS as a health policy analyst.

My timing in entering the health policy arena couldn't have been better. In a time of crisis, everyone looks to the government for support. My first major assignment was the HITECH Act of the American Recovery and Reinvestment Act, signed into law by President Obama in 2009. The HITECH Act authorized Medicare and Medicaid to provide incentive payments to hospitals and clinicians who demonstrate "meaningful use" of electronic health records (EHR), which drove large gains in EHR adoption in the following decade. Also in 2009, the discussions about a major piece of legislation to expand health insurance coverage heated up. Analyzing various draft provisions before the Affordable Care Act was passed gave me a glimpse of the federal law making process.

Fast forward a decade later, I found myself working at the Association of American Medical Colleges as a director of payment policy research and analytics. While attending a HIMSS annual conference, I noticed that all the sessions on artificial intelligence (AI) were incredibly popular. To secure a seat, one had to arrive at least 10 minutes early. During my graduate studies, I took a class on neural networks, a method in AI. A classmate once told me, after a test run using neural networks in her capstone project, "AI is too big a tool. It felt like firing a missile at a fly." She was referring to the fact that it often took hours to do a simple test run back then, which made AI not very functional to use.

What had happened in the field of AI over the past decade? This question piqued my interest and led me to discover advancements not limited to AI but also genomics and precision medicine. It was a rekindling of my first passion for science and medical innovation. Before the pandemic, I had been contemplating and writing about alternative payment models for precision medicine.

While the pandemic derailed my original plans, it propelled me towards a career change in the consulting world. I have worked with MedTech companies, hospitals, and trade associations on complex reimbursement issues. However, the fast-paced nature of consulting engagements often leaves little room for delving into the intricacies of the vast reimbursement ecosystem, which planted the seed for the book.

Completing this book has brought a sense of fulfillment and completion to my journey. It has let me connect the dots in my career path, merging my passion for science and health policy. It draws upon my previous research and writings while also uncovering new insights along the way. Writing the book has been a collaborative effort, shaped by the feedback and suggestions of former colleagues and healthcare experts who generously shared their knowledge. I express my deepest gratitude to all those who have contributed to the development of this book, as acknowledged in the dedicated section.

The primary audience I had in mind when writing the book was healthcare innovators and investors. Through my experience as a consultant, I saw their struggles with navigating the complexities of healthcare reimbursement, especially for academics turned entrepreneurs. Suggestions on the potential audience from friends, former colleagues, and healthcare experts who helped review the draft book indicate that healthcare reimbursement may be a maze for a much larger audience. Interestingly, even friends without experience in healthcare reimbursement found the book easy to follow.

This feedback suggests that the book has the potential to help a wider range of people. As I conclude this preface, I am filled with anticipation. I look forward to sharing the contents of this book with readers from diverse backgrounds, including healthcare innovators and investors, researchers and educators, healthcare providers, healthcare incubators, and anyone interested in understanding the intricacies of healthcare reimbursement. I hope that this book will not only inform but also inspire conversations and actions that contribute to the improvement of the healthcare reimbursement ecosystem.

Thank you for joining me on this journey. I invite you to delve into the following pages and turn the healthcare reimbursement maze into an amazing journey of possibilities.

Susan Xu

Rockville, Maryland

June 10, 2023

INTRODUCTION

WHAT IS HEALTHCARE REIMBURSEMENT?

An average American born 200 years ago could expect about half of your friends and neighbors to die before turning 40. In a *Slate* article, *Why are you not dead yet*, Laura Helmuth asked around and came up with a small sample of what would have killed our friends and us:

- *Adrian's lung spontaneously collapsed when he was 18.*
- *Becky had an ectopic pregnancy that caused massive internal bleeding.*
- *Carl had St. Anthony's Fire, a strep infection of the skin that killed John Stuart Mill.*
- *Dahlia would have died delivering a child (twice) or later of a ruptured gall bladder.*
- *David had an aortic valve replaced.*

- *Hanna acquired Type 1 diabetes during a pregnancy and would die without insulin.*
- *Julia had a burst appendix at age 14.*
- *Katherine was diagnosed with pernicious anemia in her 20s. She treats it with supplements of vitamin B-12, but in the past she would have withered away.*
- *Laura (that's me) had scarlet fever when she was 2, which was once a leading cause of death among children but is now easily treatable with antibiotics.*
- *Mitch was bitten by a cat (filthy animals) and had to have emergency surgery and a month of antibiotics, or he would have died of cat scratch fever.*

Medical advances have dramatically improved our lifespan and healthspan with life expectancy doubled in the past two centuries. Medical breakthroughs, such as anesthesia, antibiotics, germ theory, insulin, X-ray, vaccines, blood transfusion, and immunology, enable us not to die from illnesses that killed many in the past. Often the stories of medical advances centered on the dogged pursuit of the researchers and their research discoveries, and rightly so. However, this storyline inadvertently gives an illusion that the road from medical discovery to medical practice is a guaranteed onward march.

A 2019 documentary film, *"Jim Allison: Breakthrough,"* highlights some twists and turns along the long, bumpy road to bring a research discovery to market. Jim Allison is an immunologist who spent decades studying how the immune system reacts to cancer cells. In 1996, he reported that mice injected with an antibody that slowed a T-cell inhibitory molecule (known as CTLA-4, whose function is like a brake on the immune system) showed a rapid reduction in tumors. What's even more astonishing is that the mice treated with the injection showed immunity when injected with new cancer cells.

However, pharmaceutical companies met the illuminating research findings with skepticism. Several clinical trials of immunotherapy drugs for cancer since 1980s had ended in devastating disappointments, which led some to believe immunotherapy would never work. The risk of failing is high when it comes to developing oncology drugs: 9 out of 10 drugs that work on animals do not work on humans, and the attrition rate is 70% in Phase II clinical trials and 59% in Phase III trials. It doesn't help when the proposed new drug takes a different approach that few can comprehend. In about two years, Dr. Allison pitched several pharmaceutical and biotech companies to fund the development of the drug and clinical trials to test the safety and efficacy of the new drug. Sadly, the answer always came back the same – no.

The challenges Dr. Allison encountered, unfortunately, are not unique. The term "the Valley of Death" refers to the early stages of transitioning original scientific research to marketable products. Uncertainty and lack of funding are commonly cited factors that make this phase difficult to survive. In the case of Dr. Allison, persistence and perseverance brought a stroke of luck and provided the strength to overcome plentiful curveballs during the clinical trials. In March 2011, more than a decade after the publication of the initial discovery, the new drug ipilimumab (Yervoy) was approved by the Food and Drug Administration (FDA) to treat metastatic melanoma. The film's postscript stated that "Ipi and successor immuno-oncology drugs have treated nearly a million patients worldwide." In 2018, Dr. Allison was awarded the Nobel Prize in Physiology or Medicine along with Tasuku Honjo.

The film didn't mention that the Centers for Medicare and Medicaid Services (CMS) started reimbursing ipilimumab in 2011. Even though the move by CMS, the largest payer for healthcare in the US, is somewhat expected, it's not insignificant for expanding access to cancer immunotherapy drugs. In 2012, about 1,200 Medicare fee-for-service (FFS) beneficiaries received ipilimumab treatment and Medicare paid nearly $68 million for ipilimumab administered in doctors' offices alone. By 2019, the number of immuno-oncology drugs reimbursed by Medicare increased to 12, and the total Medicare payments for these drugs administered in a doctor's office were close to $2 billion in 2019.

INTRODUCTION

Payers, including private health plans and public programs, account for a large share of medical technologies/services purchases. Reimbursement, the policies and practices that define a health plan or a public payer's terms of coverage and payment for a medical technology, not only affects market access for new healthcare products/services, but also influences the kinds of innovation that venture capitalists (VCs) choose to invest. The influence or perceived influence of payer's reimbursement policy may derive from different aspects, for example:

- Reimbursement policy may specify patient population and coverage criteria for a medical innovation (e.g., only patients with advanced cancers who failed first and second-line treatments can receive the treatment), which may affect a medical innovation's market size.

- Payment rate established through reimbursement policy might affect product pricing (e.g., payment rate for a surgical procedure might set an upper limit for any implantable devices to be used in the procedure)

- The established payment rate for one product/service relative to that of other comparable products/services might influence healthcare providers' and patients' choice of care.

Before a new medical innovation can be covered and reimbursed, the description of the new drug, equipment, test, medical service, or procedure must be translated into universal medical alphanumeric codes either through asking for a new code or identifying existing codes. Like a musical score that uses standard symbols to indicate the melody, tempo, and intensity of a musical piece, medical coding transforms diagnosis, procedures, medical services, and equipment documented in medical records, such as physician notes and laboratory results, into standard medical codes so that healthcare providers can bill private or public payers for their services. In the case of ipilimumab, for example, CMS first created a temporary code (C9284) for the injection of ipilimumab at a dose of 1mg, effective on July 1st, 2011, and then replaced it with a permanent code (J9288), effective on January 1st, 2012. It's the responsibility of product developers to request coding changes and provide evidence to support such changes, which adds another layer of complexity on the path to reimbursement.

Even with insurance coverage and favorable payment rate, it's ultimately the decision of healthcare providers to incorporate a new medical advancement into clinical practice. Usually, healthcare providers are the direct purchasers of medical products, such as new drugs and new medical devices, and then receive reimbursement from payers when using these new products in a patient encounter. In this scenario, reimbursement is a chain of events involving healthcare providers and payers, and different value propositions and economic models are needed for different stakeholders.

Healthcare providers' clinical decisions are also influenced by clinical practice guidelines developed and maintained by specialty societies, government agencies, and other entities. Being recognized as part of the standard of care shows the impact of a medical innovation and ensures its long-term success. In melanoma, for example, since the introduction of ipilimumab in 2011, several new treatments have been approved for treating metastasis melanoma, and melanoma survival improved rapidly. In 2019, the American Society of Clinical Oncology (ASCO) convened an expert panel and developed ASCO guidelines on melanoma treatment, which includes recommendations on ipilimumab and other drugs for metastatic melanoma.

Briefly, healthcare reimbursement refers to the complicated and intertwined process where a medical product or service is paid for. It consists of coding, coverage, rate-setting by payer, and the value translation to healthcare providers. FDA approval allows a new medical product for sale and marketing in the US. Getting marketing approval, however, is not a guarantee of market access when a medical product is used in patient care. Ensuring reimbursement for innovation is essential for a successful launch into the market and the long-term success and impact of the innovation.

So, how may healthcare reimbursement influence venture capitalists' decisions on what innovations to invest? To shed light on this, I sought the expertise of Dr. Ajit Singh, a partner at the venture capital firm Artiman. Dr. Singh is known for early-stage technology and life science investments. I had the opportunity to interview Dr. Singh almost two decades ago for the Chinese magazine *International Medical Devices* when he served as the CEO of Siemens' Oncology Care Systems Group.

Dr. Singh delves into the concept of 'product-market fit,' which is important when evaluating early-stage startups. Coined by Andy Rachleff, the founder of Benchmark Capital, product-market fit entails meeting an unmet need within a specific market segment where willing users are ready to adopt and pay for the product.

Dr. Singh emphasizes that in healthcare, the concept of product-market fit becomes more intricate due to the involvement of various gatekeepers. These stakeholders, such as clinicians, patients, and insurance companies, each have different perspectives and expectations. "This creates an additional layer of complexity for VC investors in due diligence because the criteria, or a metric of success, across different stakeholders are never identical, especially when the outcomes are measured in statistical terms. While there is no readymade answer or template for these types of assessment, there are frameworks for clinical and economic utility that can be employed," elaborated by Dr. Singh.

An essential aspect of both the reimbursement process and VC's investment assessment lies in providing convincing evidence. While proof of efficacy is relevant universally, more evidence is needed for different stakeholders. FDA's mandate is to ensure products on the US market are "safe and effective." Following FDA approval, CMS determines whether a product is "reasonable and necessary" for the care of Medicare patients and may ask for more evidence, for example, on clinical benefits or subpopulation. Besides clinical evidence, private payers may require cost-effectiveness analysis to assess the gains in health outcomes relative to the cost of the innovation and budget impact assessment on their covered population. Providers will want to know whether a new product improves the quality of care compared to the alternatives or standard of care, whether it's easy to use, and whether it will boost their facility's bottom line.

A medical breakthrough often represents the culmination of decades of exploration, involving wandering in the unknowns, formulating hypotheses, and verifying them through experiments. Healthcare reimbursement is a man-made ecosystem with interconnected parts managed by various organizations, each with its own history, purpose, structure, organizational constraints, internal and external dynamics, and idiosyncrasy.

This book aims to provide a detailed account of the healthcare reimbursement ecosystem. However, healthcare reimbursement encompasses a wide spectrum of medical innovations provided in various care settings. CMS alone has over ten payment systems for services rendered in different care settings or by different types of healthcare providers. Each payment system represents a smaller reimbursement ecosystem within the broader ecosystem, with its own processes, methods, and requirements. This book primarily focuses on services provided in three common care settings: inpatient hospital, outpatient hospital, and doctor office.

While the book uses examples to illustrate technical procedures or complex methods used in the reimbursement process based on publicly available information, it's important to note that every medical innovation is unique and may follow a different reimbursement pathway. The reimbursement pathways discussed in the book may or may not be applicable to other medical innovations, depending on factors such as care setting and type of medical innovation.

Healthcare is one of the most regulated and debated topics, and healthcare reimbursement, including coverage determination and rate-setting for public programs like Medicare and Medicaid, is no exception. The book presents different viewpoints and competing interests of stakeholders within the ecosystem, as they all play a role in the reimbursement journey. This includes instances where their involvement may cause delays or detours. The author does not advocate for any position but aims to provide a fair account of different viewpoints.

This healthcare reimbursement ecosystem is constantly evolving, with annual updates and tweaks, and major changes implemented every now and then, often triggered by legislative actions. The information presented in the book reflects the author's best knowledge at the time of writing. However, verifying the most current policies and procedures is crucial when developing reimbursement plans. Still, the comprehensive account of the ecosystem provided in these pages can help you understand and prepare for the challenges ahead.

The book is organized around key parts of the healthcare reimbursement ecosystem. The first chapter introduces payers and providers, the central players of the healthcare ecosystems, and traces their historical paths in shaping the US healthcare systems as we know it today. The next three chapters delve into coding, payment systems, and coverage determinations, which are separate but interconnected aspects of healthcare reimbursement. The following two chapters explore the various roles that providers play within the healthcare reimbursement ecosystem, and the evidential and value expectations from payers and providers. Finally, the book concludes with a discussion on strategies to navigate the healthcare reimbursement maze.

PART ONE

MARKET ACCESS GATEKEEPERS

In addition to Medicare and state Medicaid programs, US payer market also includes over 1,000 private health plans. Healthcare services are provided by over 6,000 hospitals, nearly a million doctors, 15,600 nursing homes, and other types of facilities and professionals.

Generally, the term "consumer" refers to an individual who purchases and uses goods or services for personal use. This concept typically encompasses three roles: paying for the purchase, selecting the desired product or service, and using the acquired good. However, within the context of the healthcare market, the idea of a consumer becomes more complicated due to the introduction of gatekeepers, resulting in a unique reimbursement ecosystem.

In the US healthcare market, various entities assume the roles of consumers. Payers, including private insurance plans and public programs, play a substantial role by covering much of the cost of healthcare services using funds collected through premiums or taxation. The coverage decisions made by payers often revolve around determining whether a service, procedure or item is reasonable and necessary for diagnosing or treating an illness, injury, condition, disease, or symptom. The clinical judgement of a doctor plays a crucial role in determining medical necessity. Additionally, the FDA mandates that certain drugs, devices, and medical treatments require a prescription from a doctor for access. Healthcare providers' prescriptive authority is regulated and authorized by states through licensure. Consequently, patients' access to new medical innovations is regulated by both payers through coverage policies and healthcare providers through prescriptive authority, with a framework of legal, regulatory, and financing requirements.

The US healthcare market exhibits unique characteristics that set it apart. Often viewed as a fragmented system of contrasts, the US payer market consists of many private insurance plans in competition with one another, and with public programs. Paradoxically, this high level of competition does not translate into more affordable, high-value care, as shown by the country's exceptionally high healthcare spending as a percentage of GDP. On the side of healthcare delivery, the authority held by doctors manifests in distinct arrangements, such as the separate billing for hospital and physician services for a hospital stay.

This chapter aims to trace the historical development of America's health insurance market, the transformation of healthcare delivery system, the evolution of medical discoveries and breakthroughs, and the rise of medical authority. It sets the stage for future chapters as you will meet the key players, CMS, FDA, AHA, and see how their roles have evolved to become who they are and how they function today. By providing this comprehensive background, we seek to illuminate the intricate reimbursement ecosystem that characterizes our present time.

THE DEVELOPMENT OF PRIVATE HEALTH INSURANCE

Healthcare providers played a crucial role in the development of health insurance models in the US. In 1929, Justin Ford Kimble was appointed Vice President of Baylor Health System when the Great Depression had severely affected the Baylor University hospital. Occupancy rates dropped from 71.3% to 64.1%, receipts fell from $236 to $59 per patient, and charity care increased by 400%. Kimble observed that many unpaid bills were from Dallas educators and developed a prepayment plan in which a person could pay $0.50 a month ($6.00 per year) to cover the cost of a 21-day hospital stay starting from one week into the hospital stay. Fees incurred within that first week would cost $5.00 per day above the prepaid coverage. The plan did not cover doctor bills, but subscribers were entitled to hospital care and services rather than cash indemnity, which improved their ability to pay for doctor bills. The Baylor plan was popular among Dallas educators, with 75% of Dallas teachers enrolling.

The hospital prepayment model spread to other hospitals, and community-wide plans gradually outpaced the growth of single-hospital plans. In 1933, the American Hospital Association (AHA) board of trustees endorsed the principle of voluntary hospital insurance as a "probable solution to the problem of the distribution of the costs of hospital care," and AHA established its Committee on Hospital Service to approve plans. This committee became the AHA Hospital Service Plan Commission in 1936 and the AHA Blue Cross Commission in 1946. Blue Cross coverage was available in almost every state by then, and over twenty million subscribers were enrolled.

A similar prepayment model for doctor services, the Blue Shield programs, developed in parallel with a different origin story. The Blue Shield idea emerged from lumber and mining camps of the Pacific Northwest where workers facing hazardous work conditions organized to finance medical care for job-related injuries. In 1917, the Pierce County Industrial Medical and Surgical Service Bureau was formed in Tacoma, Washington, the first major group health insurance provider. The organization comprised groups of doctors who contracted with employers to care for compensable injuries, which eventually extended to include care for ordinary sickness.

These pioneer programs provided the basis for the first statewide plan sponsored by a state medical society in California in 1939, known as California Physicians Services. In the next few years, similar plans were started in New York, Pennsylvania, and other states. At the end of 1945, subscribers of medical society-sponsored plans totaled about three million. In 1948, a group of nine Associated Medical Care Plans informally adopted the Blue Shield symbol. These groups eventually became the National Association of Blue Shield Plans.

Health insurance has been closely tied to employer sponsored benefits since its inception. During World War II, the US government imposed wage control measures, which spurred the spread of employer-based health insurance. In 1942, the War Labor Board decided that fringe benefit up to 5% of wages would not be considered towards wage ceiling. Employers began offering more generous health plans to attract and retain workers. In 1943, the Internal Revenue

Service ruled that employer-based healthcare should be tax-free. After World War II, 63% of Americans had hospital insurance by 1953. A second law in 1954 made tax advantages even more attractive.

Offering health insurance through employee groups also removed two long-standing barriers to commercial insurers, which fueled its rapid growth. One barrier is adverse selection, where sick people are more likely to buy health insurance. Another is the administrative cost of selling individual policies. The total covered only by commercial insurers in 1949 was estimated at 28 million, compared to over 31 million enrolled in Blue Cross. Commercial insurers were then far ahead of Blue Shield in coverage of surgical bills (22.7 versus 12 million people). By 1953, commercial carriers had also surpassed Blue Cross in hospital coverage, providing hospital insurance to 29 percent of Americans, compared to 27 percent by Blue Cross.

MEDICARE, MEDICAID, AND THE FRAGMENTED HEALTH INSURANCE MARKET

On July 30, 1965, President Lyndon B. Johnson signed into law the bill that led to the creation of Medicare and Medicaid programs, which provide health insurance coverage for the elderly and poor. Although most Western democracies had adopted some form of national healthcare program, national compulsory health insurance had been a losing cause for decades in the US up to 1965 due to fierce opposition, most noticeably from the American Medical Association (AMA) whose membership represents the majority of US physician workforce. In 1963, 71% of the US population had hospital insurance coverage, mostly through employment.

Retirees and the unemployed/low-income were left out, and the problem of lack of insurance coverage was acute, especially among the seniors. Only 54% of the population over 65 had hospital insurance in 1963, compared to 72% among those under 65. Among those over 65, however, one in six would have one hospital stay in a year and stayed, on average, twice as long as someone under 65. Even with social security benefits, most seniors could not afford the cost of hospitalization, which had doubled in the 1950s.

Over the years, Congress has expanded coverage for both Medicare and Medicaid programs. Before the pandemic, Medicare covers 62.5 million beneficiaries, including beneficiaries who meet the age threshold, have a disability, or have End-Stage Renal Disease (ESRD). By the end of 2019, 70.9 million low-income Americans enrolled in the Medicaid program, including eligible low-income adults, children, pregnant women, the elderly, and the disabled. The

Medicaid enrollment number also includes those enrolled in the Children's Health Insurance Program (CHIP), a program designed to cover uninsured children in families with modest incomes.

The formation of Medicare and Medicaid programs and legislative actions in the following decades to fill the gaps of insurance coverage left by employment-based coverage create a piecemeal insurance system in the US. Private health insurance, largely employer-sponsored insurance, is still the predominant source of health insurance in the US, covering about 65% Americans in 2020. Each of the two public programs, Medicare and Medicaid (CHIP), provides healthcare coverage for about 18% of the US population (with some beneficiaries eligible for both programs). The military provides healthcare services for military servicemembers, veterans, and their dependents. This piecemeal approach leaves out about 9% of the US population with no health insurance coverage.

A pervasive issue with the US health insurance system is instability, with tens of millions of Americans constantly gaining and losing their health insurance coverage due to changes in employment status. This was evident during the COVID-19 pandemic, where many individuals lost employer-sponsored health coverage due to layoffs. It's estimated that by June 2020, 7.7 million workers and 6.9 million dependents were affected. Enrollment in Medicaid, a means-tested program for low-income population, surged by nearly 20 million between 2020 and 2022, reflecting both economy trends and temporary pandemic relief policies enacted by Congress. Besides economic cycles, demographic changes and disruptive policy shifts create a rather dynamic payer market in the US. For instance, over 15 million baby-boomers are projected to shift from employer-sponsored health insurance to Medicare by 2031.

Despite the creation of Medicare and Medicaid, the US keeps a pluralist framework for reimbursement decision-making. Although the federal government being the largest single purchaser of healthcare services, reimbursement decisions for over 100 million Medicare and Medicaid beneficiaries are shared among hundreds of payers. Instead of a centralized governance body to evaluate health technologies and guide coverage and pricing decisions, hundreds of private insurance plans and public payers use their own assessment approaches, creating a fragmented and often confusing reimbursement environment with duplicative and opaque processes for coverage and payment determination.

The Centers for Medicare & Medicaid Services (CMS), a federal agency under the US Department of Health and Human Services (HHS), administers the Medicare program and collaborates with state governments to manage Medicaid and CHIP. CMS determines coverage and payment decisions for beneficiaries enrolled in traditional Medicare programs based on congressional authorization. State Medicaid agencies play a key role in reimbursement decisions for Medicaid beneficiaries.

Among the 62.5 million Medicare beneficiaries in 2019, 62% enrolled in traditional Medicare programs administered directly by the federal government, and 37% enrolled in Medicare Advantage plans, sometimes called Medicare Part C or MA plans. Medicare Part C was created in 1997 to provide beneficiaries with additional choice and improve Medicare efficiency by bringing in private competition. MA plans are run by Medicare-approved private insurance companies. They must offer coverage that meets or exceeds the standards set by the traditional Medicare program, but they need not cover every benefit in the same way. Reimbursement decisions for health services provided to Medicare MA beneficiaries are largely decided by private MA plans.

Nearly three out of four Medicare beneficiaries also had Part D prescription drug coverage. Part D drugs are generally medications that patients self-administer at home. Drugs provided during an inpatient hospital stay, at a doctor office, or at an outpatient department are covered under the traditional Medicare program or Medicare Part C. Medicare Part D was created in 2003. It's a voluntary prescription drug benefit for Medicare beneficiaries provided through private insurance companies contracted with the federal government. Stand-alone Medicare prescription drug plans and MA plans with prescription drug coverage make reimbursement decisions for Medicare prescription drugs.

THE TRANSFORMATION OF THE US HEALTHCARE DELIVERY SYSTEM IN THE 20TH CENTURY

The emergence of health insurance was inseparable from the rise of medicine and of the medical profession more generally. In the early 20th century, medicine transformed from "a relative weak, traditional profession of minor economic significance" to the modern-day doctor who "offers a kind of individualized objectivity, a personal relationship as well as authoritative counsel." However, the dominance of the medical profession extends considerably beyond its rational foundation of specialized knowledge, technical procedures and professional competence enabled by the advances of modern medicine. "The profession has been able to turn its authority into social privilege, economic power, and political influence." Several intertwined developments at the turn of the twentieth century fueled this transformation.

The medical licensing movement of the late nineteenth century was not unique for doctors but reflected a general occupational licensing trend pursued by many other professions, such as plumbers, barbers, and horseshoers, against the backdrop of the transition from agrarian to industrial society. Many states strengthened their medical licensing requirements incrementally, first requiring only a diploma, then imposing more requirements of school approval, and finally mandating state examination.

The U.S. Supreme Court decision in the Case of *Dent v. West Virginian* in 1888 solidified the legitimacy of medical licensing. Delivering the Supreme Court's unanimous opinion, Justice Stephen Field noted that "Few professions require more careful preparation … than that of medicine." But "comparatively few can judge of the qualifications of learning and skill which he (a doctor) possesses." "Reliance had to be placed on the assurance given by a license. Reasonable considerations, therefore, might prompt a state to exclude people without licenses from practicing medicine." By the turn of twentieth century, state examination was required by 25 states and the District of Columbia, and no jurisdiction in the US was without a licensing statue of some sort.

Concurrently, medical education experienced a major revamp and profound transformation. Many forces acted to lay the foundation for a science-based medical training system that has made the United States the recognized leader in medical education and medical research today. "Much of the credit for this transformation has been appropriately attributed to Abraham Flexner and his … Flexner Report of 1910."

After founding and directing a college-preparatory school in his hometown of Louisville, Kentucky, Flexner pursued an MPhil at Harvard in philosophy and journeyed to Europe, where he visited schools in Great Britain, France, and, particularly, Germany. "It was out of his practical experience as an educator in America and his exploration of pedagogical strategies in Europe that he distilled" his critical assessment of the state American educational system in his book, *The American College: A Criticism*. His work attracted the Carnegie Foundation to commission an in-depth evaluation into medical schools in the US and Canada.

The Flexner Report called on American medical schools to enact higher admission and graduation standards and to embrace scientific knowledge and investigation as the foundation of clinical training. Medical schools were categorized into one of three categories based on whether they could be compared favorably to Johns Hopkins. Flexner's recommendation for the third group, rated poorly in his report, was straightforward: they ought to be extinguished.

In the decade following the Flexner Report, the number of medical schools fell from 133 to 85, and graduates cut by half. The actions of state medical licensing boards to deny recognition to poorly rated schools put teeth into the indictments of the Report. The new medical education system greatly increased the homogeneity and cohesiveness of the medical profession.

A repercussion was the closure of all but two "negro" medical schools, and the reversion of American universities to male-only admittance programs as the admission pool shrunken significantly. Another criticism is that in the passionate pursuit of science the Report overlooked the ethos of medicine as trusted healers. As we have entered an era in which patients suffer longer, the question of a doctor as a scientist vs. healer and the focus of medicine on disease vs whole person is ever more present.

The American hospitals as we know it today emerged in a matter of decades around the turn of the twentieth century with a radical transformation from religious and charitable refuges mainly for the homeless, poor, and insane to credible institutions where regular folks sought medical treatment and even cures. From being charities dependent on voluntary hours donated by doctors, hospitals evolved into market institutions increasingly financed out of payments from patients. They became what doctors viewed as their workshops for all types and classes of patients.

Gradually, hospitals opened their doors to more doctors with access "privilege" so they could follow their patients into the hospitals and continue to attend them. This access, granted to private practitioners without becoming employed doctors, became one of the distinct features of medical care in America. Hospitals became an integral and necessary part of medical practice and played an important role in medical education and research. By 1912, 75 to 80 percent of graduates were estimated to be taking hospital internships. The rise of hospitals as the hub of medical practice, training, and specialization created greater interdependence among doctors and a stronger sense of shared identity compared to solo practitioners.

TWO CENTURIES OF SCIENTIFIC BREAKTHROUGHS – THE FUEL OF HEALTH SYSTEM TRANSFORMATION

The engine that fueled all these sweeping changes was scientific advancements. Scientific breakthroughs revolutionized medical care from a mixture of science, home remedies, and quackery in the early 19th century to the scientifically based and statistically approved diagnostic and therapeutic system what we now call modern medicine. The notable impact of scientific discoveries led to the growing acceptance of medicine as a science, which facilitated the emergence of key elements of modern medicine, including physicians' medical authority and hospitals as credible centers for treatment.

The antiseptic technics to sterilize surgical tools and environment, and asepsis practices to maintain sterile conditions sharply reduced the mortality from operations and increased the range of surgical work. Several medical discoveries in the 19th century contributed to the improved surgical outcome:

- Louis Pasteur, the French chemist, and microbiologist who is regarded as one father of germ theory, demonstrated in many experiments that diseases could be prevented by killing and stopping germs.

- William Thomas Green Morton, an American dentist, demonstrated the use of inhaled ether as a surgical anesthetic using a novel delivery instrument he invented. Supported by anesthetic, surgeons could perform longer, and more complex surgeries on patients.

- Hungarian surgeon Ignaz Semmelweis introduced chlorine hand wash in medical practice to reduce childbed fever.

- Similarly, having noted the poor condition of hospitals where soldiers were placed during the Crimean War, Florence Nightingale, an English statistician, and founder of modern nursing, collected extensive data regarding the number and cause of death of these soldiers over a two-year period. In her most famous book, *Notes on Nursing*, which was promptly re-published in the U.S., Nightingale recommended aseptic techniques to reduce hospital mortality, including implementing hand washing and other hygiene practices, maximizing light and ventilation, and improving drainage to combat water-borne diseases (e.g., cholera and typhoid).

- Antiseptic surgery was pioneered by Joseph Lister, a British surgeon and medical scientist, when he used phenol as a disinfectant to sterilize operating theatre and surgical tools.

- Robert Koch, a German doctor, and microbiologist, demonstrated through his work with anthrax and tuberculosis that diseases resulted from the presence of specific microorganisms within the body. His discoveries strongly reinforced the work of Louis Pasteur and aseptic practice.

The diffusion of Pasteur and Koch's discoveries also made a notable impact on public health by reducing water-borne and food-borne diseases. "Sand filtration of the water supply, introduced in the 1890s, was far more effective in preventing typhoid than earlier sanity reform; regulation of the milk supply dramatically cut infant mortality." Before 1908, 17 American cities had death rates from typhoid fever of 30 or more per 100,000 population; 18 had death rates between 15 and 30 per 100,000. After water filtering systems were put in place, only three of the same cities had rates exceeding 15 per 100,000. Science was seen as a more effective means of achieving desirable social goals. W. T. Sedgwick, consulting biologist for Massachusetts, declared, "before 1880 we knew nothing; after 1890 we knew it all; it was a glorious ten years."

In 1909, a Report on *National Vitality* by the economist Irving Fisher gave equal weight to public hygiene, "semi-public hygiene" (medical research, medical practice), and personal hygiene. Fisher noted, "Antiseptic surgery has in the last century been the greatest triumph of the medical profession and has given it a greater prestige than ever before." In the late 19th century, three so-called "Nightingale" nursing schools began operations in the US and their success led to proliferation of similar nurse training programs. "The presence of trained nurses with their emphasis on cleanliness, orderliness and close observation of patients successfully transformed hospitals into scientific institutions of caring."

New diagnostic techniques "added a highly persuasive rhetoric to the authority of medicine." In the mid-1800s "a series of new diagnostic instruments – the stethoscope, ophthalmoscope, laryngoscope – began to expand the physician's sensory powers in clinical examination." Another wave of diagnostic technologies populated science and medicine, including the microscope and the X-ray, chemical and bacteriological tests, and diagnostic devices such as spirometer and electrocardiograph, producing objective data about patient physiology independent from a patient's narrative. More accurate diagnosis and the knowledge powered by microbiology to identify the sources of infection for the first time "permitted physicians to link causes, symptoms, and lesions systematically."

The success of science led to the growing recognition of the inadequacy of "the unaided and uneducated sense in understanding the world," but the other side of the coin was the growing acceptance of medical authority and dependence on physician's medical judgement. Doctors benefited financially from their rising influence. Physicians' incomes increased substantially in the early twentieth century. Even though doctors' earnings fell during the Great Depression, they remained high relative to other occupations. Average annual net income of doctors was about four times the average earnings of a worker for the years 1929 to 1934. Medicine became a highly desirable career choice, which is reflected in the high medical school admission rejection rate.

THE RISE OF MEDICAL AUTHORITY

The collective organization of doctors, the American Medical Association, played a vital role in the rise of medical authority and later in the defense of physician autonomy as large organizations and government threatened to intervene. AMA was founded in 1847 at a time that medicine was not a sought-after profession among "educated talent." While seeking protection against the competition of irregular and untrained practitioners might be the impetus for convergence that created the organization, the influence of the organization during its first half century was somewhat tempered because of conflicts of competing parties within the profession. As of 1900, the AMA had only eight thousand members, representing less than 10% of American doctors. As a writer who reported these figures wrote, "the profession was in 'wretched condition' as a political force."

In 1901, the AMA revised its constitution and reorganized its structure, with central authority shifted to a House of Delegates, a board of trustees, and executive offices. The House of Delegates was modeled after the United States House of Representatives, with its representatives primarily drawn from state medical societies in proportion to their membership. A rapid transformation quickly took place at the state level with reorganizations on a uniform plan. The results were immediate and positive. In a decade, AMA's membership shot up to seventy thousand, half the doctors in the country.

Before the creation of Medicare and Medicaid, both President Roosevelt and President Truman initiated health reforms aiming to provide access to healthcare and health insurance for all. Historians debate the many reasons national health insurance proposals failed, including the complexity of the issues, ideological differences, and the decentralization of Congressional power. "The AMA's battle against health insurance is often cited as a premier case of interest group political influence." From the standpoint of the AMA, the main concern about compulsory health insurance was that doctors would lose their autonomy, unable to choose where to work, who to treat, and how their services would be compensated.

The AMA looked guardedly upon the rapid expansion of voluntary hospital insurance, on the alert to any incursions into its territory. Though the AMA endorsed voluntary health insurance as a preferable alternative to compulsory insurance and even promoted it as the "American way" to warn off some health reform proposals, it warned that "these (hospital) plans should confine themselves to provision of hospital facilities and should not include any type of medical care." Hospitals and doctors accommodated each other's interests by splitting off hospital and medical insurance.

Even though the Blue Cross and Blue Shield consolidated eventually and most health insurance offerings in our time include both hospital and medical coverage, many structures AMA fought to preserve physician autonomy continue to this day, such as separate bills for hospital and physician services for a hospital stay, and the split of "two lines of authority" (clinical vs administrative) in hospital management.

Since its founding, the AMA has been conflicted with the circus of patent medicine business and has made several attempts to regulate the advertisement of patent drugs. To call most of the 19th-century drugs "patented" is a misnomer as they were just technically proprietary with unknown ingredients and trademark names, such as Lydia Pinkham's Vegetable Compound, Hamlin's Wizard Oil, Kick-a-poo Indian Sagwa, and Warner's Safe Cure for Diabetes. Even though state licensing laws gave doctors the authority to write prescriptions, a prescription was not required to obtain almost any drugs.

Patent medicine makers were prolific and hyperbolical advertisers, accounting for roughly half of newspapers' entire advertising income. The "success" of Microbe Killer in the late 1880s exemplifies how patent medicine operated. Exploiting new scientific discoveries by Pasteur and Koch, William Radam, an ingenious Texan, promoted Microbe Killer, which was made up "nearly entirely of water, except for traces of red wine, hydrochloric and sulphuric acid." Microbe Killer was advertised as a cure-all for all diseases by destroying germs inside the body. Ironically, when doctors were beginning to understand many diseases, Radam's business exploded with seventeen factories producing the Killer.

In the early 20th century, investigative journalists joined the crusade against patent medicine with the series of exposé of deceptive medicine makers who sold dangerous and addictive drugs. The most famous investigations of the drug industry were *The Great American Fraud* by reporter Samuel Hopkins Adams, whose reports began appearing in Collier's weekly in October 1905. The AMA distributed over 150,000 copies of *The Great American Fraud.*

Following these exposé and Upton Sinclair's novel, *The Jungle,* which exposed health violations and unsanitary practices in the American meat packing industry, Congress passed the Pure Food and Drug Act in 1906. The primary objective of this legislation was to provide consumers with more information through product labeling, rather than premarket approval. Also, no detail of a drug label could be false or misleading, a loophole addressed by Congress through Sherley Amendment in 1912. This amendment prohibited labeling medicines with false therapeutic claims intended to defraud the purchaser. In 1927, Congress passed the Caustic Poison Act, lobbied for by the AMA, which required product labels to list the presence and amount of eleven dangerous substances, including alcohol, heroin, and cocaine.

In 1905, the AMA established a Council on Pharmacy and Chemistry to set drug manufacturing and advertising standards. As part of this effort, it set up a laboratory and maintained close contact with the federal Bureau of Chemistry, the forerunner of the FDA. That same year, the AMA began a voluntary program of drug approval, which remained in effect until 1955. Drug companies had to show proof of the effectiveness of their drugs to be advertised in AMA's journal. The council would not approve any drugs that were directly advertised to the public because "the AMA regarded self-medication as a threat to the medical profession." The council's publication, *New and Nonofficial Remedies,* became widely used by medical journals in setting advertising policies and by doctors in prescribing.

In the 1930s, FDA officials tried to expand federal authority over drugs. To help illustrate the many shortcomings of the 1906 law, the FDA assembled a collection of some of the most egregious products, dubbed by a reporter as the "Chamber of Horrors." In addition to the American Chamber of Horrors, the FDA drew on support from women's groups and organized consumer unions. The legislative process, though, languished in Congress for five years. The final push came in 1938 from a policy tragedy with over 100 deaths – mostly children.

Sulfanilamide, a drug used to treat streptococcal infections, had been used safely for some time in tablet and powder form. The pills themselves were bitter tasting, so at the request of doctors and patients, the Massengill Company in Bristol, Tennessee, developed a liquid form of the drug called elixir sulfanilamide. The company experimented and chose diethylene glycol, a sweet-tasting liquid, to dissolve the sulfanilamide compound, even though diethylene glycol was known to cause damage to the blood, kidneys, nervous system, and liver. The new formula was not tested for toxicity before 240 gallons of elixir sulfanilamide were shipped, as there were no requirements for safety studies at that time.

The first reports of death from the elixir came from the AMA. On October 11, 1937, the president of the Tulsa, Oklahoma, County Medical Society, Dr. James Stevenson, sent a telegram to the AMA Chemical Laboratory stating that six people had died after taking the elixir. The AMA Chemical laboratory tested a sample of the elixir provided by the Massengill Company. Preliminary laboratory tests concluded that it was the solvent, diethylene glycol, and not sulfanilamide, that had caused the deaths. The Journal of the American Medical Association issued a public warning on October 18, 1937, and the press reported the story in the following days.

The FDA learned of the deaths on October 14 and began the arduous recall process. Almost the entire field force of 239 FDA inspectors and chemists was assigned to the task. State and local health officials joined the search. One headline from the New York Times read: "Near End of Chase for Deadly Elixir, Government Agents Hope to

Recover Today the Last of 700 Bottles." In the four following weeks, the FDA recalled about 90 percent of the original shipment, but in the end, the death toll reached 107.

Again, in the aftermath, a public uproar prompted rapid approval of the 1938 Food, Drug, and Cosmetic Act (FDCA), which required, for the first time, that drugs had to be proven safe and to receive the FDA's approval before being marketed. The FDCA of 1938 dramatically shaped drug development and sales in the US. For the first time drug companies had to produce scientific safety tests. "While initially intended to protect the public, the new law precipitated a shift that ultimately created the drug development industry we know today."

The post-war period saw a blossoming of pharmaceutical invention, with breakthroughs in the development of synthetic vitamins, sulfonamides, antibiotics, hormones (thyroxine, oxytocin, corticosteroids, and others), psychotropics, antihistamines, and new vaccines. Complete new classes of pharmaceuticals were introduced, including oral contraceptives, β blocker, ACE inhibitors, benzodiazepines, and a wide range of novel anti-cancer medicines. Even though both penicillin and insulin were identified and manufactured, albeit at a modest scale, in the 1920s and 1930s, wartime demands from the US government provided a major stimulus to the expansion of the pharmaceutical industry, with requirements for the large-scale manufacturing of analgesics and antibiotics and increasing demands from governments to undertake research to identify treatments for a wide range of conditions.

Prior to the passage of the Durham-Humphrey Amendment in 1951, drug manufacturers decided for themselves whether their drugs could be sold with or without the supervision of medical professionals. The lack of a clear distinction between prescription and over the counter (OTC) drugs led to confusion by both consumers and pharmacists, and variations in how drugs were categorized. The Durham-Humphrey Amendment established two classes of drugs – prescription and OTC – and created a statutory definition of prescription drugs to include those habit-forming, and unsafe for use except under the supervision of a healthcare practitioner.

The amendment also authorized both written and oral prescription from a doctor, and the refilling of prescriptions. The Durham Humphrey Amendment is viewed by some to discourage patient self-diagnosis and self-administration of complex and potentially harmful drugs. After the Amendment became law, more drugs were sold by prescription, which also reflected increased drug specialization and expansion of insurance coverage that provided more stable market for prescription drugs. These developments coincided with the AMA's long-held goal to secure more control by doctors over the use of pharmaceuticals. The Medical Device Amendments to the Federal Food, Drug, and Cosmetic Act of 1976 extended FDA's oversight authority to medical device.

When Medicare was created in 1965, borrowed from a health insurance policy Aetna offered, the language of the Medicare Act specified that Medicare's scope of coverage is limited to items and services that are reasonable and necessary for the diagnosis or treatment of illness or injury. This language has remained unchanged and is the language that dictates how Medicare makes coverage determinations for new medical technologies and procedures. In the 1960s, state courts heard many cases requiring judges to interpret close variants of the statutory language, and these courts consistently interpreted the health insurance contract language as giving broad discretion to the recommendation of the covered person's treating physician.

To rein in the escalating cost of healthcare, Health Maintenance Organizations (HMOs), a type of managed care health plan, gained popularity in the early 1990s. Utilization control practices, such as gatekeeping and preauthorization, represented a departure from the hands-off approach to doctors' decisions sanctioned by the courts. Even though utilization control practices are perceived as an erosion of physician autonomy, physician's clinical judgement still plays a key role in defining the necessity of a service or procedure imum# PART TWO

MEDICAL CODING

THE CODE TO

REIMBURSEMENT

There is no shortage of codes. The Current Procedure Terminology codeset has over 10,000 codes to report professional and ambulatory services. There are about 8,000 Healthcare Common Procedure Coding System codes to report healthcare equipment, supplies, and services. The International Classification of Diseases, 10th edition includes about 70,000 Clinical Modifications codes to report patient diagnosis in all care settings, and over 70,000 Procedure Coding System codes for reporting hospital inpatient procedures.

Identifying and understanding appropriate coding for a medical innovation is a vital aspect of developing a successful reimbursement strategy. Obtaining a new code serves as one of the entry points to begin the reimbursement journey. However, it is important to note that obtaining a new code does not automatically imply coverage or payment by any payer, as coding is distinct from payment and coverage determination. In some cases, a new code may receive separate payment, while in other instances, providers or patients may bear the full cost of utilizing a medical innovation due to payment rules under specific payment systems or coverage determinations.

In response to Congress's inquiry about the integration of new medical procedures and devices into Medicare, The General Accountability Office (GAO) explained that Medicare covered approximately 99 percent of the procedures and devices assigned new codes by an American Medical Association panel or a committee of insurers in 2001. However, only three quarters of these new codes had specific coverage policies outlining the circumstances or restrictions for Medicare coverage, including a quarter affected by national coverage policies and the rest affected by local coverage policies. Another quarter were introduced into the program without explicit coverage policies. GAO's estimate was based on a tally of 320 new Current Procedure Terminology (CPT) codes in 2001.

According to GAO, CMS determines whether new codes created by AMA committees fall into existing Medicare benefit categories and if they are deemed "reasonable and necessary" for Medicare payment. CMS then communicates payment policies for new codes with Medicare

Administrative Contractors (MACs). Occasionally, CMS or its MACs create coverage policies, known as national coverage determinations (NCDs) or local coverage determinations (LCDs), to specify conditions of coverage for a specific procedure or device.

One common misconception about the reimbursement process is assuming a fixed sequence of coding, coverage, and then payment in Medicare. However, Medicare's reimbursement process does not always follow this linear sequence. Depending on the coding system involved, CMS may provide coding and payment instructions for newly covered services, sometimes by assigning an existing code that describes a similar item or service and sometimes by creating a new code for payment purposes.

Some may argue that it's more efficient not to initiate a coverage decision process for every one of the 320 new codes. Nonetheless, the current approach has a downside of uncertainty and unpredictability at each individual code level since the rule does not clearly define which reimbursement pathway might apply. CMS's Innovators' guide advises that "Payment for many technological advances can be made under one of Medicare's payment methodologies without being preceded by an explicit coverage determination, coding change, and/or payment decision by CMS," which aligns with GAO's findings but does not provide any additional clarity.

This chapter provides an overview of the various coding systems used in the US to report services provided in different care settings and facilitate reimbursement for different types of providers. Since all coding systems are maintained by either federal government agencies or national organizations, such as the AMA, CMS and Centers for Disease Control and Prevention (CDC), coding changes occur at the national level. In addition to outlining the history and background of each coding system, this chapter offers insights into each code set, highlights recent coding updates to accommodate new technologies, and focuses on coding change requirement and process.

HISTORY AND STATUTORY AUTHORITY FOR CODING USE

The medical coding sets used every day in medical billing to create claims were adopted by the Health Insurance Portability and Accountability Act (HIPAA) of 1996. When HIPAA was passed, medical transactions began moving from paper to electronic. While electronic transactions (like claims) were faster, cheaper, and less error-prone, there were also concerns about the privacy of the personal medical information. HIPAA Administrative Simplification Rules addressed these concerns by setting national standards for electronic transactions and HIPAA code sets to maintain the privacy and security of protected health information.

HIPAA Administrative Simplification Rules direct HHS to adopt specific code sets for diagnoses and procedures that health plans, clearinghouses and providers must use when conducting business electronically to ensure uniformity in the communication of administrative information among stakeholders. The adopted code sets and corresponding transactions where the code sets are used are:

- ICD-10 – International Classification of Diseases, 10th edition. ICD-10 includes Clinical Modifications (CM) and Procedure Coding System (PCS). ICD-10-CM is used for reporting patient diagnosis and ICD-10-PCS for reporting hospital inpatient procedures.

- CPT – Current Procedure Terminology. CPT is used to report ambulatory services/procedures, including services provided by clinicians or in hospital outpatient settings.

- HCPCS – Healthcare Common Procedure Coding System. HCPCS is used to report healthcare equipment and supplies and services not covered by CPT codes.

- CDT – Code on Dental Procedures and Nomenclature. CDT is used to report dental procedures.

- NDC – National Drug Codes. NDC is used to report drug products.

Medical Coding has become a staple in healthcare. But where did these codes come from?

Medical coding history goes back centuries. The official coding of diseases began in the 17th century in England, known as the London Bills of Mortality. "The Bill of Mortality, to our griefs, is encreased 399 this week, and the encrease general through the whole city and suburbs, which makes us all sad," noted Londoner Samuel Pepys on Nov 9,

1665. The grief and the anxious tracking of a plague's death toll in the 17th century resonate with our time and bring us back to the early days of the COVID-19 pandemic. The sad moments in human history share striking resemblance. Published by the Worshipful Company of Parish Clerks in London, UK, the weekly Bill of Mortality was a single sheet of paper that listed mortalities by causes of death for each of the 130 parishes of London. For example, the Bill of Mortality for Oct 31 to Nov 7, 1665, referred to in Pepys' comment, reported that, among other causes, 1,414 people died of "Plague", 61 of "Consumption", and that one was "Found dead in the Fields at St. Mary Islington".

A more systematic classification of disease came more than a century after the London Bills of Mortality, when William Farr, the first appointed statistician of the General Register Office of England and Wales, went before the newly formed International Statistical Congress and proposed a uniform classification system based on anatomical site in 1853. In 1900, this system evolved into the first ICD – International Classification of Diseases. The first version of ICD had 179 groups of causes of death and an abridged classification of 35 groups.

In 1946, the responsibility to update the ICD system was entrusted to the World Health Organization (WHO), which issued the sixth and succeeding revisions. Over time, the ICD has become a global tool for morbidity and mortality statistics, reimbursement, health management, and automated decision support in healthcare. The current version, the 11th Revision, was accepted by WHO's World Health Assembly in May 2019 and officially came into effect on January 1st, 2022.

In a parallel effort, the United States Public Health Service adapted the ICD to index hospital records and classify surgical procedures, resulting in the publication of the ICD, Adapted (ICDA) in 1962. The Public Health Service published an eighth revision of the ICD, specifically focused on the unique needs of the United States known as ICDA-8. The ICD-9 published in 1977 was an important transition to increased granularity.

The ICD-9-CM was the next expansion in the US to allow diagnostic coding of inpatient, outpatient, and clinician use. It was developed by the National Center for Health Statistics. The CM expansion provided an opportunity to capture enhanced morbidity data and to update more often. In 1983, when the Medicare program adopted the Inpatient Prospective Payment System to pay for hospital care, ICD-9-CM was used for assigning cases to the Diagnosis Related Groups, under which the payment amounts were determined.

The creation of Medicare program in 1965 highlighted the need for a common language of medical procedures to facilitate efficient and effective determination of physician reimbursement. The AMA, working with multiple specialty societies, developed an iterative coding system for describing medical procedures and services. This system was named the Current Procedural Terminology (CPT) coding system. It systematically lists descriptive terms and identifies codes used to describe physician services.

The first edition of CPT released in 1966 for the most part focused on surgery, with limited sections on medicine, radiology, and laboratory procedures. The second edition, published in 1970, expanded CPT's scope by adding codes for diagnostic and therapeutic procedures in surgery, medicine, and specialties. The code length was expanded from four to five, which is still used today. In the mid- and late 1970s, the third and fourth editions of CPT were released. The fourth edition was a major update and introduced a system for periodical updates to keep pace with the rapidly changing medical environment.

In 1983, the Healthcare Financing Administration (HCFA), the forerunner of CMS, established a three-part procedure labeling system, HCPCS, to identify services covered in the Medicare Part B program. CPT was designated as the level I of HCPCS codes and continued to be maintained by AMA. The level II of HCPCS was built on a coding system established by HCFA in 1978. It includes primarily non-physician services such as ambulance services and durable medical equipment and represents items and supplies not covered by level I of HCPCS codes. The level

III of HCPCS was developed by state Medicaid agencies, Medicare contractors, and private plans for specific programs and jurisdictions, which was discontinued in 2003 to adhere to HIPAA's consistent coding requirements.

The creation of the HCPCS system mandated the use of CPT to report services for Part B of the Medicare program. In 1986, the HCPCS was adopted by Medicaid. A short time later, the Omnibus Budget Reconciliation Act of 1987 mandated using HCPCS codes (including level I or CPT codes) for outpatient procedures.

CPT – DESCRIBE WORK BY CLINICIANS AND AI

The CPT is a coding system consisting of descriptive terms and codes used primarily to identify medical services and procedures provided by physicians and other qualified healthcare professionals. Developed and maintained by the AMA, the CPT coding system is updated annually. The 2023 update for CPT codeset contains over 10,000 codes that describe the medical procedures and services available to patients. This update includes 393 editorial changes, comprising 225 new codes, 75 deleted codes and 93 revised codes. The new CPT code set went into effect on January 1, 2023.

To help with navigation within the extensive range of services and procedures, CPT codes are classified into several categories:

- CPT Category I: This is the largest category, encompassing codes commonly used to describe medical procedures or services.

- CPT Category II: Theses codes are supplemental measurement tracking codes used for performance management. They are used to facilitate quality data collection and are not associated with any reimbursement.

- CPT Category III: They are temporary codes used to report emerging technology and experimental services and procedures.

- Proprietary laboratory analyses (PLA) codes: These codes describe proprietary clinical laboratory analyses and can be provided by a single ("sole-source") laboratory or licensed or marketed to multiple providing laboratories (e.g., cleared or approved by FDA).

Category I CPT codes are typically denoted by five-digit numeric characters and are clustered together to help navigate the coding system. The six main sections of CPT Category I codes are:

1. Evaluation & Management (99202–99499)
2. Anesthesia (00100–01999)
3. Surgery (10021–69990) — further broken into smaller groups by body area or system within this code range

4. Radiology Procedures (70010–79999)

5. Pathology and Laboratory Procedures (80047–89398)

6. Medicine Services and Procedures (90281–99607)

Many physician services consist of a professional component and a technical component (TC). The professional component covers the costs of professional services for their time and expertise, such as the interpretation of a CT scan result by a radiologist. The TC component addresses the use of equipment, facilities, non-physician medical staff, supplies, and so on. For instance, most clinical laboratory category I CPT codes only have a TC, while most surgical pathology category I CPT codes consist of both a professional component and TC.

An Independent Diagnostic Test Facility (IDTF) is a facility independent of a physician office and of a hospital that performs diagnostic tests. When imaging services are carried out by an IDTF, the IDTF imaging center can bill the TC component of those services. Some services offered by an IDTF include magnetic resonance imaging, ultrasound, x-rays, and sleep studies. Although certain IDTF services can be performed remotely, such as pacemaker monitoring, most require a patient to be present at an IDTF facility.

With the proliferation of AI intervention, a new type of IDTF is emerging. The IDTFs perform diagnostic services via computer modeling and analytics, or other forms of testing not involving direct patient interaction. The service is often performed by a technician who conducts a computer analysis offsite or at another location where the patient isn't present. CMS refers to them as indirect IDTFs and defines the two key features of tests provided by these facilities: the tests don't involve direct patient interaction and the tests involve off-site computer modeling and analytics.

The number of AI-related CPT codes is limited compared to the over 300 "Software as a Medical Device (SaMD)" products received FDA authorization to legally market via 510(k)clearance, de novo process, or pre-market approval. To embrace the evolving implementation of modalities of digital medicine, the AMA determined that a "more comprehensive code set is needed." The Digital Medicine Payment Advisory Group (DMPAG) was initiated in late 2016. One example of the group's achievement was the creation of a taxonomy for using AI.

The "Taxonomy of Artificial Intelligence for Medical Services and Procedures" became part of the CPT code set effective January 1, 2022. Appendix S provides language to describe the "work done by machines" in relation to the work of the physician. The new AI taxonomy provides guidance for classifying various AI-powered medical service applications, such as expert systems, machine learning, or algorithm-based solutions, into three categories: assistive, augmentative, or autonomous, with a goal to standardize code descriptor and facilitate "labeling, valuation, coverage, and payment."

The Category I code for an AI diabetic retinopathy diagnostic test, IDx-DR, was one of the codes that DMPAG reviewed. IDx-DR is the first SaMD authorized by FDA for marketing that provides a screening decision with no clinician to interpret the image or results. FDA granted IDx-DR Breakthrough Device designation and permitted its marketing through their de novo regulatory pathway in 2018.

When AMA approved the first Category I CPT code for the AI test in 2019, the CPT panel used the term "automated" to describe the code CPT92229 because there was no precedent for autonomous as a descriptor. The word "Automated," the DMPAG group believes, doesn't capture the clinical decision-making process – interpreting data, drawing conclusions, and offering diagnosis and/or management options – that AI systems like IDx-DR are providing. Shortly after the release of Appendix S in 2022, the CPT Editorial Panel considered and revised the code descriptor of CPT 92229 by replacing the word "automated" with "autonomous".

Receiving a Category I CPT code is a significant milestone for autonomous AI, as the bar is set fairly high. A proposal for a new or revised Category I code must meet all these criteria:

- All devices and drugs necessary for a procedure or service must have received FDA clearance or approval.

- The procedure or service must be performed by many physicians or other qualified healthcare professionals across the United States. However, there is no definition of "many." Opinions from the relevant specialty societies whose members would use this code are crucial here. This requirement creates a chicken-or-egg conundrum because obtaining a new code requires demonstrating volume for the procedure or service. However, achieving such volume requires a code and predictable reimbursement to ensure clinicians are adequately reimbursed for providing the procedure or service.

- The procedure or service must be performed with a frequency appropriate for the intended clinical use.

- The procedure or service must be consistent with current medical practice.

- The clinical efficacy of the procedure or service must be well-proven and documented in U.S. peer-reviewed literature. For new technologies, the minimum literature requirement is at least two peer-reviewed publications with no overlapping patient populations or authors, and at least one article is a systematic review of randomized controlled trials, a study from an individual randomized controlled trial or a systematic review of cohort studies.

Requesting a new Category I CPT code for a new test, procedure, or service is a complicated and lengthy process. The first step is to apply to the AMA through the CPT Smart App online system before one of the deadlines. AMA/CPT staff review the application to evaluate their coding suggestions. If they determine that the request is a new issue, or significantly new information is received on an item that the CPT Editorial Panel reviewed previously, the request is referred to appropriate members of the CPT Advisory Committee and the Health Care Professionals Advisory Committee (together the CPT/HCPAC Advisory Committee or "CPT Advisors") – representatives of national medical specialty societies.

Applicants are encouraged to work with the relevant specialty societies whose members would most likely provide the requested procedure or service and/or contact them prior submission. Most specialty organizations have dedicated representatives/staff involved in the CPT process and are knowledgeable resources for innovators to navigate the CPT process. In the case of IDx-DR, the code application was submitted by the American Academy of Ophthalmology (AAO) supported by IDx "(now known as Digital Diagnostics)". Applicants will be notified if their applications have received no CPT Advisor support before each CPT Editorial Panel meeting.

Panel deliberation takes place three times yearly at the CPT Editorial Panel meetings. The panel comprises 21 members, including 12 physicians nominated by national medical specialty societies; 5 representatives from the Blue Cross Blue Shield Association, America's Health Insurance Plans, the American Hospital Association, an at-large organizational member, and an umbrella organization representing private healthcare insurers; and 2 members of the CPT HCPAC. CMS have two non-voting liaisons to the CPT Editorial Panel. Five panel members serve as an executive committee that supervises the work of the full Editorial Panel. Applicants disputing a decision from the Editorial Panel can request an appeal. Each year, the panel evaluates about 350 code changes, including adding new codes, revising, or deleting existing codes.

TEMPORARY CPT CODES FOR EMERGING TECHNOLOGY AND REIMBURSEMENT

Category III codes are temporary codes within the CPT coding system that serve the purpose of collecting data for emerging technologies, services, procedures, and service paradigms. Introduced in 2001 and first published in 2002, Category III codes provide a means of tracking and gathering information for innovative medical advancements, and the data collected may be used to substantiate widespread usage in the FDA approval process. It is expected that some of the temporary III codes will eventually be converted to Category I CPT codes.

Unlike Category I CPT codes, which are grouped anatomically and by service type, Category III codes are assigned a sequential number with five characters. These codes consist of four numbers followed by the letter "T." For instance, 0509T, represents the electroretinogram (ERG) with interpretation and report, pattern (PERG).

While Category III codes are primarily intended for data collection and service tracking during the FDA approval process, they can also play a role in facilitating payment. In CY 2023, there are five temporary codes with assigned Relative Value Units (RVUs) or national payment rates as published in the Physician Fee Schedule (PFS) final rule data files. These codes are associated with three types of medical devices or services. Considering there are over 300 temporary codes in the PFS final rule data file, national payment assignments for the five codes is relatively rare. A closer examination of the three medical innovations associated with these codes can provide insights into the pathway to reimbursement for Category III codes.

Eversense Continuous Glucose Monitoring System

The Eversense Continuous Glucose Monitoring (CGM) system, which received FDA approval in June 2018 with expanded indications in June 2019, represents a significant advancement for glucose monitoring. The idea of implantable glucose sensors has been promulgated for more than 40 years, and the first implantable glucose sensors received FDA approval in 1999. Eversense is the first FDA-approved CGM system with an implantable glucose sensor that can be worn for up to 90 days. The system provides real-time monitoring of glucose levels. By displaying glucose values, trends, and alerts on a patient's mobile device, it eliminates the need for frequent finger pricking before insulin treatment. To help with the reporting of clinical trial data for this innovative technology, three Category III codes were created in 2017: CPT 0446T, 0447T, 0448T.

Pattern Electroretinogram

The ERG is a diagnostic test that measures the electrical activity of the retina in response to a light stimulus. Since its inception in the 1940s, ERG has played a role as a diagnostic tool for retinal disease and has become a standard tool for the assessment of retinal function. AAO's guideline recommends ERG — both full field ERG (ffERG) and multifocal ERG — for clinical assessment of patients with inherited retinal degenerations.

PERG uses reverse contrast pattern stimuli (e.g., sinewave gratings or checkerboards) to assess macular retinal ganglion cell activity. Researchers have been interested in the early detection of glaucoma and PERG has been explored as a potential modality. In the CY 2019 PFS final rule, the single CPT code 92275 ERG was deleted and replaced with three new codes — 92273, 92274 and 0509T — to distinguish between the different types of ERG testing. Unlike other Category III codes, CPT 0509T for PERG received a RVU assignment right away.

HeartFlow Fractional Flow Reserve CT

The story of HeartFlow follows a Silicon Valley start-up model, with Stanford at the epicenter of innovation. Both founders are Stanford faculty: one is an expert in computational fluid, and another chaired the vascular surgery department. Fractional Flow Reserve – Computed Tomography (FFRCT) is a software that applies computational fluid dynamics to the available anatomical data from coronary CT angiography (CCTA) to produce a 3D model of coronary blood flow and pressures, which helps determine how severely the blockages impede blood flow to the heart.

FFRCT offers a non-invasive option to help assess for instance whether a patient with stable chest pain may need a surgical procedure. Studies have shown that most patients do not benefit from a coronary artery by-pass graft or coronary angioplasty. However, instead of a population-level statistic, clinicians need to case-by-case determine whether the patient in front would benefit from a surgical procedure and what the risks are without a surgical procedure. FFRCT meet a critical need in clinical care.

Since the company's inception in 2010, the software went through iterations with improved diagnostic accuracy, and clinical thresholds were confirmed through clinical trials conducted in multiple centers across the globe. In 2014, HeartFlow's FFRCT received FDA de novo 510(k) clearance. A set of new Category III CPT codes for FFRCT were created in 2017 and went into effect in 2018. The code application was cosponsored by the American College of Cardiology, the Society of Cardiovascular Computed Tomography, and the Society for Cardiovascular Angiography and Interventions.

To accelerate the availability of CPT Category III codes, the AMA releases new category III codes twice a year. The full set of Category III codes is then included in the next published edition of the CPT codeset. The quick cycle is possible because Category III codes are not reviewed by AMA's Relative Value Update Committee (RUC) for valuation by the CMS. This means under the regular CPT rate setting process temporary codes do not receive payment assignment. What the five Category III codes with national payment assignments all have in common is that they had LCDs and received payment assignments through PFS rulemaking process.

For Eversense CGM, several MACs issued LCDs in October 2020 specifying justifications and conditions for Medicare coverage. The LCDs relied heavily on findings from one pivotal European trial, two pivotal US clinical trials under one investigational device exemption (IDE), and two post-market registry studies, plus guideline and consensus statements from specialty societies.

Medicare's reasoning for coverage is because therapeutic CGMs for patients on intensive insulin therapy (meeting certain criteria) have been covered by Medicare, and clinical trial findings have shown that the implantable CGMs are comparable to FDA-approved non-implantable therapeutic CGMs. Therefore, coverage of implantable CGMs is in line with exiting CGM criteria.

Also in 2020, CMS proposed and finalized policies to establish national payment amounts for the CGM codes in the CY 2021 PFS rules. Back in 2019, CMS requested information to help establish national payment rates for these codes due to significant confusion over contractor pricing of these codes, which had led to limited access to these services for Medicare beneficiaries. With no major objections received during the public comment period, CMS adopted the proposed policy for CGM codes in the CY 2021 PFS final rule.

Although CMS typically assigns contractor pricing for Category III codes, an exception was made for PERG in the CY 2019 PFS final, where a national rate was established for this temporary code. CMS explained that in cases where there is an unusually high volume of services to be performed under a Category III code, they may assign RVUs to the code prior to the creation of formal CPT code. For CPT code 0509T, it was estimated that about 100,000 services, accounting for around 80% of the services reported under the previous CPT code 92275, would be billed under this temporary code.

In 2022, CGS Administrators, a MAC, initiated an LCD process to review evidence on ERG for glaucoma. Although reports of using ERG for glaucoma management began to emerge in the 1950s, a 2011 report by AAO concluded advances in technology had yet to produced definitive guidance on the diagnosis and management of glaucoma, rendering the test "not ready for widespread clinical use." A systematic review published in 2020, analyzing studies published after 2013, showed growing but not definitive evidence of ERG in glaucoma.

In addition to the literature review, CGS convened a formal Contractor Advisory Committee (CAC) meeting with ophthalmology and optometry CAC members to evaluate and vote on the evidence. Despite the CAC panel voting for robust clinical evidence supporting ERG for glaucoma, CGS cited the lack of "high-quality randomized controlled trials" and studies comparing ERG with the current standard test in literature search as the reason for considering ERG investigational for glaucoma. Consequently, Medicare does not cover ERG for the detection of glaucoma. This means the Category III code 0509T can't be reimbursed specifically for detecting glaucoma, an area where the test shows significant potential, but it can be reimbursed for other covered indications.

Several MACs issued first LCDs on FFRCT for ischemic heart disease in 2020. In 2019, Noridian, a MAC, convened a formal CAC meeting with subject matter experts to review literature. Based on the consensus reached through the literature review, it was concluded that FFRCT is a valuable modality for guiding and assessing stable coronary artery disease, which led to the implementation of the initial LCDs in 2020. In the CY 2022 PFS final rule, CMS finalized a national payment rate for FFRCT. Following the updated guideline for the Evaluation and Diagnosis of Chest Pain in 2021, Medicare's coverage for FFRCT were updated in 2022, incorporating revised coverage criteria.

Temporary codes are typically priced by Medicare contractor. Some of the 300 temporary codes without assigned national payment rates may receive payments case by case from Medicare contractors or be covered under LCDs in relevant jurisdictions. This explains how both CGM and FFRCT could receive reimbursements before CMS established national payment policies for them. While the reasons behind CMS's decisions to establish national payment policies for the three diagnostic services may differ, it is evident that temporary codes can facilitate the establishment of payment policy and coverage determination. These various reimbursement pathways highlight the independent and interconnected relationships between coding, payment, and coverage determination.

Approval for Category III codes does not require FDA approval or proven clinical efficacy but merely having a relevance for research, either ongoing or planned, or the need to be tracked to evaluate the frequency of use. Specifically, criteria used by the CPT/HCPAC Advisory Committee and the CPT Editorial Panel for evaluating Category III code applications include:

- The procedure or service is currently or recently performed in humans AND

- At least one of these additional criteria has been met:
  - The application is supported by at least 1 CPT or HCPAC Advisor representing practitioners who would use this procedure or service (or)
  - The actual or potential clinical efficacy of the specific procedure or service is supported by peer-reviewed literature which is available in English for examination by the CPT Editorial Panel (or)
  - There is:
    - At least 1 Institutional Review Board-approved protocol of a study of the procedure or service being performed
    - A description of a current and ongoing United States trial outlining the efficacy of the procedure or service or
    - Other evidence of evolving clinical utilization

Category III codes usually remain active for five years. The expectation is that after five years, a Category III code will be replaced by a Category I code. A Category III code can be renewed after five years if needed. CPT notifies the original requestor of the upcoming expiration. The requestor can submit a proposal to ask for conversion of the Category III code to Category I, or an extension of the code with Category III status. A specialty society or industry representative may request extension of Category III status. The request needs to show the continued need for a Category III code and list the Category I criteria that the code doesn't meet for a conversion to a Category I code. There is no defined duration of a Category III code. A requestor may ask to cancel a Category III code. A Category III code will be archived if no request is received after 5 years.

MORE CODES TO TRACK MOLECULAR DIAGNOSTIC TESTS – PLA, MAAA, U CODES, AND Z CODES

Molecular diagnostics tests (MDTs) detect genomic variants and have become increasingly common in various areas of laboratory medicine, including oncology, infectious diseases, clinical chemistry, and clinical genetics. By combining laboratory testing with the precision of molecular biology, MDTs have revolutionized the diagnosis of infectious diseases, cancers, and many inherited diseases. With the rapid growth of MDTs, reported to be over 75,000 on as of 2018, several more code sets have been developed to track MDTs.

The Proprietary Laboratory Analyses (PLA) codes, an addition to the CPT code set, was created by the AMA in 2015 to accommodate requirements established by the Protecting Access to Medicare Act (PAMA) of 2014. PAMA created a new subcategory of Clinical Diagnostic Laboratory Tests (CDLTs) known as Advanced Diagnostic Laboratory Tests (ADLTs). ADLTs must have a unique CPT code or identifier to describe only that specific test. Most Category I CPT codes are used to describe multiple lab tests. The CPT PLA code set enables laboratories or manufacturers to precisely identify and track their test.

To qualify as an ADLT under CMS regulations, the test must be covered under Medicare Part B and be offered and provided exclusively by a single laboratory. The test must not be sold for use by any other laboratory except the single laboratory or a successor owner. Additionally, the test must meet either Criterion (A), involving the analysis of multiple biomarkers of DNA, RNA, or proteins, or Criterion (B), being cleared or approved by FDA. PAMA established different reporting and payment requirements for ADLTs.

PLA codes are alpha-numeric CPT codes accompanied by descriptors. For example, PLA code 0224U is for a COVID-19 antibody test from Mount Sinai, and its code descriptor is "Antibody, severe acute respiratory syndrome coronavirus 2 (SARS-CoV-2) (Coronavirus disease [COVID-19]), includes titer(s), when performed." PLA codes are in a non-Category I subsection of the Pathology/Laboratory CPT codes. The PLA Code section includes (but is not limited to) ADLTs and CDLTs. These analyses may encompass various medical laboratory tests, such as Multianalyte Assays with Algorithmic Analyses (MAAAs) and Genomic Sequencing Procedures.

The criteria for approving PLA codes are less stringent compared to those for category I/III codes, as they do not require clinical evidence, trial study, or sponsorship from specialty society sponsorship. The AMA simply requires that tests with PLA codes must be performed on human specimens and requested by the clinical laboratory or manufacturer offering the test. Applications for PLA codes are reviewed quarterly, and code submissions are accepted throughout the year.

The PLA code application process begins with the submission of a formal application through the PLA Portal. Once a completed application is received, it undergoes review by the Proprietary Laboratory Analyses Technical Advisory Group (PLA-TAG). The PLA-TAG serves as an advisory body to the CPT Editorial Panel and consists of representatives from the CPT Editorial Panel, the Pathology Coding Caucus, the Molecular Pathology Advisory Group, payer organization(s), commercial labs, proprietary labs, academic labs, registries, and private practice. After review, the PLA-TAG provides recommendations to the CPT Editorial Panel for further action.

In cases where tests have been granted ADLT status by CMS or have obtained FDA clearance or approval as CDLTs, if the test has not obtained a PLA code and has not applied for a unique CPT code to AMA, CMS will assign a unique level II HCPCS code, referred to as the U-codes (i.e., Uxxxx). Applications for U-codes are reviewed quarterly, and an approved new code typically becomes effective in the following quarter.

If a specific PLA code or U-code is not listed, the test may be reported using either a CPT Category I laboratory code or an administrative MAAA code, which is separately listed in Appendix O. MAAAs are tests that incorporate results from a panel of tests that include two or more biomarkers, along with patient demographics and clinical information, into an algorithm to generate diagnostic, prognostic, or predictive information for a disease.

Like PLA, administrative MAAA codes in Appendix O are for proprietary MAAA tests provided by a single clinical lab or manufacturer and are alpha-numeric CPT codes. For example, MAAA code 0004M has the code descriptor "Scoliosis, DNA analysis of 53 single nucleotide polymorphisms, using saliva, prognostic algorithm reported as a risk score," which describes the brand name ScoliScore test from Tansgenomic, Inc.

The Molecular Diagnostic Services (MolDX) Program was created in 2011 by MAC Palmetto GBA to identify, establish coverage, and facilitate reimbursement for molecular diagnostic tests. One crucial aspect of the program is the registration and identification of MDTs. In the MolDX model, each individual molecular assay is tracked by a unique Z-identifier code, and all tests falling under the program's scope must include the designated Z code on claims.

The Z codes are unique alphanumeric tracking codes comprising of five characters. They are used to identify and track individual molecular diagnostic laboratory test, facilitating transparent tracking of relevant utilization. For example, in 2019, Natera, a genetic testing developer, announced the assignment of two Z-codes for its Signatera test: DEX Z-Code Identifier ZB8DC for Signatera Recurrence Monitoring Whole Exome Design and Plasma Test, and ZB8DD for Signatera Recurrence Monitoring Single Plasma Test.

The registration of tests is carried out through the Diagnostics Exchange™ (DEX), an online test catalog. DEX is a web-based service designed to identify tests and promote transparency in evidence-based coverage for these tests. During the registration process, comprehensive information about the test is collected, including its name, performing laboratory, intended use, analytes measured, and methodologies employed. This tool enables laboratories to confidentially share test information with MolDX through an online platform. The test registry catalog is available for reference and review by other stakeholders within the healthcare system.

When submitting claims for reimbursement, test providers must include the Z code along with the most accurate CPT and/or HCPCS code that describes the specific test performed. If a test does not have a specific code assigned, an unlisted code is used (e.g., CPT 81479 for unspecified molecular pathology procedure). The Z code bridges the detailed information associated with the test on file and the claim details submitted for adjudication. This allows payors to understand the specific service rendered, facilitating accurate and automated claim adjudication. The unique Z code identifier reduces the need to provide more information about the test on each claim. Tests billed using the following CPT codes will require a Z-Code:

- Molecular Pathology Tier 1 – 81105-81112, 81120-81121, 81161-81383

- Molecular Pathology Tier 2 – 81400-81408

- Genomic Sequencing Procedures (GSP) – 81410-81471

- Molecular Multianalyte Assays (MAAA) – 81493-81595
- Administrative MAAA Code – MAAA codes for molecular tests only
- Microbiology – 81513-81514, 87154-87801
- PLA – PLA codes for molecular tests only
- NOC (Not Otherwise Classified) codes – 81479, 81599, 84999, 85999, 86849, 87999

The MolDX Program covers multiple jurisdictions, some of which are overseen by other MACs. A total of 28 states are part of the MolDX Program. All private, reference, and hospital laboratories that perform molecular diagnostic testing in these states are required to submit Z codes for Medicare reimbursement. Several private plans, such as UnitedHealthcare, have also adopted the program.

Note that obtaining a Z-code doesn't guarantee that the test is covered or reimbursed. Laboratories requesting a Z code can submit validation documentation and references for technology assessment, which is reviewed by Palmetto as part of its coverage determination process. Coverage determination and payment will be discussed in later chapters.

LEVEL II HCPCS CODES FOR MEDICAL PRODUCTS

HCPCS Level II is a standardized coding system primarily used to identify drugs, biologicals, supplies, and services that are not included in the CPT code set, which is primarily for reporting healthcare professional services. It includes ambulance services and durable medical equipment, prosthetics, orthotics, and supplies (DMEPOS) when used outside a physician's office. There are about 8,000 HCPCS level II codes. Suppliers of medical products, such as drugs, biologicals, supplies, and durable medical equipment, often use HCPCS Level II codes to help with reimbursement.

HCPCS Level II codes are also alpha-numeric codes because they consist of a single alphabetical letter followed by four numeric digits. HCPCS Level II coding system classifies medically similar products into categories for efficient claims process, and code chapters group related codes together based on the type of service or item being coded. The letter that begins the HCPCS Level II code represents the code chapter to which the HCPCS code belongs. For example, HCPCS level II code G0463 is for a hospital outpatient clinic visit, A-codes for ambulance services and radiopharmaceuticals, and J-codes for injectable drugs. Each code has descriptive terminology identifying a category of like items manufactured by different suppliers.

The HCPCS level II codes are maintained by CMS, which is responsible for adding, revising, and deleting HCPCS level II codes. Applications for code changes, including new codes, should be submitted to CMS through the electronic application intake system, Medicare Electronic

Application Request Information System™ (MEARIS™). HCPCS level II code applications are reviewed by a group comprising federal government employees who represent the major parts of CMS, as well as other federal agencies such as the Department of Veterans Affairs and the Department of Defense.

Drugs and biologicals are reviewed quarterly, while non-drug and non-biological products are reviewed at least bi-annually. CMS also hosts bi-annual public meetings that allow interested parties to make oral presentations and/or submit written comments in response to CMS's preliminary HCPCS level II coding decisions. These meetings allow stakeholders to give feedback on CMS's preliminary coding decisions and help shape the final coding determinations.

CMS's coding determination is primarily guided by policies and policy changes. While cost and pricing are not considered when making coding determination, CMS considers clinical effectiveness, regulatory guidelines, and other factors when making coding decisions, and these decisions are essential for accurate claims processing and reimbursement. For example, since 2018, CMS had issued unique HCPCS level II code (J-codes) for individual biosimilar products and these codes differ from their reference products, while generic drugs are generally reported using the same code for their referenced products. This coding arrangement facilitates Medicare's payment policies for biosimilar and generic drugs. However, recently, to ensure accurate separate payment for single-source drugs and biologicals, CMS added or revised at least 40 HCPCS level II codes to separately identify drugs approved by FDA through 505(b)(2) pathway usually reserved for modified innovator drug and the drugs were later not rated as therapeutically equivalent to corresponding innovator drugs. This policy change affects some generic drugs.

When any of the following criteria are met, CMS deems no new code is needed for a new item, including:

1. No new or modified code is established if an existing code adequately describes the new item. "Adequately" means the existing code describes items:

   - Functions like the new item.
   - No significant therapeutic distinctions from the new item.

2. If an existing code describes items that provide almost the same functionality with only minor distinctions from the new item, the new item may be grouped with that code and the code descriptor changed to reflect the distinctions.

3. A code is not established for an item that is used only in the inpatient setting (use ICD-10 codes and most items are packaged) or for an item that is not diagnostic or therapeutic.

4. A new or modified code is not established for an item that has not been cleared or approved by FDA.

5. Applications for non-drug items that are not regulated by the FDA and not yet available in the U.S. market will be considered incomplete and will not be processed.

Three examples from 2022 HCPCS level II coding requests and decisions illustrate how CMS uses these criteria in making coding determinations.

Feelix stethoscope

Sonavi Labs requested a new HCPCS level II code to identify Feelix stethoscope, a device that collects recordings of patient body sounds (e.g., cough) and allows physicians to review recordings remotely, as well as run diagnostic and prognostic algorithms for specific respiratory diseases (e.g., chronic obstructive pulmonary disease, pneumonia, asthma, and cystic fibrosis). The Feelix Stethoscope is a prescription-only device that has obtained FDA 510(k) clearance, which indicates its safety and effectiveness. The applicant believes no existing code defines devices used to telemeter, analyze, and diagnose body sound recordings.

CMS believes that the Feelix Stethoscope can be reported using existing remote monitoring CPT codes, including CPT 99453 "Remote monitoring of physiologic parameters, initial set up and patient education on use of equipment," 99454, "Remote monitoring of physiologic parameters, supply with daily recordings or programmed alert transmission, each 30 days," and 99457, "Remote physiologic monitoring treatment management services, 20 minutes or more of clinical staff/physician/other qualified healthcare professional time in calendar month requiring interactive communication with the patient/caregiver during the month."

<u>Oxyband Wound Dressing Matrix</u>

Oxyband requested a new HCPCS level II code to identify Oxyband Wound Dressing Matrix, which received FDA 510(k) clearance. CMS's preliminary coding recommendation was to use the exiting HCPCS code A6204 for the OxybandTM Wound Dressing Matrix. In response, OxyBand cited the unique design of their Wound Dressing Matrix and published studies showing healing of non-healing, chronic wounds, and regeneration of tissue as justifications for a new code.

CMS finalized its decision as proposed and pointed out that in the FDA 510(k) notification letter, the OxyBand Wood Dressing was stated to be substantially equivalent to another brand of dressing, which is currently coded under A6204. CMS recommended that OxyBand approaches the FDA and asks about the most appropriate classification of the OxyBand Wound Dressing considering the new information provided.

<u>Cooler Heads Cooling Cap</u>

Cooler Heads requested a new HCPCS level II code to identify Cooling Cap used with the Portable Scalp Cooling System, which is for adult patients undergoing chemotherapy for solid tumor to prevent chemotherapy-induced hair loss. The treatment can be administered by the user, their caregiver, or a nurse in a chemotherapy treatment center, for a home setting and during transit to home from the treatment center. The system received FDA 510(k) clearance.

CMS believes the Cooling Cap is not suitable for coding in HCPCS level II because this product, if covered, would be expected to be included within the payment for the professional service.

Even for a new technology that has received Medicare coverage determination, it's possible that no new code is created. The new technology might be assigned to an existing code if CMS determines that the new technology is already identified by an existing HCPCS code. For HCPCS Level II codes for DMEPOS, new technology developers should submit a code verification request to CMS' contractor for Pricing, Data Analysis and Coding (PDAC), which has been Palmetto GBA since 1993, to seek clarification on whether an existing code is appropriate or a new code is justified. CMS does not have to create a new code or product-specific code for a new technology if an existing code is available, even though it's up to interpretation what is as "identified." For example, in the case of Feelix stethoscope, there might be different thoughts on whether sound recording is "identified" by recording of physiologic parameters.

Under certain circumstances, assigning a new technology to a miscellaneous code may be possible. A few "miscellaneous/not otherwise classified" codes are available under various headings throughout the HCPCS level II code set. When a new code is appropriate, but the change cannot be implemented and incorporated into billing and claims processing systems right away when the coverage determination is made, an unclassified code may be assigned meanwhile until a new code can be implemented. This allows claims to be processed for the new technology.

Miscellaneous codes are important because they let suppliers begin billing immediately for a service or item when it is cleared or approved by the FDA, even though no distinct code that describes the service or item yet. Insurers may assign a miscellaneous code for use when a request for a new code is being considered under the HCPCS review process. Using miscellaneous codes also helps avoid creating distinct codes for items or services rarely used or for which few claims are expected to be filed, thus maintaining a more manageable coding system size. Additionally, miscellaneous codes enable suppliers to submit claims to private or public insurers when CMS decides not to create a specific code for a new technology.

Obtaining a code is necessary for a medical product to receive separate payment, although coding assignment is not a guarantee for coverage or payment. Once a new code is created, it's used to submit claims for the new technology. However, until national Medicare coverage and payment guidelines have been established for a new code, the

Medicare coverage and payment determinations for these items may be made based on the discretion of the Medicare contractors processing claims for these items.

ICD-10 DIAGNOSIS AND PROCEDURE CODES

The US version of ICD-10 consists of two medical code sets—ICD-10-CM and ICD-10-PCS. ICD-10-CM is a diagnosis code set used for all healthcare settings, while ICD-10-PCS is a procedure code set used only in hospital inpatient settings. Responsibility for maintaining the ICD-10-CM and ICD-10-PCS is divided between two agencies under the HHS. The National Center for Health Statistics (NCHS) within the CDC maintains the classification of diagnoses, while the CMS maintains the classification of procedures.

Compared to the previous ninth version, the granularity of ICD-10-CM and ICD-10-PCS is vastly improved, which offers greater specificity in identifying health conditions. The number of diagnosis codes increased from below 15,000 in the ninth version to about 70,000 in the tenth version, while the number of procedure codes jumped from fewer than 4,000 to over 70,000. The transition to ICD-10-CM and ICD-10-PCS occurred on October 1, 2015.

ICD-10-CM codes are three to seven characters long and the first 3 characters are the general categories, representing a disease or group of related diseases and conditions. For example, C00-D49 are for neoplasms, while Z00-Z99, commonly called the z-codes, are new additions to report social determinants of health, which refer to adverse social conditions that negatively affect a person's health or healthcare, including transportation insecurity (Z59.82) and material hardship (Z59.87).

The following four to seven characters in an ICD-10-CM code can be numbers or letters, with each additional character providing more specific diagnostic information. As an example, dementia is classified in ICD-10-CM using categories F01, F02, and F03, based on the etiology and severity (unspecified, mild, moderate, or severe). Here are examples of vascular dementia ICD-10-CM codes and the corresponding conditions they represent:

- F01: Vascular dementia
- F01.A: Vascular dementia, mild
- F01.A1: Vascular dementia, mild, with behavioral disturbance
- F01.A11: Vascular dementia, mild, with agitation

ICD-10-CM codes are used in claim reporting for all care settings to provide information about the clinical context in which a service or procedure is performed. Payers assess whether a patient's circumstances meet the coverage criteria for a service or procedure based on the ICD-10-CM codes reported on the claim. Coding instructions often accompany payers' coverage determinations. For example, when it comes to the coverage determination for ERG, MACs issued articles specifying the patient diagnoses required to support the medical necessity for billing ERG codes. The articles list the exact ICD-10-CM codes for claims, such as E11.3511-E11.3513 for Type 2 diabetes with proliferative diabetic retinopathy with macular edema and G45.3 for transient visual loss.

But ICD-10-PCS is a seven-character alphanumeric code system used to describe procedures performed in inpatient hospitals. While it is part of ICD-10, the coding structure of ICD-10-PCS is distinct from that of ICD-10-CM. It does not resemble CPT – the other procedural code set used to report hospital outpatient procedures.

In hospital inpatient admissions, payment amounts are tied to the diagnosis-related group (DRG), which categorizes patients based on similar diagnosis and resource use. The assignment of patients to DRGs relies on ICD-10-CM and ICD-10-PCS codes reported on claims, and several patient factors. As discussed in later payment chapter, the DRG grouping logic first assigns a case to major diagnostic categories (MDCs) based on the principal diagnosis reported using ICD-10-CM. It then allocates the case to either medical or surgical categories within an MDC based on the presence of surgical procedures reported using ICD-10-PCS. Further DRG assignment is based on ICD-10-CM codes for cases in medical categories and ICD-10-PCS codes in surgical categories.

The coding structure of ICD-10-PCS resembles a Powerball with multiple options for each of the seven characters. The choice of a number or alphabet for each character positions is not random but follows logical and intuitive rules. Each of the seven characters corresponds to a specific aspect of a procedure, including section, body system, root operation, body part, approach, device, and qualifier. ICD-10-PCS codes are not arbitrary numbers but structured descriptions of procedures, with each code value explaining one feature of the procedure.

The first character offers 17 sections to choose from, represented by the numbers 0–9 and the letters B–D, F–H and X. Most medical and surgical procedure codes are found in section 0, which encompasses most ICD-10-PCS codes. Sections 1–9 cover medical and surgical related procedures, such as obstetrical procedures, administration of substances, and measurement and monitoring of body functions. Sections B–D and F–H are for ancillary sections, including imaging procedures, nuclear medicine, and substance abuse treatment. Section X is dedicated to new technology procedures.

Character two to seven provide 34 values to choose from, including numbers 0-9 and the letters of the alphabet (excluding O and I to avoid confusion with numbers zero and one). The 34 possible character values for each of the six-character positions give ICD-10-PCS immense potential, as the same value in a different position conveys a different meaning.

Section X was introduced based on public comments regarding the classification of new technology procedures. The medical coding community generally opposes creating new codes for specific drugs, devices, or supplies used in inpatient setting because these services are typically bundled into episodes of inpatient stay under the DRG system. Section X was established to provide a separate category for certain new technology procedures and has been in recent years, primarily utilized for the New Technology Add-on payment, a transitional payment adjustment for new technologies.

Section X codes maintain consistency with other sections in ICD-10-PCS by using the same coding structure and value definitions. For example, the new procedure for COVID-19 vaccine injection can be represented by the ICD-10-PCS code XW013U6, suggesting the introduction of COVID-19 vaccine into subcutaneous tissue, percutaneous approach, new technology group 6. The code starts with X, denoting the new technology section, followed by body system "W" for "anatomic regions," which is often used when no specific body system is identified. Root operating "0" corresponds to introduction – putting in or on a therapeutic, diagnostic, nutritional, physiological, or prophylactic substance except blood or blood products. Body part "1" refers to subcutaneous tissue, and approach "3" is for percutaneous. Device "U" is for COVID-19 vaccine.

In section X, the seventh character is used exclusively to indicate the new technology group, which is updated yearly when new technology codes are added to the system. For example, new technology codes added in the first year have the seventh character value 1 for new technology group 1. So, qualifier "6" simply means new technology group 6.

New technology developers can request new ICD-10-PCS codes or coding changes through the MEARIS system. Proposals for new codes must describe the requested code and the reasoning behind the need for the new code. Supporting references and literature may also be submitted. Proposals need to adhere to the structure and conventions of the classification system.

The ICD-10 Coordination and Maintenance (C&M) Committee, co-chaired by representatives from NCHS and CMS, holds public meetings twice a year, generally in spring and fall, to discuss proposed revisions. The C&M Committee plays an advisory role. They recommend proposed code revision during the meetings, but no decisions are made at these meetings. The Director of NCHS and the Administrator of CMS make all final diagnosis and procedure coding decisions, respectively.

PART THREE

PAYMENT SYSTEMS AND MEDICAL INNOVATIONS

Medicare employs over ten distinct payment systems. In fiscal year 2020, Medicare spent $104.1 billion on inpatient services covered under the Inpatient Prospective Payment System, $52 billion on hospital outpatient care paid under the Outpatient Prospective Payment System, and $64.8 billion for physician and other health professional services paid under the Physician Fee Schedule.

We encounter daily payment systems designed under different ideas. For example, in a restaurant or café, when the dishes on a menu — appetizer, entrée, and dessert — are priced item by item, we are paying for the food under a fee for service model. Sometimes, a restaurant offers lunch/dinner specials — a three-course meal for a fixed price, for example. Medicare often uses bundled payment approaches in its payment system design. There is also an all-you-can-eat buffet, where the fee is charged per capita instead of per item.

How payment arrangements influence consumer choices: would you order and eat different items under different payment arrangements? For example, would you order appetizer or dessert if they are charged separately instead of as a part of a bundled meal? Now imagining that 80% or so of the charge for the meal would be paid by payer instead of out of your own pocket, would you order something entirely different? This is a main concern of third-party payers, and adjusting payment arrangement is one of the tools payers use to incentivize or disincentivize certain behaviors.

How healthcare providers are reimbursed by payer for their services is one of often-debated and often-legislated topics in America's healthcare due to the providers' role as gatekeepers in regulating healthcare service consumptions. It's also a critical product-to-market question for entrepreneurs and venture capitalists, as the answers to which decide the likelihood of establishing a sustainable and successful business and mission enterprise in the healthcare industry from a medical innovation. For a new medical technology, reimbursement is the primary driver to profitability as it assumes the all-important revenue stream that keeps a company viable.

The US healthcare payment systems have evolved over time with increasing complexity and sophistication in response to competing priorities. The design of payment system aims to incentivize efficient care delivery and minimize unnecessary costs, while at the same time the objectives of payment design also include providing adequate compensation for healthcare providers to ensure patient access to care and not penalizing healthcare providers for caring for sicker, more complex, and high-cost patients. Public payers, like Medicare, also have a responsibility for stewardship of public funds.

The description and discussion of payment systems in this chapter will focus on Medicare programs. The creation and updates of Medicare payment systems are required to go through public rulemaking and commenting process, which provides ample information for reference. Because of Medicare's size and influence, private payers often adopt the same or similar payment policies. For example, many BCBS plans utilize Medicare-like diagnosis related groups for hospital inpatient care reimbursement, and Medicare's physician fee schedule creates a platform around which private insurers and physicians often negotiate.

This chapter will start with an overview of the revolutionary changes in Medicare's payment system, followed by a summary of key design features across different payment systems, before diving into three most frequently used Medicare payment systems – inpatient PPS, outpatient PPS, and physician fee schedule. The examination of payment arrangements for new technologies will be organized around common issues facing new technologies and discussed by bringing in recent examples.

THE REVOLUTION OF HEALTHCARE PAYMENT SYSTEMS

The landscape of healthcare payment systems in the United States has seen significant paradigm shifts over the past century. Payers have transitioned from passive role to pursuing various payment system designs aimed at improving the quality and efficiency of care delivery. The evolution of healthcare payment design has transformed the way providers are reimbursed, moving from retrospective cost-based reimbursement to prospective payment models that incentivize efficiency, and more recently, to value-based payment models. Understanding the revolution in healthcare payment systems is crucial for comprehending how new medical innovations are reimbursed and funded in healthcare.

In the early 20th century, the precursor to modern health insurance was established through Blue Cross and Blue Shield plans, which employed a reimbursement system known as "cost plus." Under this payment scheme, doctors were reimbursed based on their self-determined "reasonable and customary charges," while hospitals received reimbursement based on a percentage of their actual costs plus a percentage of their working and equity capital.

Critics often pointed out that these rate-setting approaches provide no incentive for healthcare provider to control cost or charge. Between 1950-1964, per-patient day hospital expense rose by a staggering 166%. The cost growth also reflected the increasing intensity of hospital services enabled by new technologies (e.g., kidney transplant, intensive care) and increasing staffing levels. During the same period, both hospital rates and physicians' fees increased more than any other major part in the "Consumer Price Index," such as food and housing.

When Medicare was first established, to appease healthcare providers, Medicare modeled its payment systems on prevailing private insurance plans, such as Blue Cross and Blue Shield plans and Aetna's plan for Federal employees (later becoming the model for Medicare Part B). Hospitals could nominate an intermediary, such as Blue Cross and Blue Shield companies, to process billing claims and serve as the primary contact point.

Payment methods for facilities (hospitals, nursing home, and home health) were based on reasonable costs determined retrospectively. Payments for doctors and other suppliers were based on the lower of a local calculation of "customary, prevailing and reasonable" fees or their own customary or actual charges. Leveraging existing payment models and using insurance companies for payment processing helped with the smooth implementation of the Medicare program, which was up and running in a year.

With professional self-control being the only control, escalating healthcare cost became a growing national concern. Healthcare fraud and abuse became an easy target, which dominated several senate hearings in 1969. In response, the Nixon administration proposed a "Health Cost Effectiveness Amendments of 1969," which had provisions to strengthen administrative controls over program payments and experiment with prospective payment methods.

John G. Veneman, the undersecretary of what was then the Department of Health, Education, and Welfare, made a blunt and prophetic declaration: "In the past, decisions on healthcare delivery were largely professional ones. Now, the decisions will be largely political." The Social Security Amendments of 1972, signed by President Nixon on July 1, 1972, introduced price controls for the first time, establishing Medicare payment limits for hospitals and doctors. This marked the beginning of a pattern of periodic legislative responses to contain healthcare spending growth that has continued to the present day.

In 1983, Congress adopted the most significant change in the Medicare program since its inception by approving a prospective payment system (PPS) for hospital inpatient services. Under the new inpatient PPS, Medicare establishes payment rates prospectively, instead of based on hospital actual cost retrospectively. The predetermined rates pay for an entire hospital stay and are the same for patients assigned to the same diagnosis-related group (DRG), regardless of whether a patient stays in the hospital 5 days or 10 days.

The inpatient PPS heralded the era of PPS, which continues to day. The PPS family now includes outpatient PPS, home health PPS, hospice PPS, inpatient psychiatric PPS, inpatient rehabilitation PPS, long-term care PPS, and skilled nursing PPS. Nearly all Medicare payment systems (with some unique exceptions, such as payment for organ acquisition) have transitioned to a rate-setting process that establishes payment rates prospectively.

The Balanced Budget Act (BBA) of 1997 included extensive legislative changes aimed at combating double-digit rates of annual healthcare inflation in the early 1990s. In addition to reducing payment increases to providers, the BBA established Medicare+Choice, later renamed Medicare Advantage, to offer a new array of managed care and other health plan choices for seniors. A financial journalist summarized the popular understanding of Part C's purpose as "to incorporate the cost-saving measures of 'managed care' into the Medicare Program."

Health maintenance organizations (HMOs), a type of managed care plan, gained popularity in the early 1990s, fueled primarily by employers wanting to control healthcare costs. By 1995, most Americans with employer-sponsored health insurance had enrolled in some form of managed care plans. In addition to utilization control practices, such as gatekeeping, utilization review, clinical practice guidelines, and selective physician contracting, HMOs commonly used capitation as a payment model to incentivize doctors to exercise greater financial discipline.

Capitation is a prospective payment often as a flat fee per patient per month or year, where a payer makes a fixed payment for a defined set of services, regardless of the amount of services actually provided. Under this arrangement, doctors bear greater risk for the quantity and intensity of health services consumed by a patient. Although HMOs succeeded in controlling premium hikes, the constraints provoked resistance from patients and doctors, leading to a retreat from some of the more severe managed care policies, such as capitation and narrowing provider network.

Despite these reforms that helped slow down spending growth temporarily, per capita health spending continued to outpace personal income growth consistently, and total U.S. health spending steadily increased as a share of gross domestic product (GDP). In his 2006 book, *Redefining Health*

Care: Creating Value-Based Competition on Results, Harvard professor Michael Porter proposed a new strategic framework for transforming healthcare value. Value was defined as patient-relevant outcomes divided by costs. Although the primary aims of the Affordable Care Act (ACA) of 2010 were to expand health insurance coverage, it also had various provisions to shift Medicare from paying for volume to value.

The ACA introduced a range of hybrid payment models and established the Center for Medicare & Medicaid Innovation (CMMI), an innovation lab within CMS, to test new payment models. Under the general setup of new payment models, a certain percentage of traditional fee for service payments under Medicare's existing payment systems would be at risk based on whether a healthcare provider compares favorably with a set of value targets. Specifically, ACA kicked start pay-for-performance programs that tie Medicare payment to performance on a set of quality measures and alternative payment models that hold providers accountable for spendings beyond a siloed care setting and/or the duration of one payment unit (e.g., one visit or inpatient admission).

The establishment of pay-for-performance programs was driven by initiatives and pilot testing in response to recommendations by the Institute of Medicine (IOM) in its 2001 report, *Crossing the Quality Chasm: A New Health System* *for the 21st Century.* The ACA created three hospital quality programs, including the Hospital Value-Based Purchasing Program (HVBP), the Hospital-Acquired Condition Reduction Program (HACRP), and the Hospital Readmissions Reduction Program (HRRP).

Later legislations, including the Protecting Access to Medicare Act (PAMA) of 2014 and Medicare Access and CHIP Reauthorization Act (MACRA) of 2015, established pay-for-performance programs for skilled nursing facilities and physicians. Quality performance targets are often based on national benchmarks with risk adjustments to account for a provider's unique patient mix. Since the benchmarks are routinely updated, achieving financial success in the quality programs often requires a provider to consistently outperform the rising tide of the benchmark.

Since its inception in 2010, CMMI has launched over 50 models that cover a wide array of settings (e.g., hospital, skilled nursing, and primary care), patient conditions (e.g., oncology, diabetes, chronic kidney disease, and cardiovascular conditions), and model designs (e.g., episode-based, and population-based). Approximately 40% of Medicare traditional fee-for-service payments, 30% of commercial payments, and 23% of Medicaid payments are made through some form of value-based arrangements.

Despite these impressive numbers, only six of the tested models delivered significant financial savings, with net savings (after subtracting bonus paid to providers) ranging between 1 and 3%. Some model design issues may have reduced the amount of saving Medicare could have achieved. Many models adjust the patient risk profile when setting financial benchmarks, which creates "opportunities for potential gaming and upcoding among participants — and reduced savings for Medicare." Upcoding refers to the practice when a healthcare provider submits codes for more severe and expensive diagnoses or procedures than the provider diagnosed or performed.

Provider participation in alternative payment models is generally voluntary. To attract more participation, many models offer the option of one-sided or upside-only model, in which providers share in savings if spending is below the benchmark but are not responsible for losses if spending exceeds the benchmark. It's a delicate balance because when the administration dialed up the pressure towards two-sided risk models there was a noticeable withdrawal of participation.

In CMMI's refreshed vision and strategy for the next 10 years, the center aims to address these issues based on lessons learned. Along with improving its methods, the strategy refresh also signifies a change in thinking. While reducing costs to improve accessibility remains a strategic aim in line with the center's statutory mandate, the refreshed goals include assessing the success of models not only on their ability to save Medicare money, but also on whether they promote transformation in other dimensions of the health system, such as equity, care delivery, patient outcomes, and/or market characteristics.

KEY DESIGN FEATURES OF MEDICARE PAYMENT SYSTEMS

Medicare employs over ten distinct payment systems and reimbursement methodologies to compensate for services provided by different types of healthcare providers in various care settings. In addition to the PPS family, Medicare also utilizes several fee schedule systems. These fee schedule systems establish a list of maximum fees used to reimburse doctors, providers, and suppliers fee-for-service. While there are many payment systems within Medicare, each of which has its own unique history, design, and annual rate-setting process, we will focus on the common design features that can be found across many of these systems, using the three most common payment systems – inpatient PPS, outpatient PPS, and physician fee schedule – as illustrative examples. By examining these systems, we can better understand the general design of Medicare's payment framework and updating process.

Most Medicare payment systems include three key components:

- A system to differentiate and quantify relative costs/resource use of different services, procedures or bundles of services/procedures covered under a payment system. This system usually involves attaching a relative weight to each service, procedure, or bundle of services/procedures. The relative weight creates a subtle shift from focusing on payment accuracy and adequacy of each service to parity among different services.

- A base rate or conversion factor to convert service weight to payment. As updates to base payment rate are often the result of legislative interventions, overtime, payment accuracy and adequacy have become an across-the-board policy issue.

- Provider level rate adjustments to account for differences in some provider characteristics, such as geographic location. Most payment systems include some form of wage adjustments to account for geographic variations in labor costs.

Now, let's examine the inpatient PPS, outpatient PPS and PFS to see how the components work together.

Under the inpatient PPS, each inpatient admission is assigned to a DRG. The experience with cost-based reimbursement has shown that it promoted a near-maximum growth rate and demand for new technology. The PPS design adopts a bundled approach with a payment unit encompassing a whole inpatient stay, rather than just an item provided during an inpatient stay. This approach provides incentives for more selective use of expensive treatment options.

Each DRG has a payment weight assigned to it based on the average resources used to treat Medicare patients in that DRG. For example, the DRG weight for Chimeric Antigen Receptor T-Cell (CAR-T) and other immunotherapies is 36.14 for 2023. When DRG A's weight is twice as that of DRG B, it indicates that, on average, the treatment costs for patients grouped into DRG A are double that of DRG B.

The inpatient PPS base payment rate is divided into an operating and capital portion. Taking 2023 as an example, the base payment rate is $6,859 (excluding any applicable penalties due to quality reporting or meaningful EHR use requirements), including $6,375 for operating and $484 for capital. The national payment rate for a particular DRG is the product of its DRG weight and base rate. For example, the payment rate for CAR-T is $247,884, which is the product of DRG weight 36.14 and the national base rate of $6,859.

The inpatient PPS is built on an "averaging" concept. At an individual case level, the payment may be more or less than the estimated costs, but on average, it is expected to be enough to cover hospital costs. To incentivize efficiency, the inpatient PPS system sacrifices payment accuracy for individual cases. Inpatient PPS has several provider-level payment adjustments to offset some systematic provider-level cost differences, including the provider wage index to account for geographic wage differences, indirect medical education (IME) add-on payments for teaching hospitals, and disproportionate share hospital (DSH) add-on payments for hospitals with a higher share of low income and Medicaid patients. There are also special payment arrangements for certain rural hospitals under inpatient PPS.

Conceptually, the justification for IME and DSH add-ons is the uneven distribution of high-cost cases among hospitals, even though it's not always possible to separate the drivers of higher costs (e.g., patient complexity vs. overutilization). Significant underpayment may occur when some hospital characteristics attract a higher share of patients with above-average treatment costs, which justifies add-on payments, even though there is no denying the influence of politics at play in the creation of payment add-ons.

The design of outpatient PPS mirrors that of inpatient PPS but with a simpler base rate and fewer provider level payment adjustments. Services paid under the outpatient PPS are classified into groups called Ambulatory Payment Classifications (APC). Services in each APC are clinically similar and require similar resources. A weight is established for each APC.

The outpatient PPS conversion factor is a national dollar multiplier converting APC weights to payment rates. National APC payment rates, without geographic and provider-level adjustments, can be computed by multiplying PPS conversion factor with the APC weight. The wage index used in the inpatient PPS is also applied in the outpatient PPS to adjust for geographic wage differences. Under outpatient PPS, the only available provider-level adjustment is a 7.1% payment increase for certain rural hospitals.

Unlike inpatient and outpatient PPS, PFS is a fee schedule system where each service is paid individually without bundling for most services. RVUs define the value of each service or procedure relative to all services and procedures paid under PFS. This scale is based on a complex formula that gauges the amount and intensity of physician work, clinical and nonclinical resources needed to perform this service, factoring in the cost of overhead and malpractice insurance.

Like outpatient PPS, a PFS conversion factor is used to convert RVU to a national payment rate for each service or procedure. Geographic Practice Cost Indices (GPCIs), like the wage index used in inpatient and outpatient PPS, adjust for geographic cost variations. However, GPCIs have their own definition, data, and methods.

Injection or infusion drugs administered in hospital outpatient department or doctor office can be reimbursed under Medicare Part B through the outpatient PPS or PFS, respectively. The payment amount for drugs is not determined by the APC weight or PFS RVU. Medicare payment for Part B drugs is set at an average sales price (ASP) plus six percent based on sales data submitted by pharmaceutical companies quarterly.

The ASP methodology captures price changes over time but does not exert control over them. However, under the Inflation Reduction Act (IRA) of 2022, drug companies must pay rebates to Medicare if their prices rise faster than inflation for drugs used by Medicare beneficiaries. IRA also requires that the federal government begins negotiating prices for certain high-impact drugs covered under Medicare.

The maintenance and updates to the payment systems are managed through annual federal rule-making cycles. Each payment system has its own annual updating schedule. The general process is CMS first issues a proposed rule and then give the public a period, usually 60 days, to submit comments. CMS then incorporates public comments and makes decisions in the final rule. The standard timeline, with occasional exceptions, requires that the final rules are released before a new fiscal/calendar year starts, as per statutory deadlines.

Unless urgent, such as when mandated by Congress with an implementation deadline, in a final rule, CMS normally does not propose new policies or make final decisions on policies not proposed. This is because CMS must provide the public with an opportunity to provide feedback. New issues raised in comment period but not proposed often are addressed in the next or future rulemaking cycles. This sometimes disappoints commentators who expect to see immediate changes in the final rule in response to their comments or communication with CMS during the proposed rule comment period.

Payment rate updates are a routine part of the annual rulemaking process to implement legislative mandate with established methods and data. However, they often attract a lot of public attention. Under inpatient and outpatient PPS, annual payment updates are based on a CMS market basket, which measures the change in price over time of the same mix of goods and services used in providing healthcare from the base period. The market basket is used to update payments in various PPS payment systems.

Payment update is also a tool used by Congress to control spending growth. For example, the ACA of 2010 includes a market basket reduction for inpatient and outpatient services starting from 2010 and extending for 10 years and beyond. Another example is the Medicare sustainable growth rate (SGR) introduced by the BBA of 1997, under which a cross-the-board reduction would be triggered if physician service spending grows faster than the rate of economy growth using a complicated formula. Since

2002, Congress would pass short-term legislation yearly to avert the SGR payment reduction. In 2015 The SGR payment reduction would have accumulated to more than a 20 percent cut for professional services when Congress finally fixed the SGR permanently in the MACRA of 2015. Under MACRA, however, there is a zero percent update of the fee schedule from now to 2025. Physicians can either earn a bonus by participating in Alternative Payment Models (APMs) or receive a performance-based payment adjustment in the Merit-based Incentive Payment System (MIPS).

Even though CMS does not review the assignment of every DRG/APC/RVU annually, the DRG/APC/RVU weights are recalibrated every year using the most recent input data available. One guiding principle of annual DRG/APC/RVU weight recalibration is that it must be budget neutral. Generally, the aggregate Medicare payments, including all the changes to the DRG/APC/RVU assignments and weights, must be kept at the same level as if no changes were made. This creates a zero-sum game situation where payment increase for some services would be at the expense of payment decrease for other services.

Each payment system has its own methods of implementing budget neutrality. Under PFS, for example, a budget-neutral adjustment is applied to the conversion factor to offset any payment changes due to RVU updates. One recent case is that in CY 2021, CMS increased work RVU for the majority EM services, resulting in nearly an 11% reduction to the PFS conversion factor. Although some specialties are likely to experience major improvements in Medicare PFS payments, the reduced PFS conversion factor could result in substantial reimbursement reductions for other specialties. Congress stepped in with several annual temporary fixes to smooth the impact.

Due to the data lag, there is a time lag in capturing the costs of new technologies in the weighting system. Taking the fiscal year (FY) 2023 inpatient PPS rule as an example, the final rule was released in 2022, and by then, the most recent data available were 2021 billing claims data and 2020 hospital cost report data, which were used for the recalibration of the FY 2023 DRG weights. If a new medical innovation started being billed by hospitals in 2021, its costs should be captured and reflected in FY 2023 DRG weights but not in FY 2022 or FY 2021 weights. Time lag is a common issue, not limited to inpatient PPS.

However, whether a new medical innovation will significantly affect DRG weights depends on various factors, including the pricing, volume, distribution of the new technology across different DRGs. Since DRG weights measure relative resource use, a technology widely used in many DRGs won't affect relative cost between different DRGs.

WHY MOST REQUESTS TO CREATE A NEW DRG ARE DENIED?

Creating new DRGs or modifying existing ones is a crucial part of the annual rulemaking process. Recognizing the adaptable nature of hospital resource use across different DRGs due to changes in treatment patterns, technology, and other factors, Congress mandates the adjustment of DRG classifications and relative weights at least once a year. While not every DRG is modified, many of the hundreds of pages of inpatient PPS rule each year is dedicated to changes and updates to the DRG systems, including the introduction of new DRGs and revisions to existing ones.

MedTech companies sometimes submit requests for new DRGs, typically to increase payment rates for DRGs associated with specific devices or treatments. However, these requests are rarely accepted by CMS, primarily due to a limited understanding of the DRG grouping logic and CMS's analytical approach. On a broader level, the design of the DRG system, a patient classification system, aims to achieve three key goals:

- Clinical coherence that aligns with clinicians' medical judgement on patient classification

- Meaningful measurement of resource intensity by grouping patients with similar resource utilization patterns, and
- Management simplicity by maintaining a manageable number of DRGs

The current Medicare Severity Diagnosis Related Groups (MS-DRG) system includes over 700 DRGs, with the majority falling within one of 25 mutually exclusive major diagnostic categories (MDCs) or transplant pre-MDC. Each MDC corresponds to a single organ system (e.g., the nervous system and the respiratory system) or cause and is generally associated with a specific medical specialty. While most MDCs focus on a particular body system, five MDCs involve multiple body systems, including injuries, poison, and toxic effect of drugs (MDC 21), burns (MDC 22), factors Influencing health status and other contacts with health services (MDC 23), multiple significant trauma (MDC 24), and human immunodeficiency virus infection (MDC 25).

The DRG assignment starts by classifying a case into one of the 25 MDCs based on the principal diagnosis. The diagnosis codes are based on the ICD-10-CM. Organ transplant cases are not assigned to MDCs but are immediately classified based on the procedure to one of the pre-MDC DRGs, recognizing the high cost associated with these procedures. One nuance about transplant DRGs is that the inpatient PPS payment only reimburses costs associated with the transplant operation. Organ acquisition costs are reimbursed separately using a cost-based approach.

Once a case has been assigned into an MDC, the case is determined to be either medical or surgical based on the presence of a surgical procedure code. The medical-surgical distinction in most MDCs reflects that surgical procedures, which require the use of the operating room, tend to use more hospital resources (e.g., operating room, recovery room, anesthesia). The distinction is also useful in further defining the clinical specialty involved.

Patients are considered surgical if they have a procedure performed in the operating room. The claims data submitted do not specify whether a procedure is performed in an operating room. Surgical patients are identified based on the procedure codes submitted, which are based on the ICD-10-PCS. Surgical procedures were identified by physician panels based on whether the procedure would, in most hospitals, be performed in the operating room.

Once divided into the medical or surgical categories, surgical patients are further classified based on the precise surgical procedure performed, while medical patients are classified based on the precise principal diagnosis for which they were admitted to the hospital. In the surgical category, a case can be classified based on the type of surgical procedure (e.g., percutaneous or bypass) and devices used in the procedure. Since a patient can have multiple procedures in one operation or during an entire inpatient stay, a surgical hierarchy in each MDC ensures that a patient is assigned to only one DRG, which is based on the highest hierarchy of all the procedures performed. In the medical category, usually, each MDC would include a class for neoplasms, symptoms and specific conditions relating to the organ system involved.

Besides the principal diagnosis, the current MS-DRG system uses up to 24 secondary diagnosis codes, and for a few DRGs, also age, sex, and discharge status in DRG assignment. Depending on their severity, these other diagnoses may be designated as complications and comorbidities (CCs) or major complications and comorbidities (MCCs), which are conditions considered to significantly increase hospital costs for treating patients with the same principal diagnosis. The current CC and MCC lists primarily comprise significant acute disease, acute exacerbations of significant chronic diseases, advanced or end-stage chronic diseases, and chronic diseases associated with extensive debility. About 12 percent of all diagnoses were classified as a major CC and 24 percent as a CC. Medicare updates the lists of CCs and MCCs yearly. For FY 2019, 335 base DRGs are subdivided into a total of 761 two or three sub-level DRGs based on the presence of MCC or CC, with higher weight assigned to DRGs with MCC/CC.

Among Medicare patients admitted to inpatient hospitals, many have more than one CCs and/or MCCs. An

Office of Inspector General (OIG) analysis shows that among the 8.7 million inpatient hospital stays, about 40% or 3.5 million stays were billed at the highest severity level, generally with at least one major complication. Nearly half of the $109.8 billion that Medicare spent on inpatient hospital stays in FY 2019 was for stays at the highest severity level.

CMS evaluates requests for new DRGs in line with the fundamental logic of DRG design to ensure clinical and resource use coherence. CMS's clinical advisor typically assesses a new DRG request for clinical similarity. An analytical approach often involves examining the distribution of principal diagnosis codes associated with a medical device or treatment. Clinical similarity is often determined based on the clustering of diagnoses that describe a patient population clinically. Indicators such as length of inpatient stay and treatment cost are commonly used to evaluate resource use. Patients are often grouped into different cohorts based on DRG, principal diagnosis, and a medical device or treatment to assess whether creating a new DRG will improve resource use consistency within a DRG and enhance resource use differentiation between DRGs.

Under the inpatient PPS, most devices, treatments, and medical innovations are bundled into the DRG payment and do not receive separate reimbursement. Hospitals buy the devices, therapies, and medical products for providing various services and then bill Medicare after each patient encounter. When hospitals submit claims to Medicare for reimbursement, the UB-04 medical billing form requires them to include information such as a patient's diagnosis codes, procedure codes, and hospital charges at each revenue code level – revenue code indicates hospital settings a service is provided or charged, such as emergency room or intensive care unit. Charges submitted in claims are converted to costs using cost to charge ratios derived from hospital cost report data, which are used in recalibrating DRG weights annually.

While the use of medical technology during an inpatient stay rarely changes the reimbursement for a specific case, the costs associated with the technology will be considered in the recalibration of DRG weights in future years if hospitals report them in their claims. However, the inability to influence immediate reimbursement serves as a disincentive to report services and procedures that do not impact DRG payment, often leading to the depreciation of a DRG's weight overtime.

For new medical innovations, it typically takes 2-3 years to capture the costs of new technologies/treatments due to data time lag. Once the billing claims data become available, it can be analyzed to understand the patient population, hospital resource use, and DRG payment distribution. The findings should be reviewed from both a clinical perspective and statistical perspective.

To support a request for a new DRG or DRG modification, it's necessary to demonstrate substantial higher costs among cases with a medical device or treatment than those without in the same DRG(s). While it may seem a good selling point to have a separate DRG associated with a specific device or treatment, it does not always increase total DRG payments if a device or treatment is used across a wide range of DRGs with drastically different DRG payment rates. Simulating the potential DRG weight/payment rate for a new DRG and evaluating potential payment redistributions are possible once the criteria are specified. Special attention should be given to cases that are likely to experience reduced payment compared to the DRG rates under the existing payment arrangement. There have been instances in the past that DRG modifications initiated by MedTech manufactures were later reversed due to objections from the provider community.

NEW TECHNOLOGY ADDON PAYMENT

The New Technology Add-on Payment (NTAP) has gained significant attention since CMS granted NTAP for Viz ContaCT (Viz LVO) by Viz. ai, Inc, an applied artificial intelligence (AI) healthcare company. It marks the first time an AI-based technology has received such a designation. The number of NTAP applications and technologies covered has been on the rise, with 18 technologies granted NTAP for fiscal year 2020, compared to fewer than 10 in the first 10 years since its inception. The increase reflects CMS's policy changes in recent years to expand NTAP eligibility criteria and NTAP payment amount in response to public criticism.

The NTAP was created by Congress in 2000 to address the 2-3 year time lag for capturing the costs of a new technology in the inpatient PPS rate-setting process. Its primary goal is to support the timely adoption of new technologies. Although the NTAP designation lasts for about 2-3 years, it provides the recognition a new technology needs for a successful market launch, partly due to the high standards established by CMS for the NTAP designation. Studies on the impact of NTAP have shown a small but significant influence on the uptake of new technologies.

For a technology to be eligible for an NTAP designation, CMS requires compliance with three specific criteria, as mandated in the statute. These criteria are:

- Newness criterion. The medical service or technology must be new, typically within 3 years of receiving FDA approval. It must also not be "substantially similar" to any existing technology. CMS specifies that a technology would be considered not "new" for NTAP if a technology meets all three of the following criteria when compared to existing technology aimed at achieving a therapeutic outcome:

a.   Use the same or a similar mechanism of action.

b.   Be assigned to the same MS-DRG.

c.   Treat the same or similar types of disease and patient population.

Generally, the newness criteria exclude FDA 510k clearance and most generic drug approval, as these products have no clinically meaningful differences compared to an existing product approved by FDA.

- Cost criterion. The medical service or technology must be sufficiently costly to render the existing MS-DRG rate inadequate. To qualify for NTAP, the expected average charges for cases involving the new technology must exceed a threshold set for each MS-DRG. CMS provides step-by-step instructions on how the data and calculations of case costs are determined and annually releases the MS-DRG cost thresholds for NTAP.

- Substantial clinical improvement criteria. The medical service or technology must show a substantial clinical improvement over existing services or technologies. Substantial clinical improvements can be demonstrated in various ways, such as introducing a new treatment for a patient population without current treatment options, developing a new diagnostic tool that can detect an undetectable condition or detect a condition faster with meaningful impact on care management, or providing a technology that offers significantly improved outcomes in terms of mortality, morbidity, and health resource utilization.

In recent years, CMS has established alternative pathways that link FDA special designations and NTAP qualifications. Specifically, products that receive FDA Breakthrough Device status, Qualified Infectious Disease Product (QIDP) designation, or Limited Population Pathway for Antibacterial and Antifungal Drugs (LPAD) pathway are assumed to meet the criteria for newness and substantial improvement. The Breakthrough status, QIDP, and LPAD programs, formalized by the FDA, provide expedited pathways, such as priority review and fast-track designation, for the approval or clearance of devices, infectious disease products, and antibacterial and antifungal drugs that address high clinical unmet needs.

Once a new technology receives NTAP designation, hospitals can include the specific ICD-10-PCS code for the new technology when billing Medicare for inpatient stays where the technology is used, potentially enabling them to receive the new technology add-on payment. For example, in the case of inpatient cases involving Viz LOV, hospitals can include procedure code 4A03X5D in the billing form.

The NTAP payment amount is calculated case by case for each eligible discharge that includes the technology. NTAP payments are made only when the estimated cost of a case exceeds the standard MS-DRG payment, which includes all the provider addon payments (e.g., IME and DSH) but does not include high-cost outlier payment. It's important to note that the estimated case costs include only operating costs and do not include capital costs. Consistently, the NTAP pays to cover operating costs but does not cover capital-related expense. Devices that require capital investment, such as large imaging equipment, are not eligible for NTAP.

The NTAP payment amount is equal to the lesser of 1) 65% of the technology costs, or 2) 65% of the pay cap between the costs and the standard MS-DRG payment. For Viz LOV, the NTAP payment under formula 1) is calculated to be $1,040 (based on a 50% reimbursement rate), which sets an upper limit for Viz LOV's NTAP payment amount. The rate of reimbursement has been increased to 65% in recent years, up from 50%, in response to criticism of inadequate reimbursement for high-cost new technologies such as CAR-T therapies. For QIDP or LPAD products, the reimbursement rate is 75%.

However, not every case that uses Viz LOV would be eligible to receive the maximum NTAP payment amount or any NTAP payment. While subscribing to Viz LOV may add new cost to inpatient stays, any reduction in the consumption of other resources, such as a shorter length of stay or a shorter intensive care unit (ICU) stay, could keep the total costs below the payment, resulting in no NTAP payment. A study evaluating the impact of NTAP policy has shown significant variability in terms of NTAP amount received, both within a technology and between different technologies.

THE DILEMMA OF PAYING FOR CAR-T-LIKE HIGH-COST THERAPIES UNDER INPATIENT PPS

With launch prices ranging from $373,000 to $475,000, CAR-T therapies presented a unique challenge to the bundled and imprecise DRG payment system and serve as a test case for future high-cost new products. CAR-T therapies are genetically altered versions of a patient's own white blood T cells with improved ability to identify and attack cancer cells. The FDA approved two CAR-T therapies, tisagenlecleucel (Kymriah®) and axicabtagene ciloleucel (Yescarta®), in 2017 for patients with relapsed and refractory cancer. In 2019, CMS issued a national coverage decision and began covering CAR-T therapies when provided in healthcare facilities enrolled in the FDA risk evaluation and mitigation strategies (REMS) for FDA-approved indications.

In contrast to traditional cancer treatments such as oral anticancer agents, intravenous chemotherapies, or immunotherapies administered in the outpatient setting, CAR-T therapies are typically administered during inpatient stays, and hospitals are reimbursed under the inpatient PPS. As first, CMS assigned CAR-T cases to an existing MS-DRG – DRG 016, autologous bone marrow transplant with CC/MCC or T-cell immunotherapy, which has an average national rate (with no payment adjustments) of less than $45,000. CMS also granted CAR-T NTAP status and raised NTAP reimbursement ratio from 50% to 65%.

When DRG payment plus NTAP are not enough to cover treatment costs, hospitals may receive more payments through high-cost outlier payment, another part of the inpatient PPS system intended to reduce financial risk to hospitals for treating exceptionally costly cases. To qualify for outlier payment, a case must have costs above the sum of adjusted MS-DRG payments (incl payment adjustments and add-on payments), NTAP, and a fixed loss threshold, which is updated annually and reaches $38,859 in FY 2023. The high-cost outlier payment reimburses the payment gap where costs exceed Medicare payments plus a fixed loss threshold at a rate set at 80%.

At the conclusion of the NTAP period, CMS created a new MS-DRG, DRG 018, specifically for patients receiving CAR-T immunotherapies, and expanded the MS-DRG to cover other immunotherapies in the subsequent year. The national payment rate for DRG 018 is about $250,000 for 2023. One might question why the DRG rate is so much lower than the costs associated with CAR-T therapies.

Understanding this apparent disparity requires a ride down memory lane in the history of hospital "charge master." The charge master is essentially a comprehensive list of prices or charges for procedures and products, often comprising thousands of items. It was originally developed and widely used for payment negotiations when hospital rates were based on individual services. When Medicare transitioned to the inpatient PPS system, charges reported on claims were used for calibrating DRG weights for many years. Hospitals routinely update and inflate charges annually. Over time, charges became disconnected from costs or payments under the PPS system, as a more nuanced review aimed at aligning charges with costs tends to focus on new or highly competitive services.

Recognizing the disconnection between charges and costs and its potential impact on DRG weight, CMS shifted to cost based DRG weights in FY 2007. A major concern regarding cost estimates centered on "charge compression," which refers to hospital practices that assign a lower markup to relatively higher-cost items and a higher markup to lower-cost items. Although charge compression is widespread, its impact is pronounced in DRGs where one or two exceptionally high-cost items account for a large part of average per-case costs.

The substantial gap between Medicare's national payment rate for CAR-T DRG and the cost of CAR-T therapy exemplifies the impact of charge compression. The national average cost-to-charge ratio for the drug/pharmacy cost center is less than 0.2. This means that for a charge of $400,000 for CAR-T therapy, the recognized cost averages less than $80,000. To accurately reflect a purchasing price of $400,000 for CAR-T therapy, the charge needs to be inflated to $2 million, a figure that would undoubtedly attract media attention.

To address concerns about inadequate payment for CAR-T therapy, various payment arrangements were discussed, with stakeholders expressing different perspectives during the public commenting process. It is fairly common for payment policy discussions to involve different viewpoints and positions due to the inherent complexity of the issues at hand. With multiple facets to consider, any changes can have significant financial implications for different stakeholders, often requiring a longer timeline to reach consensus or solutions.

In a letter to CMS, the Medicare Payment Advisory Commission (MedPAC) recommended separately paying for CAR-T therapies instead of bundling them into the standard DRG payment. MedPAC is a nonpartisan independent congressional agency established by the BBA of 1997 to advise the U.S. Congress on issues affecting the Medicare program. MedPAC suggested assessing CAR-T therapies' cost separately based on ASP, an approach used by outpatient PPS for determining payment for Part B drugs. Treating CAR-T therapies as separate pass-through cost is an approach already adopted by the majority of private plans, although many view it as a temporary solution rather than a long-term sustainable option.

Because "the prices of drugs and biologics generally do not vary" geographically or based on hospital characteristics, MedPAC believed that "it would be inequitable to apply" wage index and other inpatient PPS payment adjustments (e.g., IME and DSH) to the CAR-T part of the MS–DRG. CMS echoed such reasoning by pointing out that "these percentage add-on payments could arguably result in unreasonably high additional payments for CAR T-Cell therapy cases unrelated to any significant empirical way to the costs of the hospital in providing care."

While there is a broad consensus that the full costs of CAR-T therapies should be recognized whether to include or exclude add-on payments became a point of contention. Strong opposition to the add-on carve-out approach came from hospitals that view add-on payments as an integral part of the DRG payment system. With over $10 billion in IME payments at stake, their main concern was about setting a precedent that lets CMS carve out high-cost items from applying add-on payments.

The underpayment for CAR-T cases for now might not be as severe as suggested by comparing national DRG rate with the price tag of CAR-T therapies because of various payment adjustments under inpatient PPS, outlier payment, and other exceptions. Nearly all the hospitals enrolled in FDA's REMS and allowed to provide CAR-T treatments are teaching hospitals. Teaching hospitals tend to locate in inner city areas with high geographic wage adjustment, namely, wage index. Major metropolitan areas such as Boston, New York city, and San Francisco, receive 25~90% payment increases from wage index adjustments.

Even though IME adjustment varies among teaching hospitals, major teaching hospitals (with resident-to-bed ratios greater than 0.25) see additional 10~75% bump to their wage index adjusted DRG rate. In addition, 11 cancer hospitals, including the University of Texas M.D. Anderson Cancer Center and Dana-Farber Cancer Institute, are exempt from the inpatient PPS. The current DRG payment rate for CAR-T may discourage certain types of hospitals or hospitals in certain geographic areas from offering CAR-T treatments.

The reimbursement challenge for CAR-T and other high-cost therapies has not been resolved. When new therapies enter in volume and more patients receive new treatments, the budget impact will come into view. With the rapid proliferation of novel health technologies – 26 FDA-approved cell and gene therapies, 50 more expected to be launched in 2024, 109 late-stage gene therapy clinical trials underway - the National Bureau of Economic Research predicts over one million Americans will benefit from these new therapies in the coming decade and the spending on new therapies is expected to reach $25 billion annually.

It remains to be seen, though, whether competition from new therapies may negatively impact pricing. Would medical innovation and Medicare insolvency collide to create a budgetary crisis in the coming decade? Would major changes to the DRG payment system be in the cards? The issues will only intensify with the advent of powerful and expensive new treatments.

WHICH IS THE APPLICABLE PAYMENT SYSTEM: INPATIENT OR OUTPATIENT?

The existing payment structure – Medicare's 10+ payment systems – is largely organized around care settings and type of providers, such as inpatient, outpatient, and doctor. The starting point to identify payment systems under which a product is reimbursed is the care setting where a product is provided and the type of healthcare providers who use it. However, due to various payment rules, delineating care settings in payment systems may not be that straightforward.

Viz LVO NTAP payment is a good example to understand the complex relationship between the place of service and payment system. When a patient arrives at an

Emergency Room (ER) with stroke-like symptoms, a computed tomographic angiogram (CTA) scan is often ordered and then reviewed by a neurologist and interventionalist before a patient is admitted to surgery to remove the blood clot in a large vessel that goes to the brain. Time is of the essence to prevent irreversible damage to the brain.

Viz.AI software module Viz LVO analyzes and detects a large-vessel occlusion (LVO), one of the most common strokes, on a CTA, and alerts doctors of potential LVO patients to speed up the process so patients can get into surgery quicker. Even though Viz LVO is deployed in an ER, a hospital outpatient department, the NTAP payment is a part of the inpatient PPS payment. To understand the connection, it's helpful to tour the early days of the PPS and the creation of the three-day rule.

The preadmission policy – treating outpatient services provided one day before admission as part of inpatient stay – had been in place from the start in 1966. When the inpatient PPS was introduced in 1983, the DRG payment also covered preadmission nonphysician outpatient services (such as radiology, other diagnostic tests, or laboratory services) provided on the day before admission to the same hospital.

After adopting the inpatient PPS, the noticeable shift of physician services, supplies, and diagnostic procedures from inpatient to outpatient confirmed what many had expected: "PPS would shift many test and other preparations for surgery or medical treatment to hospital outpatient clinics and would shift many surgical and other admissions to outpatient clinics, freestanding ambulatory surgical centers, and other outpatient settings." In practice other factors, such as increased scrutiny by peer review organizations (PRO) for inpatient admission necessity, might have also contributed to the shift.

In 1990, Congress expanded the DRG payment window to three days prior to the date of admission to curb further unbundling of services. Outpatient services covered by the DRG window policy include diagnostic services and admission-related non-diagnostic services provided by the admitting hospital or its subsidiaries. Recommendations have been raised to expand the DRG payment window further but have not been adopted till now due to concerns over increased "health risk for beneficiaries."

In the case of Viz LVO, even though a patient was first admitted to the ER, and a CTA scan and Viz LVO alerts all happened before inpatient admission because all these outpatient services were diagnostic services or admission-related non-diagnostic services happened at the admitting hospital within the three-day preadmission policy window, they were bundled into and paid under the DRG payment for the stroke patient's inpatient stay. That's why Viz LVO is eligible for NTAP under the inpatient PPS, even though the AI tool can also detect stroke among patients already admitted into inpatient hospital.

The preadmission window isn't the only issue that blurs the line between inpatient and outpatient. Observation stays, a hospital stay that isn't an inpatient hospital stay, are another issue that causes a great deal of confusion. A typical scenario goes like this: a person with chest pain goes to a hospital ER. After a set of tests, the ER doctors determine that they aren't having a heart attack but keep them staying overnight for observation. They never were admitted as an inpatient, even though the hospital keeps them for a day or so, sometimes in an observation unit, or in some hospitals in a regular ward. There has been an enormous growth in observation stays, partly due to aggressive targeted audits of inpatient short stays by Medicare Recovery Audit Contractor (RAC).

In 2013, CMS established the "two-midnight rule" to draw a time-based "clear" line between inpatient and outpatient. Under the two-midnight rule, hospital inpatient admissions are considered reasonable and necessary for patients whose stays cross two midnights. Stays expected to span less than two midnights under the rule are generally considered outpatient. The rule requires doctors to project the expected treatment duration, which can often be difficult. The doctor must have a reasonable expectation that the patient's stay will cross two midnights and admit the patient based on that expectation.

The time that a patient spends in the ER receiving treatment, and/or the time that the patient spends in surgery, is counted as part of this two-midnight period. So, the patient's preadmission time spent in a hospital will affect whether or not they get admitted, rather than their medical condition sometimes.

The inpatient versus outpatient status has significant financial impact on both hospitals and patients. Medicare pays for inpatient and outpatient services under two payment systems, and the amount Medicare pays for a short inpatient stay is much higher than for similar outpatient observation stays.

Patient's liability differs depending on whether they are admitted to inpatient or not. Patients in an inpatient setting are responsible for payment for the Part A deductible, which is 1,600 in 2023, while patients in an outpatient setting are responsible for paying a coinsurance amount, which is on average 20% of outpatient payment rate. According to MedPAC, overall patients' financial liability is higher in the inpatient setting compared to those served in the outpatient observation status.

However, the time that beneficiaries were treated in outpatient observation does not count toward the skilled nursing facility (SNF) coverage eligibility of three inpatient days, making those who require SNF care financially liable for SNF stays. The situation has been exacerbated in recent years as CMS removed total knee and total hip replacements from inpatient-only list, thus increasing pressure on hospitals to offer the procedures in the outpatient setting.

In 2022, a federal court ruled that hospitalized Medicare beneficiaries who were switched from inpatient to observation status can appeal the decision, making it easier for them to receive coverage for subsequent nursing home care. The ruling ended more than a decade of litigation for Medicare recipients.

These complex delineation between care settings complicates the effort to map out a reimbursement strategy for new medical products. First, the applicable payment system may not be based on the care setting where a medical product is used. Second, the same service or procedure may be paid under different payment systems, such as inpatient PPS and outpatient PPS, with different reimbursement structure and rates. For example, a service or product bundled into a DRG payment in the inpatient setting may receive separate payment when provided in the outpatient setting. Third, different coding systems could be used by different payment systems. For example, inpatient PPS uses ICD-10-PCS codes for the same procedure, while outpatient PPS uses HCPCS codes. Each coding system has its own process and criteria to review and approve new code applications.

PACKAGED OR SEPARATELY REIMBURSED? PAYMENT UNDER OUTPATIENT PPS

Outpatient is one of the fast-growing care settings. Over the past decade, procedures, and services historically performed in inpatient hospitals have shifted to outpatient. Factors contributing to the rise in outpatient care include technology advancements, such as minimal invasive surgeries, cardiac catheterizations, and cataract surgeries. Additionally, patient preference and policy changes, such as the 2-midnight rule and the removal of high-volume inpatient procedures like knee and hip replacements from inpatient-only procedure list, have played a role in the transition from inpatient to outpatient care.

The outpatient PPS can be a perplex payment system to navigate. Determining whether a service, such as a CTA head scan (CPT 70496), receives separate payment under the outpatient PPS is not a straightforward matter. Unlike the inpatient PPS, where nearly all procedures and services are packaged into a single payment, the outpatient PPS presents a more complex payment system that can feel uncertain for those unfamiliar with its intricacies.

One challenge in the outpatient setting is the diverse range of services provided, encompassing over 9,000 HCPCS codes. These services range from regular outpatient visit, ER visit, imaging and lab tests, vaccine, drug, or biologic injections, to complex procedures that require anesthesia. Additionally, unlike inpatient services with clear admission and discharge dates, outpatient services do not always have well-defined starting and ending points. Besides, outpatient services can recur, and an outpatient bill can include services provided over a period of up to 30 days. This can make it difficult to establish time-based episodes.

For the first decade since its effect in 2000, the outpatient PPS was a hybrid model that combined elements of PPS and fee schedule to balance competing policy concerns such as efficiency and accuracy. The outpatient PPS underwent significant changes from 2014, aligning it more closely with a prospective payment system. This involved the creation of more and larger service bundles as payment units. CMS significantly expanded packaging and bundling policies to make APCs look more like DRGs. Packaging polices involve packaging ancillary services and items into a single payment for a primary service, while bundling policies combine multiple procedures or adjunctive procedures, services and items reported on the same claim into a single payment unit.

The APC grouping logic starts from categorizing the 9000+ HCPCS codes into three buckets: primary services, packaged services, and separately payable services. Examples of primary services include emergency department visits, colonoscopes, and surgical procedures. CMS also carves out certain services to receive separate payment, such as corneal tissue, blood and blood products, and drugs and biologics whose costs exceed a threshold ($135 per day in 2023).

Under the outpatient PPS, packaged services are items and services considered an integral part of primary service. No separate payment is made for packaged services because the costs of these items and services are included in the APC payment for the primary services. There are two types of packaged services:

- Unconditionally packaged services. They are services always packaged into the payment for other services and never receive separate payment. Examples of unconditionally packaged services include routine supplies, anesthesia, diagnostic radiopharmaceuticals, contrast agents, drugs, biologicals, radiopharmaceuticals that function as supplies when used in a diagnostic test, and procedure, and drugs and biologicals that function as supplies or devices when used in a surgical procedure.

- Conditionally packaged services. They are packaged services if occur on the same claim with certain other primary services, and otherwise can receive separate payment according to the assigned APC. There are many rules and circumstances that define when a conditionally packaged service is separately paid for and when packaged into other services. For example, on the same claim of a hospital outpatient visit (CPT G0463, a national rate of $120.86 for 2023), a wide variety of lab tests are conditionally packaged and do not receive separate payment under the clinical lab fee schedule (CLFS), ranging from low-cost tests like hemoglobin glycosylated a1c (CPT 83036, $9.71 for 2023) to tests with a price tag higher than a regular outpatient visit like insulin tolerance test (CPT 80434, $285.03 for 2023). There are exceptions, as is often the case. CMS exempts Advanced Diagnostic Laboratory Tests (ADLTs), molecular pathology tests, and cancer-related protein-based Multianalyte Assays with Algorithmic Analyses (MAAAs) from the outpatient PPS lab test conditional packaging policy.

Another approach to creating larger bundles under the outpatient PPS is through bundling multiple, significant procedures together into a single unit of payment. There are two approaches to bundle services together:

- Composite APCs provide a single payment for certain combinations of diagnostic and/or treatment services when provided on the same date of service. A single composite payment is also made when two or more related ultrasound, Magnetic Resonance Imaging (MRI), or CT services are provided in the same outpatient visit.

- Comprehensive APCs (C–APCs) provide a single payment for an entire outpatient encounter. The idea is to combine a primary service and all adjunctive services that support the primary service billed on the same claim into a single payment. However, some items and services, such as pass-through devices and drugs, are excluded from C-APCs per statutory requirements.

For services or procedures considered primary services under outpatient PPS, their payment rates are mostly determined by APC assignment. The services assigned to an APC are clinically similar and similar in terms of the resources required to provide each service. Resource use of a service is assessed using geometric mean costs of an HCPCS code, including all packaged services and items, and costs are estimated by converting charges reported on claims to costs using cost-to-charge ratios derived from hospital cost report data. One APC may be assigned to many HCPCS codes, but any individual HCPCS code can be assigned to only one APC.

When making APC assignments or reassignments, CMS compares the costs of individual services assigned to an APC to prevent violations of the two times rule. The two-times rule requires the cost for the highest-cost service within APC may not be more than two times the cost for the lowest-cost service in the APC. From time to time, though, exceptions were made in unusual cases, such as low volume items and services. The weight for an APC is based on the geometric mean cost of all the services assigned to the APC.

The assignments of HCPCS codes to APCs are updated annually, and APC weights are recalibrated yearly. The costs of services can change from year to year because of changes in hospitals' charges, changes to cost-to-charge ratios as determined by hospital cost reports, and changes in the frequency of services. So, the APC assignment of a service may change from one year to the next to meet the two-times rule requirement or to improve clinical and/or resource homogeneity of APCs. This APC reconfiguration may result in significant fluctuation in the payment rate for individual APC and for all the services assigned to the APC.

However, not all services covered under outpatient PPS are paid under APCs or based their payment rates on APC weights. For example, the payment rates for lab tests are based on CLFS if they are not packaged into other services. Durable Medical Equipment is paid through non-APC methods. Separately payable drugs are reimbursed at a rate of ASP plus 6 percent. ASP excludes rebates paid to state Medicaid programs but includes various discounts offered by manufacturers, such as volume discounts, prompt pay discounts and cash discounts, per statutory requirements.

Now, let's revisit whether a CTA head scan (CPT 70496) receives separate payment under outpatient PPS. The answer is that it really depends on what other services are provided on the claim. If the CT scan was the only service reported on a claim, it will be paid under APC 5571 for a national rate of $180.34 in 2023. However, if the patient is later admitted for inpatient care, the claim will be packaged into the DRG payment under inpatient PPS. If there is another CT scan on the claim, it may trigger a composite APC 8006 and the single payment rate for the 2 or more CT scans is $434.16 for 2023. If the patient is admitted through the ER and stays for more than 8 hours under observation, the CTA scan would be packaged into a comprehensive APC 8011 with a national rate of $2,439.02 in 2023.

The case of reimbursement for a CTA head scan shows that reimbursement under outpatient PPS is situational. The APC assignment provided at HCPCS code level in the addendum B table offers a starting point for understanding reimbursement when no other payment rules apply. The status indicator (SI) assigned to a code describes the payment logic associated with the code. For example, the SI for CPT 70496 is Q3, which indicates that the code may be paid through a composite APC. To develop a comprehensive understanding of outpatient PPS payment for a new technology, it's helpful to identify common use cases how the technology is used in hospital outpatient departments. Based on this information, a scenario-based reimbursement assessment can be developed.

PAY FOR NEW TECHNOLOGIES UNDER OUTPATIENT PPS

Like the inpatient PPS, the outpatient PPS also has special payment adjustments for new technologies, in one of two ways. The transitional pass-through (TPT) payments provide temporary additional payments for certain drugs, biological agents, brachytherapy devices used to treat cancer, and categories of other medical devices for at least two but not more than three years. For new technology services that are not eligible for TPT payment but are complete or comprehensive services or procedures "with a beginning, middle, and end" and too new to be captured in claims data, CMS assigns them to "New Technology APCs."

The assignment to new technology APCs is based only on similarity of resource use. For CY 2023, there are 52 New Technology APC levels, ranging from the lowest cost band assigned to APC 1491 (New Technology—Level 1A ($0-$10)) to the highest cost band assigned to APC 1908 (New

Technology—Level 52 ($145,001-$160,000)). An assignment to a New Technology APC is temporary and usually lasts two to three years. However, if sufficient claims data are collected in less than two years, CMS may reassign the service to a proper APC instead of New Technology APC. On the flip side, if there aren't sufficient claims data at the end of three years, CMS may keep the service in a New Technology APC longer till adequate data become available.

The 2023 New Technology APC class presents an interesting array of new technologies, including minimally invasive procedures, new imaging studies, a surgical procedure to administer a newly approved gene therapy, and Software as a Service (SaaS). Some of these technologies, such as histotripsy service – a non-invasive, nonthermal, mechanical process that uses a focused beam of sonic energy to destroy cancerous liver tumors, are still in FDA-approved investigational device exemption studies. Clinical improvement is not required for New Technology APC application. The main justification is that the technology's cost information has not been sufficiently captured by claims data.

A service or procedure does not have to have its own HCPCS code to be considered for New Technology APC. If the service or procedure meets the criteria for assignment to a New Technology APC, CMS would consider creating a Level II HCPCS code to describe the procedure comprehensively. CMS clarifies that the Level II HCPCS assigned to facilitate billing and payment through a New Technology APC is independent of approval for a national Level I or Level II HCPCS code.

The TPT payment is the outpatient version of the NTAP. Like the NTAP, the criterion for device TPT includes newness, cost thresholds, and substantial clinical improvement. For the same rationale as NTAP, capital medical equipment is not eligible for TPT. CMS has also created an alternative TPT pathway for Breakthrough Device designation, a parallel to NTAP alternative pathways.

Device TPT, though, has some unique requirements. One eligibility criterion requires that "device is an integral part of the service furnished, is used for one patient only, comes in contact with human tissue, and is surgically implanted or inserted (either permanently or temporarily), or applied in or on a wound or other skin lesion." The TPT payment is for new device categories. To justify the creation of a new device category, the proposed new category for a device must not have been appropriately described by the existing categories (either active or expired) established for TPT payments.

The device TPT payment amount is determined case by case. The hospital charge for the device with TPT status is used to calculate the costs of the device by multiplying the hospital charge with the hospital's cost-to-charge ratio. The

TPT payment amount is the computed costs of the device minus a device offset amount, which is the part of the APC payment amount associated with the cost of existing device. The deduction of device offset intends to prevent duplicate payment for the device, and CMS calculates and publishes the device offset amount. When a hospital bills for a service with charges for a device TPT, the outpatient payment for the case is the sum of the APC payment and the TPT amount.

Drugs, biologicals, and radiopharmaceuticals qualifying for TPT include orphan drugs, cancer therapy drugs and biologicals, radiopharmaceutical drugs and biologicals, and certain new drugs and biological agents. Policy packaged drugs and biologicals, including anesthesia drugs, contrast agents, diagnostic radiopharmaceuticals, stress agents, skin substitutes, and drugs and biologicals that function as supplies when used in a surgical procedure, are eligible for TPT and can receive separate payment during the 2-3 years TPT period. Once the TPT status ends, they are packaged items and not eligible for separate payment under the current policy.

Approval of a drug, biological or radiopharmaceutical for a transitional pass-through payment under the hospital outpatient PPS is not contingent on prior assignment of a national HCPCS code. If no HCPCS code is available, manufacturers can request a new code along with the application for TPT payment.

For separately payable drugs, the payment for passthrough drugs and biologicals is at ASP plus 6 percent for CY 2023, equivalent to the payment rate these drugs and biologicals would receive in the physician's office setting. In policy-packaged drugs, the pass-through payment amount equals to ASP plus 6 percent for CY 2023 minus a payment offset for policy-packaged drugs. CMS updates and releases a file that has the APC offset amount annually.

Outlier payments are available under outpatient PPS to help mitigate the financial risk associated with high-cost and complex procedures. CMS defines an outlier as a service with costs that exceed 1.75 times the APC payment rate and exceed the APC payment rate by an outlier fixed-dollar threshold ($8,625 for 2023). For a service meeting both thresholds, the outlier payment is 50 percent of the difference between the cost of providing the service and 1.75 times the APC rate. Outlier payments are financed by imposing a reduction to total projected outpatient PPS payment prospectively. CMS has set the projected target for aggregate outlier payments at 1 percent of the estimated total payments under outpatient PPS and adjusts the fixed-dollar threshold annually to meet the projected outlier payment target.

PRICING A NEW DIAGNOSTIC TEST UNDER THE PHYSICIAN FEE SCHEDULE

For the cardiac monitor maker, iRhythm Technologies, 2021 was a roller coaster ride. iRhythm started off its 2021 on a high, with its stock price soring and a new CEO taking over the company. By the summer, however, the company's stock price was caught in a downward spiral, falling nearly 80% from the start of 2021. The new CEO stepped down and a shareholder sued, accusing the company of misleading investors. At the center of the saga was Medicare's payment rates for extended Holter heart monitoring under the physician fee schedule.

An array of services is reimbursed under PFS, including office visits, telehealth visits, imaging examinations, pathology readings, and surgical procedures. These services can be furnished in all settings, including doctor offices, hospitals, clinical laboratories, independent diagnostic testing facility (in the case of iRhythm), and beneficiaries' own homes. Generally, clinicians are reimbursed under the PFS while facilities receive payment for their "facility fee" under other Medicare payment systems, including inpatient and outpatient PPS. Among the 1.3 million clinicians who bill Medicare directly, 56 percent are physicians.

CMS determines the payment rate for each service under the PFS based on RVUs that measure relative resource use of three cost components to provide clinician services, or types of RVUs. These RVU types measure:

- Work RVUs reflect time and intensity to perform a procedure for a "typical" patient. Work RVUs account for on average about 51% of the total RVUs.

- Practice expense (PE) RVUs comprise costs such as rent, equipment and supplies, consulting and professional services, and staff salaries of the practice. Practice expense RVUs account for on average about 45% of the total RVUs. When a doctor provides a service or procedure in a facility, the facility—rather than the physician practice—covers some of the direct inputs (e.g., clinical staff, disposable medical supplies, and medical equipment) and overhead costs (i.e., administrative staff, office expenses and non-medical equipment). In these instances, CMS assigns two PE RVUs to a code – a non-facility PE RVU and a facility PE RVU to differentiate payment rates for different practice settings.

- Malpractice RVUs reflect the cost of professional liability insurance based on an estimate of the relative risk associated with each CPT code. Malpractice RVUs account for nearly 5% of total RVUs.

Diagnostic services, like extended electrocardiogram involving iRhythm, generally comprise two components: a professional component (PC) and a technical component (TC). The TC is the part of the service that involves the collection of information from the patient—for example, a sample, specimen, radiological image, or interrogatory study. The PC portion involves the interpretation of the collected information by a physician or other practitioner. The PC and TC may be furnished independently or by different providers, or they may be furnished together as a global service.

As an independent diagnostic testing facility (IDTF), iRhythm can bill Medicare directly for the technical component of extended electrocardiogram (ECG) using CPT 93243 (ECG monitoring 2-7 days and reporting) and CPT 93247 (ECG monitoring for 7 - 15 days and reporting) or invoice the ordering physician who will then bill Medicare for both TC and PC. Both CPT 93243 and CPT 93247 are for technical component codes without a work RVU. The pricing of the two codes is centered around PE RVUs.

The current PE valuation methodology encompasses two categories of practice expense: direct and indirect. CMS uses a "bottom-up" approach to determine the direct PE by summing up the costs of clinical labor, disposable medical supplies, and medical equipment involved in furnishing a service to a "typical" patient. Indirect costs include expenses such as administrative labor, rent, utilities, and other forms of overhead.

CMS uses AMA's Physician Practice Information Survey (PPIS) data on indirect practice expenses per hour (PE/HR) by specialty in developing the indirect portion of the PE RVUs. The most recent version of the PPIS was conducted in 2007–2008 from self-employed physicians and selected non-physician practitioners. Supplemental surveys have been conducted for selected specialties and non-physician practitioners. Indirect PE is allocated to each service based on physician work and direct costs through a complicated analytical process.

In discussing the pricing of extended ECG monitoring codes, CMS elaborated extensively on why the clinical labor time should be 1 minute instead of 5, how long the equipment time should be, and why one pair of non-sterile gloves is needed to attach the ECGs instead of two. For clinical labor and equipment use, the driver of value is "times," while for supplies, it's the quantities.

CMS often cites recommendations from AMA's RVS Update Committee (RUC) when making assumptions about the number of minutes of clinical labor time and equipment time and the number of medical supplies involved in performing a procedure for a "typical" patient. RUC's PE recommendations often come from its Practice Expense Subcommittee, which reviews information submitted by the specialty societies about the direct PE inputs. "This information is typically generated by specialty society consensus panels of practitioners performing the service and takes into account the PE inputs for similar reference procedures."

All these debates regarding times and gloves were a usual part of the rulemaking and commenting process and wouldn't have prevented CMS from issuing national rates for the two codes for 2021. At the heart of the drama is the pricing of one new supply item – extended external ECG patch, a medical magnetic tape recorder. The traditional approach CMS relies on is paid invoices by doctors "representative of commercial market pricing" to establish a national price for a new supply or equipment item.

Instead of a traditional invoice, some proxy cost analyses were provided to CMS, including a study that estimated cost of the patch per service based on total costs of the testing facility divided by the total number of tests furnished. However, this approach was challenged by some commenters in the public comment period for including research and development costs associated with developing the patch, which are typically indirect costs under PFS' PE methodology.

Absent of a traditional invoice, CMS first proposed referencing an existing supply as a proxy price, under which the supply cost for the patch was valued over $400. The proposal set iRhythm stock soaring in the summer of 2020. However, the proposal also drew backlash from the public in the commenting process. Several commenters stated that the patch was "available for purchase at roughly $100 to $120 if bought in bulk quantities."

In the CY 2021 final rule, CMS finalized the codes but leave the pricing decision to local MACs, citing "unable to identify accurate national pricing" for the patch given the conflicting information provided. When Novitas, a local MAC, posted reimbursement rates at a range of $40-$80 for extended ECG monitoring codes in January 2021, iRhythm's stock price went into freefall, which opened a tumultuous year for the company with twists and turns trailing Novitas' pricing changes. The years-long reimbursement overhang ended in 2023 when CMS finalized national payment rates for extended ECG monitoring codes at a range of $230-250, based on 21 invoices received for the patch.

There is no doubt that the current system needs improvements. In the CY 2023 PFS final rule, CMS acknowledges a list of concerns raised by interested parties, with the PE input data being a central focus of these concerns. The direct PE RVUs are primarily based on RUC recommendations, often by comparison to a reference code. Although RUC sometimes undertakes revaluation for codes identified through screenings and CMS has refined specific PE data inputs in recent years using a combination of market research and publicly available data, there is still a significant gap between the current state and CMS's desired system where routine PE updates can be implemented.

Indirect PE data, on the other end, relies on legacy information collected more than a decade ago, before the widespread adoption of Electronic Health Records (EHRs) and other technologies. The indirect PE data may no longer reflect the cost structure of typical physician practices today. To address this, the new Physician Practice Information (PPI) Survey data collection for 2023-2024 is underway, which will provide a much-needed update in the coming years. However, implementing standard and routine updates remains a challenge.

In the CY 2023 PFS final rule, CMS sought comments on strategies to improve PE data collection and methods. The challenge for the agency is to "balance the various interest of the public, and any path forward should allow for ongoing and routine cycles of PE updates." The need to balance different public interests also makes it difficult to disregard traditions and tailor CMS's reimbursement methods to individual cases, as exemplified by the pricing saga of iRhythm's diagnostic test.

MEDICARE'S REIMBURSEMENT FOR AI

In 2020, CMS provided coverage for an AI-powered diabetic retinopathy (DR) screening, IDx-DR, under the physician fee schedule. IDx-DR is a software program that uses AI to analyze eye images taken with a retinal camera called the Topcon NW400. The images are uploaded to a cloud server, and the software can provide one of two results: (1) "more than mild diabetic retinopathy detected: refer to an eye care professional" or (2) "negative for more than mild diabetic retinopathy; rescreen in 12 months." DR is the most common cause of vision loss among the over 30 million Americans living with diabetes. Initial and regular screenings for DR are recommended for diabetic patients by the American Diabetes Association.

In 2018, IDx-DR received FDA approval for marketing. It's the first device authorized for marketing that can provide an eye screening diagnosis without the involvement of a clinician (e.g., an eye doctor), which makes it usable in primary care clinics that may not normally offer eye screening. In 2019, the AMA CPT Editorial Panel created a new Category I CPT code for IDx-DR, the first Category I code for AI.

CMS didn't finalize a national PFS payment rate for the new DR screening code in 2020 but deferred the decision to local MACs., The holdup was mainly about whether the $25 analysis fee recommended by RUC is a form of indirect PE or a separate direct PE input. CMS considers CPT code 92229 to be a diagnostic service under the PFS. Because no physician is involved, this service is PE only.

Traditionally, CMS considers most computer software and associated analysis and licensing fees (e.g., computer decision support systems) to be indirect costs tied to costs for associated hardware (equivalent to medical equipment). In the case of IDR-DX, CMS viewed the retinal camera as the hardware for remote imaging in its first 2020 proposal. This categorization was questioned during the commenting process. Commenters argued that the analysis fee should be treated as direct PE because the analysis was conducted at each patient encounter. There would be no service if the software was not used on a per patient basis.

Besides a philosophical question about the role and function of AI, the direct and indirect PE distinction also presents a technical dilemma. In current PE methodology, indirect costs – expenses such as administrative labor and office expenses – are allocated to direct PE expenses. If the analysis fee is treated as a direct supply cost, as recommended by the RUC, CMS's concern was that they would inadvertently allocate too many indirect costs for a supply item that does not require physical space in an office or administrative staff hours to maintain it. The challenge is, as acknowledged by CMS, costs associated with software, licensing, and analysis fees are not well accounted for in the current PE methodology because the indirect cost data were last collected in 2007 and 2008 before the AI-based services existed.

As is often the case, CMS resorted to crosswalk – establishing values for a new code by referencing an existing code with perceived similar resource costs – to finalize a national pricing for CPT code 92229 in 2021. Even though CMS's reimbursement decision provides some financial predictability and stability for IDR-DR, it is a temporary solution to the broad question of paying for AI or software as medical device (SaMD) or software as a service (SaaS).

The data and method issues around PE RVUs complicate the effort to create a permanent policy on AI. CMS repeatedly referred to the study that RAND is conducting to improve PE data collection process and allocation methodology as a potential solution. With more accurate and timely accounting for resource costs for innovative and emerging technologies, the hope was that CMS may not need to rely on crosswalk to value a new service.

IDx-DR also received reimbursement as a diagnostic test under the outpatient PPS, and the national payment decision came out in 2020 with no delay. At first CMS proposed to assign IDx-DR as a conditional packaged code, which meant that hospitals wouldn't receive separate payment for IDx-DR if it was provided during a hospital outpatient visit or other primary procedures or services. However, considering the possibility that hospitals might schedule the IDx-DR test on a separate day from an outpatient visit to receive separate payment, CMS categorized IDx-DR as a major service so hospitals need not schedule the test on a separate day to receive separate payment for IDx-DR.

IDx-DR is not the first SaaS reimbursed under outpatient PPS. CMS began paying for the SaaS procedure HeartFlow in 2018. The HeartFlow analysis is a coronary physiologic simulation software that provides a three-dimensional image of a patient's coronary arteries, allowing physicians to identify the fractional flow reserve to assess whether patients should undergo further invasive testing such as a coronary angiogram. On the PFS side, HeartFlow also received a national payment rate, and the PFS and outpatient PPS rates for the SaaS procedure are comparable in 2023.

Also in the CY 2018 outpatient PPS final rule, CMS provided a separate payment for the SaaS procedure, CPT 0503T, instead of packaging it into a CT scan. The code was assigned to a New Technology APC, and CMS extended the New Technology APC payment till 2022, using the low-volume payment policy, which allows CMS to base APC assignment on up to 4 years of claims data for procedures with fewer than 100 claims per year. In CY 2023, CMS collected enough data to make a clinical APC assignment for HeartFlow.

For CY 2023, CMS also finalized a policy that separately pays SaaS add-on codes instead of packaging them with a diagnostic imaging service under outpatient PPS. Unlike HeartFlow and IDx-DR, which are described by a single CPT code, for several newly created SaaS procedures, including LiverMultiScan, Optellum, and QMRCP, AMA has established two codes to describe each SaaS procedure: a primary code that describes the SaaS procedure when run on a past scan and an add-on code that describes the same SaaS service when provided along with a diagnostic imaging service.

It's a longstanding outpatient PPS principle to package add-on codes into the primary procedure. However, CMS made an exception for SaaS add-on codes because FDA cleared or approved them, and the AMA created CPT codes for these procedures. Additionally, CMS pointed out that the descriptors of these codes contradict normal definition of add-on services for the packaging policy, and in many cases, the costs associated with the add-on codes exceed the costs of the imaging services they would be billed with.

The decision was not without controversy, as MedPAC opposed "separate payment for expensive services that do not necessarily provide a substantial clinical improvement." The concern was that separate payment may "limit the competitive forces that generate price reductions among like services, lead to overuse (to the extent clinically possible), and shift financial pressure from providers to Medicare."

Even though both PFS and outpatient PPS separately pay AI services for now, we are still at an early stage of understanding the value of AI in healthcare and developing a sustainable reimbursement framework that balances competing priorities. In both the PFS and outpatient PPS rules, CMS sought comments to help formulate reimbursement solutions.

Clinical software, including clinical decision support system and computer-aided detection, has been used to aid or augment clinical decision-making for decades, and both PFS and outpatient PPS have established policies to reimburse these services. AI products can play different roles in relation to the work of clinicians, ranging from assistance, supplementation, to substitution, which makes it harder to draw a clear line between new and old clinical software.

The differentiating factors for SaaS have been FDA approval or clearance and a separate code granted by AMA. However, the 21st Century Cures Act provides a potential exclusion from FDA regulation for AI diagnostic decision support software based on explainability, i.e., whether healthcare professionals can independently review the basis for AI recommendations. This could add another layer of complexity to creating a uniform reimbursement framework for AI. The impacts of AI on healthcare, including clinician times and practice costs at a micro level, and access, quality, cost, and health equity at a macro level, are still too early to assess. It may sound cliché, but in the realm of AI reimbursement, change is an unavoidable constant.

PART FOUR

PAYER'S COVERAGE DECISION MAKING

Medicare issues on average 3-4 national coverage determinations and 37 local coverage determinations annually. In the Medicare Coverage Database, there are 349 national coverage policies, 982 final local coverage policies, and 113 proposed local coverage policies in place. In addition, there are 2,340 Articles, including 1,487 billing and coding articles and 676 responses to comments articles.

"Coverage" refers to the terms and conditions under which Medicare and private payers will (or will not) pay for a specific medical product or service. It is unquestionably the most important component of the reimbursement process and one of the primary payer tools to regulate access and costs of medical inventions. Even though coverage decision on whether and how a particular product or service is covered is determined on a case-by-case basis, payers may issue policies granting, limiting, or excluding coverage for a specific medical item or service.

Coverage decision can carry an ethical dilemma when cost containment faces off with a patient's opportunity to live. In the legal drama, Rainmaker, attorney representing a health insurance company, Great Benefit, warns that covering the bone marrow transplant for Donny Ray Black, the 22-year-old son of a middle-aged couple Dot and Buddy Black, will cause premiums to spin out of control. In response, the attorney who represents the Black family, Rudy Baylor, plays the deposition of Donny Ray video-taped several days before his death. Donny Ray tells the jury that he "had a 90% chance of living." In the movie, the jury rewarded the Black family with a stunning victory — $150,000 in compensatory and $50 million in punitive damages. New therapies offer hope of a cure for some genetic disorders are arriving, but coming with hefty price tags, which will only intensify the ethical tension between cost and choice, not merely in fictional form.

Unlike many developed countries, the U.S. does not have a centralized governance body (e.g., the National Institute for Health and Care Excellence in the U.K.) to broadly evaluate health technologies and guide coverage and pricing decisions. Each private and public payer has their own coverage criteria to determine whether and how a new product or service should be covered, although FDA clearance or approval of the product or service is most often a prerequisite. The pluralist system reflects the current U.S. political landscape as well as the fragmented payer market.

Traditional wisdom believes that the Medicare coverage policies exert significant influence on the practices of both state Medicaid programs and private payers. Our focus in this chapter will be on the Medicare program, including its benefit categories, national and local coverage determinations, and Medicare coverage for evidence development activities. This chapter will also provide an overview and selected examples of state Medicaid coverage determinations and private payer coverage decision-making. While there are similarities, the details like coverage determination criteria and process vary between public programs and private payers, and among different insurance plans.

MODEST MEDICARE BENEFIT EXPANSION IN HALF OF A CENTURY

The Medicare program was created in 1965 to provide health coverage and increased financial security for seniors who struggled to get health insurance coverage in the private market dominated by employment-based group coverage. At the time of Medicare's enactment, insurance for hospital stays was the primary insurance benefit since this was perceived as the key financial vulnerability to catastrophic losses for seniors. That was partly because physician services and prescription drugs represented only a small part of healthcare spending back then. The program first covered hospital stays (Part A) as the principal benefit for eligible beneficiaries and offered doctor and other outpatient services (Part B) as optional, supplementary insurance.

The Medicare statutory language defines benefits under Medicare Part A and Part B. However, the Medicare law does not have a comprehensive list of specific items or services eligible for Medicare coverage. Rather, it lists categories of items and services and authorizes CMS to determine which specific items and services within these categories can be covered under the Medicare program.

The program has adapted to the changing healthcare environment – including the shift from acute to chronic care – with modest expansions in coverage and eligibility after 50-plus years of campaigning, lobbying, and legislating. In 1972, Medicare eligibility was extended to individuals under age 65 with long-term disabilities or with end-stage renal disease (ESRD). In the 1980s, several benefit changes, including the removal of prior hospital stay requirements and the waiver of Part B coinsurance, made home health services more readily available to beneficiaries. In 1983, President Reagan signed Medicare hospice benefit into law, which provides coverage for palliative care and support services to terminally ill patients and their families. In 2003, the Medicare

Prescription Drug, Improvement, and Modernization Act (MMA) created a new optional prescription drug benefit, Part D prescription drug program, provided through private health plans.

Preventive services were among those categorically excluded services when the program was first established because preventive services did not "fit the traditional insurance model of providing coverage for expenses that are unpredictable (and thus cannot be budgeted) and substantial (and thus are a serious financial burden to individuals and families)." Since then, Medicare law has been amended many times to add coverage of specified preventive services, such as pneumococcal immunization and pap smears. Before the passage of Medicare Improvements for Patients and Provider Act (MIPPA) of 2008, adding a new preventive service to Medicare had to go through a legislative process. MIPPA gave the Secretary of HHS limited authority to add coverage for new preventive services administratively.

In the absence of a national health technology assessment program to guide benefit design and other policies, Congress has relied on several agencies to provide independent technology assessment. The Office of Technology Assessment (OTA) was a legislative branch agency established by Congress in 1972 to provide Congress with early indications of the probable beneficial and adverse impacts of technology applications, and the agency included a program focused specifically on healthcare. "The agency operated for more than two decades, producing approximately 750 full assessments, background papers, technical memoranda, case studies, and workshop proceedings spanning a wide range of topics." For example, in a 1993 report, OTA examined evidence on the effectiveness and cost-effectiveness of selected clinical preventive services and provided Congress with policy options on providing coverage for clinical preventive services. The OTA was defunded in 1995 amid broader efforts by the Republican-led legislature to reduce the size of government.

Following the defunding of OTA, Congress sought help from other agencies to fill a gap for objective, fair technology assessments, including the Congressional Research Service (CRS), the National Academy of Sciences, Engineering, and Medicine, and the GAO. CRS's Resources, Science and Industry division provides Congress with policy analysis on science and technology issues. For example, in 2018, CRS provided an analysis of policy options to address drugs shortages.

GAO has engaged in science and technology work for decades, and in recent years has established formal organizational structure and enhanced its capacity of technology assessment. In 2000, GAO established the Center for Technology and Engineering in its Applied

Research and Methods team to undertake efforts to develop and improve its technology assessment capabilities. This center later became GAO's Center for Science, Technology, and Engineering. The Consolidated Appropriations Act 2008 provided 2.5 million for GAO to establish a permanent technology assessment function. The Consolidated Appropriations Act of 2019 directed GAO to expand its technology assessment capacity by reorganizing its existing function and creating a "more prominent office."

In January 2019, GAO announced the establishment of a new Science, Technology Assessment, and Analytics (STAA) team. The initial plan issued in April 2019 specified that STAA's main functions include providing technology assessments and technical assistance to Congress, auditing science and technology programs within the federal government, compiling and using the best practices, and establishing an audit innovation lab.

GAO has issued several reports evaluating implications of healthcare technologies, including AI, vaccines, CRISPER gene editing and infectious disease modeling, and identifying strategies to optimize their use in healthcare. Some works were jointly conducted with other agencies, such as the National Academy of Medicine. Besides technology assessment reports, STAA teams also provide Congress with rapid responses, and in 2019, STAA launched GAO's Science & Tech Spotlight product line, a series of two-page overviews for policymakers and the public on emerging science and technology issues.

In October 2020, GAO established the Polaris Council, a group of cross-sectional science and technology policy experts to provide long-term, multidimensional advice to the agency on emerging science and technology issues. In 2021, GAO issued a technology assessment design handbook that provides guidance on key steps and considerations in the design of technology assessment – "the thorough and balanced analysis of significant primary, secondary, indirect, and delayed interactions of a technological innovation with society, the environment, and the economy and the present and foreseen consequences and effects of those interactions."

MEDICARE STATUTORILY EXCLUDED SERVICES

Medicare statutorily excluded services are services not recognized as part of a covered Medicare benefit. Legislative action is normally required to gain Medicare coverage for non-covered services; generally, they are outside CMS's authority to make coverage decisions. The Medicare non-covered list includes many services that seniors most likely need, such as hearing aids, routine dental and vision care, foot care, and custodian care.

Exceptions can be made when the services are related to a medical condition and prescribed by a doctor. For example, Medicare does not cover cosmetic surgery to improve a beneficiary's appearance. However, Medicare may cover cosmetic surgeries because of accidental injury, burns, or a car crash.

Traditionally, Medicare only covers services for the diagnosis and treatment of illness. Unlike diagnostic care, which are services ordered by doctor to confirm or rule out a certain illness when symptoms or risk factors are presented, preventive care is generally provided absent symptoms, often as part of routine physical or checkup. Over time, Medicare added various preventive services, including shots and vaccines, tests and screenings, wellness visits, diabetes-related services, counseling and therapies, and mental health services.

Medicare stature outlines specific coverage criteria for many preventive services, including types of preventive tests or services covered, target population (e.g., age and risk profiles), and frequency of test or service. For example, statutory language (42 CFR 410.23) specifies conditions and procedures for Medicare's coverage for glaucoma screening. The coverage is only for high-risk beneficiaries, including diabetic patients, individuals with a family history of glaucoma, African Americans aged 50 and over, and Hispanic Americans aged 65 and over. Screening for glaucoma is either a dilated eye examination with an intraocular pressure measure, a direct ophthalmoscopy examination, or a slit-lamp biomicroscopic examination.

For cancer screenings, Medicare specifies the tests covered for each cancer type and there are differences in the frequency of coverage and more eligibility criteria for certain cancer types. Medicare cover pap smears and pelvic exam for cervical or vaginal cancer screening, mammogram for breast cancer screening, PSA blood test, or digital rectal exam for prostate cancer screening, low-dose CT for lung cancer screening for high-risk populations, and several tests for colorectal cancer screening (including multi-target stool DNA tests, barium enemas, colonoscopies, fecal occult blood tests and flexible sigmoidoscopies). Unfortunately, most cancers do not have proven early detection screening tests, nor does Medicare cover any cancer screening tests outside the selected cancer types.

The development of multi-cancer early detection (MCED) test has generated a lot of attention recently, with Grail's Galleri MCED test named one of Time magazine's best inventions of 2022. The two MCED test developers – Grail and Thrive – raised nearly $650 million in total from investors. These tests typically rely on sequencing and detecting circulating free DNA (cfDNA) in blood shed by cancer cells. MCED tests, such as Galleri, can identify many types of cancer through a simple blood sample, including some cancer types with no recommended screening tests. FDA approves no MCED tests, but some MCED tests are available through a waiver as laboratory-developed tests – a type of in vitro diagnostic test designed, manufactured, and used within a single laboratory.

For a new cancer screening test to be covered by Medicare, in addition to pursuing legislative changes, such as the Medicare Multi-Cancer Early Detection Screening Coverage Act of 2021 introduced in the Senate, MIPPA 2008 authorizes the Secretary of HHS to add coverage of preventive services using the National Coverage Determination (NCD) process, if three conditions of the provision are met. The three conditions are:

- reasonable and necessary for the prevention or early detection of an illness or disability;
- recommended with a grade of A or B by the U.S. Preventive Services Task Force (USPSTF); and
- appropriate for individuals entitled to benefits under Medicare part A or enrolled under Medicare part B.

MIPPA also authorizes the Secretary to consider cost in determining whether to add coverage of a preventive service. With the new authority provided, CMS added HIV screening to the list of covered preventive services in 2019 using its NCD process.

The USPSTF is an independent, volunteer panel of national experts in prevention and evidence-based medicine created in 1984. The Task Force makes recommendations about clinical preventive services such as screenings, counseling services, and preventive medications. Authorized by Congress, the Agency for Healthcare Research and Quality (AHRQ) provides scientific, technical, administrative, and dissemination support to the USPSTF.

All USPSTF's recommendations are based on a rigorous review of existing peer-reviewed evidence. The Task Force does not consider the costs of a preventive service when determining a recommendation grade. Each recommendation is assigned a letter grade (an A, B, C, or D grade or an I statement) based on the strength of the evidence and the balance of benefits and harms of a preventive service. Grade A is USPSTF recommended services with high certainty that the net benefit is substantial, while Grade B is also USPSTF recommended services with high certainty that the net benefit is moderate or with moderate certainty that the net benefit is moderate to substantial.

Traditional Medicare (Part A and B) generally do not cover OTC products, such as OTC drugs and at-home tests. Medicare Advantage plans (Part C), and Medicare Part D drug plans may cover some OTC drugs. Temporary free at-home COVID-19 tests have been provided during the COVID-19 Public Health Emergency (PHE) period. In January 2022, the Biden Adrmimistration required insurance companies and group health plans to provide free at-home COVID-19 tests based on authorities in the Families First Coronavirus Response Act of 2020 and the Coronavirus Aid, Relief, and Economic Security Act of 2020.

In April 2022, the administration extended similar benefits to Medicare beneficiaries with Part B coverage till the end of PHE. In an FAQ, CMS refers the coverage expansion as an initiative allowed under the "Social Security Amendments of 1967 (42 U.S.C. 1395b-1(a)(1)(B)) to engage in demonstration projects testing the efficacy of Medicare covering otherwise non-covered services in order to conduct this initiative."

CMS notes the significance of the decision and its complexity by stating, "This is the first time in the history of the Medicare program that Medicare will be paying for any over-the-counter test without cost sharing for Medicare beneficiaries." CMS further explained the complexity of orchestrating such a program, "In addition to designing this initiative to meet statutorily required benchmarks, there are several operational changes that needed to be made to ensure this new and unprecedented pathway runs smoothly and that program integrity guardrails are established." The unprecedented circumstance, though, limits the generalizability of this coverage pathway.

Medicare Advantage plans must cover Medicare Part A and B benefits covered by traditional Medicare (except hospice or clinical trials); but may also offer coverage of more services excluded under traditional Medicare and have considerable flexibility in designing cost-sharing. Many MA plans offer coverage for Medicare statutorily excluded services, including hearing aids, routine dental, vision and podiatry benefits, and selected health education and wellness benefits, and cost-sharing may be less for these services compared to other diagnostic services and treatments. MA plans may also offer OTC allowances for members to buy certain OTC medications, first aid supplies, vitamins and other health and wellness products excluded in traditional Medicare benefits.

MEDICARE COVERAGE PATHWAYS FOR STATUTORILY INCLUDED SERVICES

The Medicare statute states that items and services provided to beneficiaries must be "reasonable and necessary" to qualify for reimbursement. Although the Medicare program determines whether an item or service is reasonable and necessary in specific cases, it also issues coverage policies as national or local coverage determinations for specific items or services. Medicare's coverage determination does not directly establish the Medicare payment rate, which is handled through applicable Medicare payment systems using established payment methods. Medicare does not use coverage as leverage to negotiate prices. Receiving a coverage determination does open the door to a more scalable and predictable approach to paying for new medical innovations.

The Medicare statute does not authorize CMS to take cost into account when making coverage determination, even though cost is CMS's unspoken and constant concern. CMS has made several unsuccessful attempts to bring cost into the "reasonable and necessary" definition in 1989 and 2000, borrowing ideas from managed care plans popular in the private market. The 1989 proposal made by the Health Care Financing Administration (HCFA) – CMS's forerunner – suggested adding cost-effectiveness as a criterion for coverage. Cost-effectiveness was explained in the proposed rule as comparing the effectiveness and costs offered by new technology or treatment against existing ones. Instead of using cost-effectiveness to make go- or no-go coverage decision, HCFA recommended factoring cost-effectiveness into establishing payment levels.

HCFA formally withdrew the 1989 proposal in 1999 and replaced it with another proposal in 2000. HCFA's 2000 proposal introduced a total cost for Medicare beneficiary criterion when the clinical benefit of a new item or service is comparable to a Medicare-covered alternative. This proposal was later abandoned. CMS has since issued several rules clarifying the national coverage determinations (NCD) process and moved towards strengthening evidence-based coverage determination.

CMS issues NCDs that specify whether a particular item or service is covered nationally under Medicare law. An NCD is a national policy statement granting, limiting, or excluding Medicare coverage for a specific medical item or service. An NCD is often written in terms of whether a particular patient population may receive (or not) Medicare reimbursement for a particular item or service. As a formal instruction regarding how to process claims – when to pay, when not to pay, pay only when certain clinical conditions are met – an NCD binds all Medicare contractors and managed care plans. These instructions have a specific effective date dictating when claims will be processed according to the new criteria.

Taking the NCD for next-generation sequencing (NGS) for solid tumors (CAG-00450N) as an example, it specifies that the coverage is only for patients with recurrent, relapsed, refractory, metastatic, or advanced stages III or IV cancer who sought further cancer treatment, and the NCD language allows only one test of the same NGS test for the same tumor. The initial NCD went into effect on January 27, 2020. The National Medicare's Coverage Determinations Manual has information about national coverage determinations, organized by categories, e.g., Medical Procedures, Supplies, Diagnostic Services.

Absent a specific NCD, coverage determinations are made locally by Medicare contractors following related national guidance. Medicare contractors can publish local coverage determinations (LCDs) to advise providers and practitioners when coverage for a particular item and service is available in the contractor's jurisdiction.

Sometimes coverage determinations are made on a claim-by-claim basis under these criteria:

- It's safe and effective;
- It's not experimental or investigational; and
- It's appropriate, including the duration and frequency in terms of whether the service or item is given according to accepted medical practice standards in a proper setting by qualified staff and right for the beneficiary's medical need.

It's worth noting that most technological advances can be reimbursed under one of Medicare's payment systems without being preceded by an explicit coverage determination. For example, IDx-DR, the AI screening tool for diabetic retinopathy, received payments from both physician fee schedule and outpatient PPS through regular rulemaking processes. CMS's decision on ipilimumab, the first immunotherapy, was one sentence in the 2022 outpatient PPS final rule – "We are adopting as final, without modification, our proposal ..." – as CMS received no comments on their proposal to provide separate payment for ipilimumab.

These payment decisions and related coding changes were communicated through Transmittals with Medicare administrative contractors. A study by Tufts Center for the Evaluation of Value and Risk in Health finds that a large majority of FDA-approved breakthrough devices have obtained Medicare reimbursement without being subject to a formal CMS coverage determination, i.e., National Coverage Determination (NCD) or Local Coverage Determination (LCD).

For services or products packaged into service bundles, such as inpatient PPS and outpatient PPS, providers serve as the direct purchaser and select items and services to be used in the payment bundle. Both inpatient PPS and outpatient PPS have transitional payment adjustments to encourage providers to adopt new technologies, including NTAP under inpatient PPS and pass-through payment under outpatient PPS. For example, Viz LVO, the AI tool helps speed up the diagnosis of stroke patients in the ER, received NTAP designation. Most Medicare payment systems, such as inpatient PPS and outpatient PPS, are designed to gradually capture the costs associated with new technologies and reflect the use of new technologies in payment rates without requiring major changes.

A National Coverage Determination (NCD) analysis, a process that allows CMS to research and review evidences, collect public feedback, and establish a national Medicare coverage policy, is more likely to be triggered "when the item or service produces significant clinical consequences for beneficiaries, when the medical community is divided about the merits of an item or service for a particular population, or when the item or service has a significant impact on the Medicare program."

Given the controversy around FDA's 'accelerated approval' of Alzheimer drug, Aduhelm, the debate among scientists and doctors whether clearing amyloid plaques – a surrogate end point in the drug's clinical trials – would slow cognitive decline, and the potential impact on Medicare spending, it's not surprising that CMS initiated an NCD analysis for monoclonal antibodies (MABs) targeting amyloid to treat Alzheimer's disease.

Both NCDs and LCDs establish policies specific to an item or service, and there is no specific order in terms of which should come first. Inconsistent local coverage policies could be a reason for CMS to initiate an NCD so that similar cases are adjudicated under uniform criteria, which was one reason CMS opened an NCD analysis for CAR-T. At the same time, LCDs may be developed absent an NCD or as a supplement to an NCD if the LCD policy does not conflict with national policy. One example is since the NCD for NGS test for solid tumors went into effect, several LCDs have been issued, for example to clarify coverage for lab-developed tests.

MEDICARE NATIONAL COVERAGE DETERMINATION

National coverage determinations are made through an evidence-based process, with opportunities for public participation. The process can take up to nine months. CMS has issued several regulations specifying the NCD process.

The NCD process starts from a request, which can be initiated internally or externally. CMS encourages external requesters – typically a Medicare beneficiary, manufacture, doctor, or trade association – to have informal communications with CMS to gain more insights into relevant materials needed for an NCD review before submitting a formal NCD request. CMS noted that a significant proportion of potential requests were incomplete and withdrawn by potential requesters after communicating with CMS. Common reasons for request withdrawal include:

- There are existing NCDs or LCDs to cover items of interest;
- The request is about coding or payment instead of a national coverage decision;
- The items of interest are a statutorily excluded service;

- The items of interest are packaged services under Medicare's payment rules and won't receive separate payment; and
- The requester realized the lack of sufficient evidence to support an NCD.

To be considered a complete, formal request, it must be a written request with clear statements of applicable statutorily defined benefit category, design, and function of the item of interest, and clinical benefits of the item to Medicare population, supported by sufficient scientific and clinical evidence. An NCD request could be establishing, limiting, or entirely removing a coverage.

The NCD request for CAR-T drugs provides an example of external request. The letter was from UnitedHealthcare which administers MA plans. The impetus for the request was a series of concerns. The request cited the complexity of the therapy, the potential for severe and life-threatening side effects, and the high cost of the therapy and associated care required as justifications for an NCD. Given the high cost of CAR-T drugs, absent an NCD, there would be variations in local coverage decisions, which also affects MA coverage decisions.

Once an NCD request is accepted, CMS will post a tracking sheet for the public to track and participate in the review process, and a request for public comments right away, as for both CAR-T and Alzheimer drug Aduhelm. On average, the NCD review process takes 6-9 months. The first step, staff review, is conducted by the Coverage and Analysis Group (CAG), responsible for developing NCD. In CMS's organizational chart, CAG is grouped under CMS's Center for Clinical Standards and Quality (CCSQ) led by CMS's Chief Medical Officer and Director. CAG also provides oversight of Medicare contractors to make sure that the LCD process is followed correctly.

A proposed decision is normally issued for public comment within six months since the start of an NCD review. And within 60 days after the close of the 30-day public comment on the proposed decision memo, CMS will issue a final NCD decision memo. The statutory timeframe, however, might be extended if CMS convenes a Medicare Evidence Development and Coverage Advisory Committee (MEDCAC) meeting to discuss the quality of the evidence.

CMS established the Medicare Coverage Advisory Committee, later renamed MEDCAC, to provide independent guidance and expert advice to CMS on specific clinical topics. MEDCAC meeting can be an integral part of the NCD process. If CMS requests recommendations from the MEDCAC, the NCD timeframe is extended from six to nine months, which happened in CAR-T's NCD review, and the MEDCAC meeting was convened to review the evidence specific to patient-reported outcomes.

The MEDCAC, composed of about 100 members, includes ten industry representatives, ten patient advocates, and experts in various fields such as clinical medicine, subspecialties, administrative medicine, biologic and physical sciences, public health administration, healthcare data and information management and analysis, healthcare economics, and medical ethics. The MEDCAC meeting panel, comprising no more than fifteen members with knowledge specific to the NCD questions, meets publicly four to eight times throughout the committee's duration. The panel reviews medical evidence related to the NCD question, listen to public testimony, and provides advice on the quality of the evidence.

Sometimes, CMS may require an external technology assessment (TA) to evaluate the available evidence before deciding on the need for an NCD. Usually, a TA follows the opening of an NCD. If CMS requests an external TA as an integral part of an NCD, the NCD timeframe is extended from six to nine months. Generally, an external TA is asked to supplement CAG's internal expertise and resources, for example, when the body of evidence to review is too massive to be completed within the 6-month statutory timeframe, or when there are significant differences in opinion among experts in medical and scientific literature, or when the review requires unique technical and/or clinical knowledge or calls for specialized methods.

CMS has an arrangement with the AHRQ for conducting TA. AHRQ may conduct the TA in-house, select an Evidence-Based Practice Center (EPC) for the task, or contract with other qualified entities. The primary focus of TA is to evaluate the clinical and scientific evidence on clinical benefits and risks, and cost is not a factor in NCD review or coverage decision, even though economic consideration may be a factor discussed in a TA.

The NCD review process for NGS for solid tumors was accelerated because Foundation One CDx participated in the FDA-CMS parallel review program. The parallel review program allows manufacturers to engage both FDA and CMS in the trial design phase so that one clinical study can satisfy both agencies' evidential needs. Additionally, both agencies will review clinical evidence concurrently. This allowed CMS to open the NCD review for NGS for solid tumors on the same day of FDA approval with a proposed decision memo, instead of spending six months to develop one.

The FDA is charged with regulating whether a device or pharmaceutical is "safe and effective," while CMS and its contractors seeks to determine whether an item or service is "reasonable and necessary." Even though both agencies make evidence-based decisions, maybe even based on the same evidence, they are guided by two evidentiary standards and seek to answer different questions. In a recent NCD,

CMS required coverage with evidence development (CED) to collect more data on clinical benefits for FDA approved Alzheimer drug, Aduhelm, which highlights the evidential difference.

However, the industry has questioned whether the parallel review shortens the time to bring innovative medical technologies to patients. Studies have shown CMS's "reasonable and necessary" standard is more stringent than the FDA's "safe and effective" one. To satisfy the evidential needs for both agencies may require longer trial time, in which case seeking FDA approval and then LCDs separately might be faster than a parallel review.

The NCD process may end in a range of possible outcomes. It may result in an NCD, a noncoverage NCD, or an NCD with limitations. For example, CMS may require a CED – the coverage of an item or service is conditioned on the participation of a clinical study, as the case of Aduhelm. CMS first proposed the CED pathway for CAR-T but reversed course in its final decision after strong pushback. For CAR-T, FDA approval requires the therapies are provided in facilities participating FDA Risk Evaluation and Mitigation Strategies (REMS) program, which already limits access to the therapy. An NCD can also limit the patients eligible for a service, frequency/duration of a service, or settings where a service can be provided. Another possibility is CMS may decide not to issue an NCD and let local Medicare contractors make the initial determination.

A final decision memo, though, differs from an NCD. The decision memo is the public document that includes a summary of public comments on the proposed decision and CMS's responses, lays out the reasons for the decision and process followed, and summarizes of the evidence considered. The NCD itself follows the decision memo, sometimes by several months, because "numerous internal, related steps" must occur before a payment change can be issued.

An NCD describes the circumstances for Medicare to cover a specific item or service, specifying covered and non-covered indications, and any coverage criteria. Before the release of an NCD, CMS must determine the codes providers will use for claim submission and the proper payment level. An NCD is often accompanied by a transmittal that instructs Medicare contractors to implement these coding and payment changes. An NCD includes an effective date – the date on which an NCD is effective – and an implementation date – the date when Medicare contractors have all the related coding and payment edits in place to implement the NCD.

Any individual or entity can ask for CMS to reconsider any provision of an existing NCD by filing a formal request for reconsideration. The requester will need to document new scientific and clinical evidence not considered in first NCD or material mistakes made by CMS in the NCD.

For example, the reconsideration request submitted by the Alzheimer's Association on the NCD for MABs directed against amyloid to treat Alzheimer's disease in December 2022 cited new clinical data from a new MAB product, Lecanemab. Specifically, the request referenced a new study published in the New England Journal of Medicine in November 2022 showing improved cognitive function besides surrogate markers and asked CMS to remove the CED requirement. CMS declined the reconsideration request and laid out evidential criteria for reconsideration in a public statement - "evidence that answers the CED questions or approval by the FDA based on evidence of clinical benefit." For NGS for solid tumors, one year after the NCD went into effect, CMS opened a reconsideration internally to evaluate coverage for another indication – germline mutations (inherited mutations).

NCD REVIEW TIMELINE

	MABs Directed Against Amyloid for the Treatment of Alzheimer's Disease	CAR-T Therapy for Cancers	NGS for solid tumors

FDA approval or clearance	6/7/2021 for Aduhelm (aducanumab)	2017 for Tisagenlecleucel (Kymriah®) and axicabtagene ciloleucel (Yescarta®) CAR T-cell therapies	11/30/2017, FoundationOne CDx (F1CDx) (FDA-CMS Parallel Review Program); approval order 12/18/2017
Formal request accepted and review initiated	7/12/2021	5/16/2018	11/30/2017
Public comment period	7/12/2021-8/11/2021	5/16/2018-6/15/2018	NA
MEDCAC meeting	NA	8/22/2018	NA
Proposed decision memo released	1/11/2022	2/15/2019	11/30/2017
Proposed decision memo public comment	NA	2/15/2019-3/17/2019	11/30/2017-1/17/2018 (extended due to FDA approval order)
Decision memo released	4/7/2022	8/7/2019	3/16/2018

Outcome	Coverage with evidence development	An NCD when administered at FDA REMS facilities	An NCD
Effective date	4/7/2022	8/7/2019	1/17/2020 (after NCD reconsideration)

MEDICARE COVERAGE FOR EVIDENCE DEVELOPMENT ACTIVITIES

The controversy surrounded the highly expected Alzheimer drug, Aduhelm, from its FDA approval to CMS's limited coverage decision, turns the spotlight on CMS's coverage with evidence development NCD pathway. While CED is neither new nor rare at CMS since its formal launch in 2005, most CEDs have been for devices or diagnostics or off-label use of approved drugs, rather than new drugs or biologics. However, CED is only one vehicle at CMS's disposal to cover evidence development activities. The other authorized programs include the investigational device exemption (IDE) and the clinical trial policy.

The MMA of 2003 authorized Medicare payment for the routine costs of care provided to Medicare beneficiaries in certain categories of IDE studies, which lowers the financial barrier for beneficiaries and trial sponsors to participate in device clinical trials. Since 2015, the review and approval of IDE studies have been managed directly by CAG. Once an IDE study has received CMS approval, Medicare will cover the routine care items and services in the trial.

When the FDA approves an IDE study, the FDA assigns the device to Category A or B based on whether the risk of the device type has been established. Category A is labeled experimental, for which "absolute risk" of the device type has not been established. Category B is labeled nonexperimental/investigational, for which the underlying questions of safety and effectiveness of the device type have been resolved, or the device type can be safe and effective because, for example, other manufacturers have obtained FDA approval. Medicare does not cover experimental or investigational devices, however, for Category B IDE studies approved by FDA, Medicare also pays for devices used, but not for Category A devices.

The current Medicare clinical trial policies are defined in a 2007 NCD for the clinical trial policy. CMS covers the "routine costs" of qualifying clinical trials for Medicare beneficiaries. These routine costs include the provision of the investigational item, but not the investigational item itself (unless Medicare already covers the item outside the clinical trial), the prevention, diagnosis, and treatment of complications, and generally all items and services that would be covered for a Medicare beneficiary absent the clinical trial, no matter whether a beneficiary is in the experimental or the control arms of a clinical study.

So, what is a qualifying trial? First, certain conditions can directly qualify a trial for Medicare coverage, including trials funded by certain federal agencies like NIH and CDC, or trials conducted under an investigational new drug (IND) application reviewed by FDA. Other clinical trials must meet all these requirements:

- The trial must evaluate an item or service that falls within a Medicare benefit category;
- The trial must NOT be designed exclusively to test toxicity or disease pathophysiology. It must have a therapeutic intent;
- Trials of therapeutic interventions must enroll patients with diagnosed diseases, not healthy volunteers. (Trials of diagnostic interventions may enroll healthy patients as a control group.)

It is generally assumed that many phase 1 trial can't meet these requirements. Besides must-have requirements, there are a list of should-have requirements, including health outcomes as trial aims, proper design, and credibility of the trial sponsor.

Medicare's clinical trial policy also covers trials under CED. Under CED policy, in addition to routine costs, Medicare also pays for promising therapeutics and services that show evidence of significant medical benefit but insufficient evidence to support a "reasonable and necessary" determination when administered in a clinical trial meeting the NCD requirements. The policy isn't limited to NCDs, as some Medicare local coverage decisions may also require data development.

However, covering treatment costs only addresses one barrier to conducting clinical trials. Conducting clinical trials requires dedicated experts from a few disciplines in an extended period, from initial design, trial recruitment and data collection, to reviewing and analyzing trial data. Most of these costs are borne by trial sponsors. There are also other operational and logistical challenges to consider. Facilitating a high-quality registry or trial requires a champion, such as a commercial entity, a patient group, or a scientific community, and this champion is best identified at the time of CED.

For example, in response to CMS's CED requirements to cover positron emission tomography with F-18 fluorodeoxyglucose (FDG-PET) for cancers, the National Oncologic PET Registry (NOPR) was established. The funding for NORP came from the Academy of Molecular Imaging (now World Molecular Imaging Society), whose leadership convinced the industry to fund this effort, and the American College of Radiology manages the registry through the American College of Radiology Imaging Network. Participating doctors were asked to fill out pre-PET and post-PET forms and pay a fee to the registry so the data could be collected and used to assess the effect of PET on referring physician's treatment plans across the spectrum of expended cancer indications (e.g., diagnosis, staging, and treatment monitoring) for multiple cancer types. Given the significant financial and operational investment needed, it's not surprising that some CED-required studies may never be started or completed.

CMS views CED as a balanced approach that "expedites earlier beneficiary access to innovative technology while ensuring that systematic patient safeguards…are in place." However, formal evaluation of the program, such as its impact on patient access to new technology and safety, is not yet available. According to CMS, CMS has issued a total of 26 NCDs requiring CEDs since 2006. CMS has approved 109 CED studies and five national registries to facilitate evidence collection for these CED NCDs, including 42 studies that produced evidence on 14 topics.

Zeitler et al examined the CED program performance by linking CED studies with published trial and registry results and found significant variability. Of the 27 CED NCDs from 2005 to 2022 examined, 7 CEDs had an approved registry, 21 had at least 1 approved clinical trial, and 4 had neither. Of the 7 CEDs with registry, 5 were related to cardiovascular therapies, of which 4 had a registry administered by the American College of Cardiology's

National Cardiovascular Device Registry suite. Of the 23 CEDs with either registries and/or trials, 20 (87%) released results publicly.

The expectation is CED NCD will produce evidence that will lead to revisions to Medicare coverage policies. A CED cycle is completed when CMS completes a reconsideration of the CED NCD and removes the CED requirement as a condition of coverage. As with any NCD, the reconsideration can be initiated both internally and externally and includes a period of public comment. According to CMS, out of the 26 CED NCDs issued, only three have had the CED requirement removed following an NCD reconsideration and received national coverage.

Zeitler et al found that of the 27 CED NCDs examined, the duration of CEDs ranged from 1 to 16 years, and, so far, only four led to the removal of CED requirements. CMS revoked 2 CEDs and deferred the coverage decision to local contractors, such as the CED NCD for home oxygen for cluster headaches, due to the "challenging to implement [CED clinical study requirements] for this treatment due to patient characteristics and care setting."

The variability in CED duration reflects the lack of clearly defined CED timeline or exit criteria. An interesting case to examine is transcatheter aortic valve replacement (TAVR also known as TAVI or transcatheter aortic valve implantation), a minimally invasive heart procedure to replace a bad aortic valve.

The initial CED NCD was issued in 2012, shortly after FDA approval. Since then, TAVR has evolved significantly with newer and safer devices, becoming the gold standard for patients at high surgical risk or considered inoperable, and preferred approach over open-heart surgery in patients at intermediate risk suitable for a transfemoral approach. The procedure experienced a tenfold increase, with annual volumes rising from fewer than 5,000 procedures at 198 sites in 2012 to over 50,000 procedures at 582 sites in 2017.

Despite this advancement, a decade later, CMS hasn't removed the CED requirement for TAVR. In 2017, CMS received a reconsideration request specifically about the non-TAVR volume criteria in the original NCD. These volume requirements for participating sites are a proxy for better outcome. The discussions and comments on CMS's proposed decision memo were less about safety of the procedure or device, or whether the procedure was reasonable and necessary, but about what facilities are better equipped to offer the procedure. The CED requirements, though, come at a price for the health system – the registry enrollment fee alone ran $25,000 in 2019, atop the staff hours collecting and reporting all the data.

The long-standing CED does not seem to dampen the growth trajectory of TAVR; however, it begs the question of what exactly the intent of TAVR CED is, how Medicare's "reasonable and necessary" standard is defined and evaluated, and what the CED exit criterion is.

MEDICARE LOCAL COVERAGE DETERMINATION

Since the inception of the Medicare program, CMS has contracted with private insurance companies to serve as intermediaries between the traditional Medicare program and healthcare providers. Medicare Administrative Contractors are multi-state, regional contractors responsible for administering both Medicare Part A and Medicare Part B claims in their jurisdiction. There are 12 Part A/B MACs and 4 Durable Medical Equipment (DME) MACs serving over 1.1 million healthcare providers enrolled in the Medicare Part A & B program, and processing claims for about 36 million Medicare beneficiaries.

MACs act on behalf of the CMS as the direct point of contact for claims submission and payment, policy establishment, and special pricing of services. Each MAC determines whether a particular use of an item or service is reasonable and necessary, and eligible for Medicare payment in its jurisdiction. Other responsibilities of MACs include call-center services, clinician enrollment, provider education, and fraud investigation.

MACs play a significant role in determining Medicare coverage. MACs are responsible for creating and updating local coverage determinations through an evidence-based policy-making process to define the conditions under which an item or service is considered reasonable and necessary, and hence covered by Medicare in their jurisdiction.

Additionally, MACs issue Articles that address local coverage, coding or medical review related billing and claims considerations. These articles may include newly developed educational materials, coding instructions, or clarification of existing medical review-related billing or claims policy. Billing and coding Articles contain information such as what clinical circumstances and diagnoses are considered medically necessary, specific documentation requirements, and how to bill for services. They serve as a tool that helps providers in submitting correct claims.

There are various reasons a MAC may want to develop an LCD. A MAC may want to establish an automated review process when there are no appropriate NCDs, or when there is a need to define further NCD conditions for a service not covered under certain circumstances. A MAC may also undertake the effort to develop an LCD to avoid issuing frequent denials. A multistate contractor may want to generate uniform LCDs across its jurisdiction. Lastly, an LCD may be needed to ensure beneficiary access to care.

The development of LCDs is led by the Contractor Medical Director (CMD), who is a physician and a leader in the provider community. The CMD's clinical expertise and judgement guide determinations regarding the need for LCDs and updates and ensure the appropriateness of LCDs. Their leadership responsibilities involve engaging the provider community in the LCD process and acting as a co-chair of the Contractor Advisory Committee (CAC).

In response to changes made by the 21st Century Cures Act (Cures Act) of 2016 to the LCD process, and public concerns about LCD process transparency and lack of stakeholder engagement, CMS significantly changed the LCD process in October 2018. The aim was to "increase transparency, clarity, consistency, reduce provider burden and enhance public relations while retaining the ability to be responsive to local clinical and coverage policy concerns." The revised Chapter 13 of the Medicare Program Integrity Manual specifies steps that MACs must follow to issue an LCD. Key aspects of the LCD development process include:

- The new LCD process introduces an option for requesting informal meetings with the MAC to discuss potential LCD requests. These meetings are for educational purposes only and are not for pre-decisional negotiations.

- For requesting an LCD, healthcare providers or MedTech companies must be conducting business in the MAC's jurisdiction.

- Like the NCD request, a complete, formal request for an LCD must be submitted in writing and include clearly defined Medicare benefit category, LCD language, justification supported by peer-reviewed evidence, and explanations of product/service design and medical benefits.

- Within 60 calendar days after receiving the request, the MAC is required to inform the requester, in writing, whether the request is complete or incomplete.

- The proposed LCD is published on the Medicare Coverage Database (MCD), allowing a 45-calendar-day public comment period.

- After the proposed LCD is made public, MACs are required to hold public meetings.

- MACs are required to respond to all comments received in the Response to Comment (RTC) Article. The final LCD and RTC Article will be published on the MCD.

- The LCD can take effect after 45 calendar days of notice period following the publication of final LCD.

The new process ensures that the public and other stakeholders have opportunities to provide feedback in the LCD process. However, the final decision on all issues related to LCDs rests with the MAC. In addition to commenting and public meeting requirements for stakeholder input, the revised Chapter 13 also requires MACs to establish one CAC per state or have the option of establishing one CAC per jurisdiction or a multi-jurisdictional CAC with representation from each state.

CAC membership often draws from doctors with each state medical specialty typically represented by one member. The revised LCD process expands CAC representation by including other healthcare professionals, such as nurses, social workers, and epidemiologists. Beneficiary representation is also required on the CAC, and CAC meetings are now open to the public.

The LCD process includes a reconsideration process to re-evaluate the evidentiary basis for an LCD decision and an appeal process to challenge applicable LCDs that result in coverage denial. Additionally, individual claims denied due to an LCD can be appealed case by case.

CMS further clarified the revised LCD process in a subsequent Q&A document. In response to concerns that the commenting process outlined in Chapter 13 may cause delays in approvals for new technologies, CMS stated that MACs typically must finalize or retire all proposed LCDs within a rolling year since the publication of a proposed LCD. CMS also clarified that for an individual LCD, it's at the discretion of the MAC whether to host CAC meetings for LCD consideration and whether to host CAC meetings before posting a proposed LCD or after the publication of the proposed LCD.

Under the new process, MACs must remove coding instructions from LCDs. This creates a bifurcated system where billing & coding information is placed in Articles instead of being part of LCDs. This approach aligns with NCDs, which have not had coding information since 2006. This separation between LCDs and coding instructions allows coverage policy to remain independent of coding changes. However, concerns have been raised by AMA and other specialty societies about the potential inappropriate use of Articles to advance policies rather than simply provide billing instructions. Articles do not have to undergo the same public notification and commenting process as LCDs, which has raised concerns about transparency and stakeholder input.

Sometimes, a single MAC processes all claims for a specific Medicare-covered item or service for all Medicare beneficiaries around the country. This typically occurs when there is only one supplier of a particular item, medical device, or diagnostic test, such as a test developed by a laboratory under the Clinical Laboratory Improvement Amendments without FDA approval or clearance. In this situation, MA plans must follow the coverage requirements or LCDs of the MAC that enrolled the supplier.

MACs typically make LCDs independently, which sometime result in inconsistencies in coverage policies. However, the MolDX program stands out as a unique initiative. It was established in 2011 by Palmetto GBA, a subsidiary of Blue Cross Blue Shield of South Carolina, specifically to address the growing number and complexity of molecular diagnostic tests (MDTs). MDTs involve the detection or identification of nucleic acid(s) (DNA/RNA), proteins, chromosomes, enzymes, cancer chemotherapy sensitivity and/or other metabolite(s). The MolDX program focuses on DNA/RNA tests, including laboratory-developed tests that are designed, manufactured, and used within a single laboratory under the Clinical Laboratory Improvement Amendments (CLIA), most often without FDA approval or clearance.

What sets the MolDX program apart is its integration of test registration, coding application (Z-code), coverage determinations, and payment into a single platform. Another distinguish feature is its substantial expertise in molecular diagnostic testing. To be considered for coverage, laboratory developers must submit a clinical dossier for technology assessment. The MolDX team, supported by subject matter experts, evaluates the analytical performance of the test as well as clinical validity and clinical utility studies submitted. The goal is to determine if an assay demonstrates clinical utility and meets the CMS "reasonable and necessary" criteria as defined in associated MolDX policies.

Several MACs have since joined the program. Through established operating agreements with Palmetto GBA, they implement and process claims using MolDX guidelines in their jurisdiction. The program covers multiple jurisdictions, encompassing 28 states. The MolDX program offers an alternative to NCDs in addressing inconsistencies in Medicare coverage policies across different geographic areas. Additionally, it can potentially improve the LCD process efficiency by avoiding redundant coverage evaluation process and fostering expertise in some highly specialized subject areas.

MEDICAID COVERAGE DETERMINATION

All states run Medicaid programs that provide comprehensive benefits. In addition to covering routine services, including hospital, doctor, laboratory and imaging, Medicaid can cover many Medicare-excluded services, such as preventive care, dental services (optional for adult), and vision care. For children under the age of 21 eligible for Medicaid's Early and Periodic Screening, Diagnostic and Treatment (EPSDT) benefits, Medicaid generally covers the costs of eye exams, eyeglasses, oral screening, and dental examination, hearing, and screening services. Optional

Medicaid benefits include prescription drugs, physical therapy, and occupational therapy. While federal Medicaid law sets out coverage parameters for Medicaid program, states may determine the type, amount, duration, and scope of services to cover for Medicaid enrollees.

In most states, staff has little guidance regarding the standards they should apply, the evidence they should consider, or the process they should follow in making Medicaid coverage determinations. Many state Medicaid programs published definitions of medical necessity, but only a few posted coverage determination standards, policies, procedures to initiate a Medicaid coverage review, and the evidence needed for evaluation. With ever-burdening budget constraints, it has been reported that in many states, the coverage decision on high-cost therapies (e.g., with a price tag $500,000 or more) requires approval from high-level officials, such as the health commissioner, the legislature, or the governor. Some states, such as Oregon and New York, have established systematic evidence-based coverage determination processes.

Oregon uses a Prioritized List of Health Services to guide coverage determinations, and only services ranked above the legislature-approved funding line on the Prioritized list are covered. The development of the Prioritized List was initiated by Oregon Legislature in 1987 to guide effective and accountable allocation of resources for healthcare. Each service is scored with explicit consideration of priority of service category, impact on both individual and population health, effectiveness, and desirableness of a service for a patient population. The ranking of service category places greater emphasis on preventive services and chronic disease management. Within each service category, services are scored based on impact in five domains, including healthy life years, suffering, population effects, vulnerability of population affected, and complication prevention. Since its adoption in 1993, over 1.5 million Oregonians have been covered under the Prioritized List.

In Oregon, the Health Evidence Review Commission (HERC) decides whether to cover a service, and HERC considers the best evidence available as well as the needs and concerns of patients and providers. The public can nominate a topic. HERC staff conduct research and work with Evidence-based Guidelines subcommittee to define the scope and draft first coverage guidance, which is the phase I of the three-phase coverage guidance process.

HERC's coverage guidance process also includes public comment periods and public meetings along the way. The HERC develops recommendations using the ideas of the Grading of Recommendations Assessment, Development and Evaluation (GRADE) system, which is a transparent and structured framework for developing and presenting summaries of evidence and making recommendations. Each identified outcome is graded based on strength of evidence, called the confidence level (e.g., low, or moderate confidence). Evidence considered includes published systematic reviews, meta-analyses, and reviews conducted by the Oregon Health Sciences University's (OHSU) Center for Evidence Based Policy. HERC also factors in cost, value compared to alternative interventions, and provider and patient preference in developing recommendations.

When New York Governor Andrew M. Cuomo created the team to redesign Medicaid in 2011, reducing costs was one explicit goal. The evidence-based benefit submission and evaluation process was borne out of the Medicaid redesign initiative, often called the Dossier Process. Stakeholders can submit requests for a coverage determination through a dossier intake process, through which the state collects information on clinical evidence, outcomes, target population, and costs.

The state conducts its own search for evidence and uses the Population, Intervention, Comparator, and Outcome (PICO) framework to help focus the evidence review on a manageable research topic. New York State has established a hierarchy of evidence structure, with systematic review at the top of the hierarchy, observational studies in the middle, and expert and case reports at the bottom. The Dossier Process integrates the use of GRADE for synthesizing evidence and determining the strength of evidence.

New York's coverage decision is based on an assessment of the net impact of a service factoring in both harms and benefits. The measurement of net impact is derived from a sophisticated multi-step quantitative approach using odds ratio, relative risk, effect size, and number needed to treat, and considers diagnostic efficacy measured by sensitivity, specificity, positive and negative predictive values, and likelihood ratios, as well as harm calculated as hazard ratio and number needed to harm. While other factors may influence the coverage decision New York Department of Health (DOH) will decline to cover interventions with any of the following criteria:

• Zero or negative net impact; or

• Very low strength of the body of evidence; or

• No evidence.

Coverage of the service under review will generally be granted when both of these criteria are met:

• A high strength of evidence; and

• A substantial or moderate positive net impact.

The Dossier Process offers a 30-day comment period to the public, during which more resources of evidence may be submitted.

The Medicaid Evidence-Based Decisions (MED) project is a collaborative initiative created to help state policymakers make the best evidence-based decisions on Medicaid coverage and benefits. The MED initiative is coordinated by the OHSU Center for Evidence-Based Policy and 27 states have joined the initiative by 2021.

Participating states may nominate topics for review, and in 2021, the center completed 18 research reports for the MED project on a range of topics, including maternal care, telehealth, COVID-19 disparity, and child immunizations. MED reports provide evidence about effective treatments, information about harmful or unnecessary services, and details on coverage and policies from state Medicaid agencies across the country. MED members meet regularly to review report findings and discuss implementation issues. Members also collaborate through workgroups that address focused areas, including behavioral health, telehealth, substance use disorders, genetic testing, and durable medical equipment.

The creation of MED was built on the experience of the Drug Effectiveness Review Project (DERP), also run by OHSU's Center for Evidence-Based Policy. It's a joint effort by 28 state Medicaid programs and public pharmacy programs aimed at supporting state drug coverage decisions. From the onset, the center was asked to conduct systematic reviews of certain classes of drugs – syntheses based on a comprehensive search of evidence. The review primarily focuses on effectives and harms of an intervention, and evidence about cost and cost-effectiveness is not included.

The reports do not have a coverage or funding recommendation, so states Medicaid programs may incorporate other factors, such as cost and provider preference, to make decisions. The multi-state collaborative defines the project's agenda by nominating and deciding on the topics DERP should research. Topics selected for the next phase of DERP review include gene therapies, spinal muscular atrophy, management strategies for hemophilia treatment, therapies to treat Duchenne muscular dystrophy, and an ongoing look at the ever-evolving high-cost drug pipeline.

To supplement standard comprehensive literature search, DERP has been soliciting both published and unpublished evidence from pharmaceutical manufacturers. A recent retrospective review shows that for the 40 systematic reviews conducted between 2006 and 2015, DERP received 160 dossiers. Out of 7360 studies/datasets submitted, 2.2% (160) were included in a DERP review, though, the ratio of submitted-to-included increased over time. Almost 42% of the studies submitted were unpublished. Most of the submitted studies were rated fair quality by the original systematic review authors, with 7.3% rated as good and 14% rated as poor quality. Out of all the literature considered for the 40 systematic reviews, 7.2% came from a dossier, and 16% of dossier studies were included in a meta-analysis. The dossier studies changed conclusions in 42% of the systematic reviews. Out of 46 unpublished unique studies in a systematic review, 25 (54%) influenced the conclusions for the manufacturers drug, 8% favored a competitor drug, and 40% favored neither.

Most states (35 of 50 reporting states) incorporate comparative effectiveness review (CER) information in drug coverage reviews. Besides DERP and MED, the Institute for Clinical and Economic Review (ICER) is another often-cited source of information. Most states (46 of 50 reporting states) reported having a preferred drug list (PDL) as of July 1, 2019, to control drug costs and offer incentives to prescribe preferred drugs. Sixteen states whose pharmacy benefit is delivered through managed care organizations (MCOs) reported having a uniform PDL between traditional Medicaid and MCOs, and eight states indicated they planned to establish or expand a uniform PDL.

PRIVATE PAYER COVERAGE DECISION MAKING

With over 1,000 registered private health insurance companies in the US, the private payer market is both exciting and overwhelming. According to a survey conducted among members of the National Association of Managed Care Physicians (NAMCP), an organization representing over 20,000 medical directors from payers, purchasers (employers), and provider systems, the coverage determination process varies at individual plan level in terms of number and nature of staff involved in the technology assessment process, where evidence is sourced, how evidence is assessed, whether external expertise is engaged, and who is involved in decision making.

Like public payer, new coverage determination can be initiated both externally (e.g., product developer, provider, or specialty society) or internally, as plans actively monitor medical technology trends, clinical practice guidelines, and Medicare coverage determinations. In evaluating benefit design, private payers also consider what employers and consumers want and will pay for.

The journey to coverage begins at the formation of an evidence or value dossier. These dossiers summarize the key clinical and economic evidence for a product and characterize dimensions of product value. The Academy of Managed Care Pharmacy (AMCP) Dossier Format was introduced in 2000 to facilitate the exchange of information between drug manufacturers and payers and has evolved through several versions since. The original AMCP Format was developed to address evidence for drugs, biologics, and vaccines. The current Version 4.0 has been updated to include guidelines on the evidentiary requirements for companion diagnostic tests. The Format can convey evidentiary requirements for medical devices, such as implantable drug delivery devices, blood glucose measuring devices, test strips, and inhalation devices, even though some areas of the format might not apply for medical device.

The benefit of submitting a dossier through the AMCP portal is that it will be made available to healthcare decision-makers (health plans, PBMs, government agencies, etc.) upon their unsolicited requests. The information can support coverage and reimbursement consideration of a new product or new indication of an existing product. The utility of AMCP dossier, though, varies widely among decision-makers.

Besides the product information, disease description, and clinical evidence, the AMCP dossier also requests information on health economics and outcomes research and economic models on budget impact and cost-effectiveness. Different payers might have different views on economic modeling. While plans do assess the impact of coverage decision, many are skeptical about rosy saving forecast and assumptions made in modeling to derive the savings.

Greater emphasis has been placed on clinical data (including harms), comparators and comparative outcome, real-world data outside of investigational settings, and pricing. The recent coverage controversy around Alzheimer drugs through FDA's accelerated approval process also shows the payer's mistrust of surrogate markers and clear preference for endpoint outcomes. The pricing consideration might be more complicated for pharmaceutical products because of the involvement of other players, like pharmacy benefit managers and group purchasing organizations, and rebate and other price concessions that might complicate the calculation of price.

Plans generally take an evidence-based approach for coverage decision-making. While coverage criteria are not always publicly available, the BlueCross and BlueShield Association (BCBSA) Technology Evaluation Center's (TEC, ceased to exist) clinical coverage criteria are generally viewed as the template many plans used to derive their own. BCBSA TEC's coverage criteria include these key elements:

- The technology must have final approval from the proper governmental regulatory bodies (when required).
- The scientific evidence must permit conclusions about the effect of the technology on health outcomes.
- The technology must improve net health outcomes.
- The technology must be as beneficial as any established alternatives.
- The improvement must be attainable outside investigational settings.

The level of health technology assessment work performed by plans varies. Some plans have internal medical technology evaluation team, while others may collaborate with external organizations. While large plans tend to have an internal technology evaluation unit, the Kaiser

Permanente Evidence-based Practice Center (KP EPC) is an exceptional example, the only one out of nine AHRQ EPCs affiliated with an insurance plan. The KP EPC has over 75 researchers. Like other AHRQ EPCs, KP EPC conducts systematic reviews or methods-related projects for many groups, including the Effective Health Care Program, the USPSTF, the CDC, the National Cancer Institute and Patient-Centered Outcomes Research Institute, besides supporting KP's own technology assessment needs.

The BCBSA has a proprietary, subscription-based web platform, Evidence Street™, to collect and analyze available peer-reviewed evidence on devices, diagnostics and pharmaceuticals and issue technology reviews to their subscribers. The influence of Evidence Street's technology assessment is not limited to independent, community-based Blue Cross Blue Shield (BCBS) plans. Large plans, like Aetna and Cigna, cite Evidence Street's assessments in their coverage decisions as well.

The Blue Shield of California takes a different approach by relying on an independent appraisal committee – California Technology Assessment Forum (CTAF), also an ICER program. CTAF convenes three public meetings each year to review evidence reports, directly engage clinicians, patients, and payers, and develop recommendations. California Blue's technology reviews are held with CTAF meetings, and the Blue Shield of California Medical Policy

Committee uses CTAF recommendations when making coverage determinations.

For national payers who maintain various plan offerings, the technology assessment process is often the same, and individual plans incorporate the technology assessment into their policy following government requirements and contractual rules. Smaller health plans have much more limited staffing and often depend on technology assessments produced by outside private or public agencies.

The influence of ICER on payers' decision-making has been growing in recent years. Founded in 2006, ICER is an independent health technology assessment organization. ICER's profile was elevated in 2015 when they started the Emerging Therapy Assessment and Pricing program, funded through a $5.2 million grant from the Laura and John Arnold Foundation (now Arnold Ventures). It becomes a price watchdog in the US, and its reviews determine cost-effectiveness of pharmaceutical drugs through incremental cost-effectiveness thresholds of $50,000 to $150,000 per quality-adjusted life year (QALY). A 2018 study by Xcenda found that 78% of payers stated that ICER recommendations influenced their coverage decisions, up from 49% in 2016.

Criticism has risen with ICER's growing reputation. Some patient groups accused that ICER's findings were used by payers to deny patient access to drugs. In addition, ICER evaluations look at cost-effectiveness for entire US patient populations, and do not offer assessment for specific subpopulations, which limits its generalizability, as private payers may be interested in targeting certain treatments or services to certain subpopulation groups.

Larger plans rely on staff to assemble evidence package for coverage review, while smaller ones may contract with a third-party. The evidence synthesis process is similar, generally involving a literature search of clinical studies, evaluation of practice guidelines, consideration of existing coverage and product fit under existing infrastructure, and consultation with doctors with expertise in the disease area.

Some plans apply a hierarchy of criteria and evidence with federal and state mandates (e.g., CMS NCDs) placed on the top of the hierarchy. Systematic reviews and randomized clinical trial results are often ranked higher in the evidential hierarchy, while clinical position papers of specialty societies and expert opinion are on the lower end., There may be special coverage requirements for Medicare MA, Medicare Part D, or Medicaid managed care programs.

Not a lot of information is available about the internal coverage decision-making process. According to a survey of private payers, medical directors participate in the medical policy review process for new technology in 96% of plans surveyed. However, only in 27% of plans, medical directors have final authority over coverage decisions. The evidence package is normally reviewed by a plan's Medical Policy or Pharmacy Policy Committee. If a drug falls under the pharmacy benefit, pharmacy director might be the one responsible for the internal review process and the coverage is managed by the plan's Pharmacy Policy Committee. Most coverage decision processes occur one or more times throughout the year.

Large plans such as UnitedHealthcare, Aetna, and Blues, maintain a library of medical coverage policies. These policies have the payer's coverage reasoning, interpretation of current medical evidence and literature, conditions of coverage, as well as billing and coding instructions. Not every technology, though, will have an individual coverage policy. Often, private payers bundle multiple technologies under a single policy in disease areas where multiple service options/treatments exist. Sometimes plans may impose more requirements on coverage such as prior authorization and step therapy.

PART FIVE

THE MULTIFACETED ROLES OF HEALTHCARE PROVIDERS

AMA's House of Delegates includes 125 national medical specialty societies that can nominate physician representatives on the Advisory Committees to the CPT Editorial Panel and RVS Update Committee. The Health Care Professionals Advisory Committee, which is represented on both CPT Editorial Panel and RVS Update Committee, include 19 organizations representing non-physician healthcare professionals such as nurses and physical therapists.

THE MULTIFACETED ROLES OF HEALTHCARE PROVIDERS

Healthcare providers play a host of essential roles in medical innovations that span from identifying unmet need, initiating innovative ideas, conducting research, designing, and validating products or solutions, to commercializing and utilizing medical innovations in patient care. Healthcare providers are at the frontline of medical innovations themselves. In fact, the model of academic medical center was built on the idea that the tripartite mission — clinical care, education, and research — integrated under one organizational umbrella would enable a seamless loop for medical innovation by identifying research topics in clinical care, testing research findings in clinical practice, and disseminating best practice through medical education of the next generation clinicians.

Since the Bayh-Dole Act of 1980, which allows federal grantees and contractors to patent and license inventions stemming from federally funded research, academic medical institutions have commercialized their intellectual property through licensing. Many leading academic medical institutions have been known as innovation powerhouses and startup hubs. Studies also show contributions of physician entrepreneurs in medical innovations.

Recognizing the important role of clinicians in medical innovations, many specialty societies invest efforts in helping build physician-innovator partnerships and encourage physician entrepreneurship. The Heart Rhythm Society convened a forum in 2015 discussing obstacles to physician's involvement in medical device innovation and potential solutions. The proceedings from the forum outlines ways professional societies can assist physician innovators. Aiming to bring better healthcare solutions to market, AMA launched the Physician Innovation Network in 2017, a match-making tool to connect physicians with innovators. Many specialty societies have their own match-making database and provide seed funds to support early-stage ventures.

This chapter will discuss key roles healthcare providers play in reimbursement decision making for medical innovations. Healthcare providers influence reimbursement decision-making for medical innovations by sharing their clinical expertise, translating research into evidence-based clinical practice, and facilitating data collection for medical research. Specialty societies and clinical experts are consulted through various channels in the coding, coverage and payment decision making process. In coverage with evidence development, specialty societies are the main sponsors of clinical data registries. Healthcare providers are also the direct purchaser of most of the medical innovations, and most institutions have built and rely on value analysis committees to make purchase decisions.

KEY INFLUENCER OVER CPT AND RUC PROCESS

The significance of the CPT Editorial Panel in coding determination and the RUC in setting PFS rates cannot be understated. The CPT Panel considers and recommends changes sought by individual doctors, specialty societies, device manufacturers or others in the over 10,000 CPT codes.

The panel may create, revise, or delete the codes. Those codes are the building blocks of payment, determining by precise description what services are rendered.

While CPT codes list the services eligible for payment, the RUC measures how many allowable separate parts compose the reimbursable service by recommending relative values for new or revised CPT codes. For the period between 1993 and 2022, RUC made over 7,400 relative value recommendations. CMS receives these recommendations from the RUC and accepts RUC's recommendations over 90% of the times. The CPT and RUC have created a process to give clinicians a voice in describing the resources required to provide professional services, and the influence of specialty societies flow through specialty advisors to the CPT panel and RUC.

CPT is a multi-specialty committee with 12 out of 21 CPT panel members appointed by national medical specialty societies. There are also two member seats for HCPAC to represent the voice of non-physician clinicians. The HCPAC comprises 19 organizations representing physician assistants, chiropractors, nurses, occupational therapists, optometrists, physical therapists, podiatrists, psychologists, audiologists, speech pathologists, social workers, and registered dieticians.

In addition, all the national medical specialty societies who are members of AMA's House of Delegates and HCPAC members are represented on the CPT advisory committee. CPT advisors review code change application before the CPT panel meeting and provide comments for the panel to review. They play a crucial role in the code creation and modification process and have a significant voice in influencing changes and ensuring the perspective of specialty societies are represented. Coding changes can have powerful effects on payment, even though the effect may not be intuitive or immediately apparent. Many code submissions require negotiation and coordination among several specialties since gain for one may mean loss for another.

Like the CPT panel, the 32-member RUC committee has 22 members appointed by major national medical specialty societies, "including those recognized by the American Board of Medical Specialties, those with a large percentage of physicians in patient care, and those that account for high percentages of Medicare expenditures." Four seats rotate on a 2-year basis, one seat reserved for a primary care representative, two reserved for an internal medicine subspecialty, and the remaining seat is open to any other specialty society not represented on the RUC committee. The HCPAC members with three physician members of the RUC comprise the RUC HCPAC Review Board, which is responsible for developing relative value recommendations for new, revised, and potentially misvalued codes primarily reported by non-physician clinicians.

Also, like the CPT panel, all the specialty societies have a seat to serve on the RUC advisory committee. RUC advisors designate an RVS Committee for their specialty, which is responsible for generating relative value recommendations using a survey method developed by the RUC. RUC Advisors attend the RUC meeting and present their societies' recommendations for the RUC committee to evaluate. They ensure the services of their specialties are effectively represented in the code valuation process.

Although support from specialty societies is not required in the CPT and RUC process, its benefits are unquestionable. In the CPT review process, applications that receive no support from CPT advisors will be notified to the applicant and presented to the CPT editorial panel for a discussion about possible solutions. The RUC process factors in societies' level of interest in developing a relative value recommendation. Specialty societies have dedicated personnel knowledgeable about the CPT and RUC process, which are valuable sources for information.

The AMA encourages applicants to seek feedback from specialty society experts before submitting a CPT change request. Most code applications are submitted by specialty societies. For example, the level I CPT code application for IDx-DR, automated point of care retinal imaging, was submitted by the American Academy of Ophthalmology, and the level III CPT code application for HeartFlow's

FFRCT was submitted collectively by American College of Cardiology, the Society of Cardiovascular Computed Tomography, and the Society for Cardiovascular Angiography and Interventions.

Inputs from clinician experts also play a key role in PE valuation, which determines PFS payment for most new technologies, as the cost of new technologies is typically reported as a type of practice expense and reimbursed through the PE RVU. The PE methodology, though, is still a work in progress. The development of resource-based practice expense component was a substantial undertaking as it requires an estimate of each physician specialty's total practice expense and the proper allocation of practice expense to individual services.

The initial direct cost inputs used in the 1999, when the transition from physician charges to resource-based PE valuation started, were based on Clinical Practice Expert Panels (CPEPs) convened in 1995. These panels included 15 experts representing physicians, nurses, and practice administrators to develop estimates of "direct inputs" (non-physician clinical labor, medical supplies, procedure-specific equipment, and overhead equipment) necessary to perform medical procedures represented by CPT codes. Implementing the resource-based method caused protracted controversy because of the redistribution of payment among different specialties under the new PE model.

CMS sought support from AMA in its ongoing efforts to improve payments. To meet this need, the AMA RUC developed a subcommittee called the Practice Expense Advisory Committee (PEAC), which was primarily responsible for the analysis and refinement of the original CPEP data. Through its last meeting in March 2004, the PEAC provided recommendations for over 7,600 codes. Now those PE-related activities are addressed by the AMA RUC PE Subcommittee.

Since 2018, CMS has engaged RAND in studies exploring how CMS might improve the PE methodology. CMS is interested in establishing an ongoing data collection system by specialty and a new framework for allocating PE to better capture variation in PE resources provided in individual services. In the CY 2023 PFS proposed rule, CMS asked for information on how to improve the collection of PE data inputs and refine the PE methodology. In the final rule, CMS indicated its intention to move to a standardized and routine approach to the valuation of indirect PE and asked about possible alternatives to AMA's Physician Practice Information Survey, which was last conducted in 2007-2008.

The RUC process is closely coordinated with the CPT and CMS's rule cycle. The initial "Level of Interest" form that identifies potentially misvalued services is based on the CPT panel's coding actions and specific CMS requests. The

RUC advisors review the form and indicate their societies' level of interest in developing a relative value recommendation. AMA staff then distribute survey instruments to interested specialty society RVS committees.

Specialty societies lead the RUC survey process of at least 30 practicing physicians. Physicians receiving the survey are asked to evaluate the work involved in the new, revised or potentially misvalued code relative to a list 10 to 20 reference services. Claims data analysis and other studies may be used to supplement the physician survey. The specialty RVS committees prepare recommendations to the RUC based on survey findings, which are distributed before the RUC meetings. The specialty advisors present the recommendations at the RUC meeting, followed by a thorough question-and-answer session. Final recommendations to CMS must be adopted by a two-thirds majority of the RUC members, and the final vote counts are released annually.

Unlike the CPT panel, which maintains an open process and convenes public meetings to solicit direct input from practicing physicians, medical device manufacturers, diagnostic tests developers, and advisors from over 100 societies, attendance at RUC meetings is by invitation only as a guest of either a specialty society or the RUC Chair. Attendees of either the CPT Editorial Panel or RUC meetings must sign a confidentiality agreement as the detailed results of the meetings are confidential until they are published by CMS in a proposed rule and released by AMA with the final CPT descriptors. The public also have an opportunity to weigh in when CMS incorporates RUC recommendations in their PFS proposed rule and seeks feedback in its comment period.

ADVISOR IN PAYERS' COVERAGE DETERMINATIONS

Medical innovations in clinical settings often involve many healthcare providers. For example, in molecular diagnostic testing, laboratory medicine professionals include molecular pathologists (typically board-certified M.D. pathologists), clinical molecular geneticists (typically board-certified Ph.D. laboratorians), and medical technologists. Often, these providers are represented nationally and regionally by professional organizations. The molecular diagnostic testing field is represented by the Association for Molecular Pathology (AMP), the College of American Pathologists (CAP), the American Society for Clinical Pathology, the American College of Medical Genetics and Genomics, the American Clinical Laboratory Association, and the American Association for Clinical Chemistry.

In the case of HeartFlow FFRCT, the technology is of great interest of doctors and nurses specialized in cardiovascular care, who are represented by the American College of Cardiology, doctors, scientists, and technologists in the cardiovascular CT community represented by the Society of Cardiovascular Computed Tomography, and invasive/interventional cardiologists and catheter lab team members represented by the Society for Cardiovascular Angiography and Interventions.

Payers turn to medical specialists for guidance about clinical effectiveness. Specialty societies and many others are actively involved in and influence coverage discussions at the local and national level. At the state level, state medical societies are normally represented in the Contractor Advisory Committee to provide feedback on evidentiary quality for local coverage determinations. These organizations also provide comments on proposed LCDs through the public commenting process. For example, the American College of Radiology (ACR), established an ACR Carrier Advisory Committee Network to help state chapters in engaging with MACs and creating a more organized and effective mechanism for dealing with coverage and payment issues. The ACR has used a combination of clinical and economic experts to develop model LCDs for use by MACs. As experts in their specialty areas, medical specialty societies are also sought by private plans to provide services that impact coverage decision.

Professional society recommendations, consensus statements or other expert opinions are often cited in both NCDs and LCDs. For example, the LCDs for Eversense implantable continuous glucose monitoring included opinions from the American Association of Clinical Endocrinologists, the American College of Endocrinology, and the Advanced Technologies and Treatments for Diabetes Congress. The American Association of Clinical Endocrinologists and the American College of Endocrinology convened a conference to review available CGM data and findings were summarized in a consensus report. Conclusions from the authors were cited in the LCD for implantable CGM.

The involvement of providers in coverage and payment issues is not limited to professional organizations. Individual professionals can influence the discussions through involvement in a wide spectrum of committees and may provide written or public comments to coverage determinations of both public and private payers. The roster of Medicare Evidence Development & Coverage Advisory Committee, established to provide guidance and expert advice to CMS on national coverage determinations, include healthcare providers in various specialty areas, many of whom are actively involved in state and/or national specialty societies.

Another way that specialty societies influence payers' coverage decisions is by developing clinical guidelines. The Institute of Medicine (IOM) – now known as the National Academy of Medicine (NAM) – defines clinical practice guidelines (CPGs) as "statements that include recommendations intended to optimize patient care that are informed by a systematic review of evidence and an assessment of the benefits and harms of alternative care options." Guidelines are also viewed as a "convenient way of packaging evidence and presenting recommendations to healthcare decision makers." While guideline development can be centralized at the national level like the UK National Institute for Health and Clinical Excellence, medical specialty societies produce most CPGs used in the United States.

CPGs translate scientific evidence into clinical practice with recommendations to improve care. The CPGs developed by specialty societies represent evidence-based, expert consensus of a profession. They are written testimonies of "accepted standards of medical practice," a criterion used by payers to draw conclusions about the "reasonable and necessary" nature of a service or procedure. CPGs are not only considered in NCDs and LCDs but also followed to initiate updates to coverage determinations.

In the national coverage determination for next-generation sequencing tests, CMS's decision memo cited

CPGs by the National Comprehensive Cancer Network and expert opinions from the American College of Obstetricians and Gynecologists and Society for Maternal-Fetal Medicine Committee. When the AHA/ACC/ASE/CHEST/SAEM/SCCT/SCMR Guideline for the Evaluation and Diagnosis of Chest Pain was updated in 2021 with guidelines for HeartFlow FFRCT as an alternative to stress test in specific clinical settings, MACs updated their LCDs for FFRCT accordingly.

Absent LCD, NCD, or CMS manual instruction, CPGs developed by national medical societies and healthcare professionals with recognized clinical expertise are often treated by payers as authoritative and reliable evidence to evaluate whether a diagnosis or treatment is furnished in accordance with accepted standards of medical practice or "reasonable and necessary."

To guide ethical relationships between specialty societies and the pharmaceutical and MedTech industries, the Council of Medical Specialty Societies (CMSS), which represents about 50 national specialty societies, adopted a Code for Interactions with Companies in 2010. The Code was introduced on the heels of a report released on *Conflict of Interest in Medical Research, Education and Practice* by the then IOM and the Physician Payment Sunshine Act adopted as part of the ACA of 2010. Several codes or opinions guiding relationships between the profession and the industries had been adopted by various organizations, including the AMA, the Accreditation Council for Continuing medical Education, the Association of American Medical Colleges, the Pharmaceutical Research and Manufacturers America, and the Advanced Medical Technology Association.

The overcharging principle of the CMSS code is to maintain society independence in all educational activities, scientific programs, products, services, and advocacy positions. On CPG development, the code requires societies to base CPGs on scientific evidence, make the development process transparent, disclose and avoid the influence of for-profit companies. Other issues tackled by the CMSS code span acceptance of donations, research funding, and sponsorship from companies, plus industry influence on society meetings, journals, advertising, and licensing. So, when engaging with specialty societies, it's important to understand their conflict-of-interest policies, processes, and primary missions.

CONVENER OF CLINICAL DATA REGISTRIES FOR CED

A clinical data registry (CDR) is a collection of information about individuals' health status and care they receive over time, usually focused on a specific diagnosis or condition. Many registries collect information about people with a specific disease or share a common reason for needing care. Unlike clinical trials, CDRs are designed to understand care and outcomes in "real-world" medical settings.

Medical specialty societies are often the best candidates to lead CDR efforts because of their access to deep clinical expertise, dedication to advancing their profession and improving care for their patients, and strong convening power across institutions and geographies. Many specialty societies have a long history of operating CDRs, including the American Society of Reproductive Medicine in 1980, the Society of Thoracic Surgeons in 1989, the American College of Surgeons in 1990, and the American College of Cardiology in 1998.

Two drivers behind the growth of registries are quality measurement and improvement movement and innovations to generate new clinical knowledge and drive better patient care and outcomes. The MACRA of 2015 requires the Secretary of the HHS to encourage the use of qualified clinical data registries for reporting measures under the quality performance category of the Merit-based Incentive Payment System (MIPS), which give providers the option of satisfying the MIPS quality reporting requirements by participating in qualifying registries. For example, the American College of Surgeons maintains several registries that qualify for CMS's Physician Quality Reporting System, including the Surgeon Specific Registry. By 2015, there were over 120 CDRs, 90% of which were offered by specialty societies.

CDRs operated by specialty societies play an important role in collecting new evidence under Medicare's Coverage with Evidence Development program. Of the 27 CED NCDs from 2005 to 2022 examined by Zeitler et al, seven CEDs had approved registry, including four that had a registry administered by the American College of Cardiology's (ACC) National Cardiovascular Device Registry (NCDR) suite. The ACC's NCDR offers seven registries, including Chest Pain - MI Registry, AFib Ablation Registry, CathPCI Registry, EP Device Implant Registry, IMPACT Registry, LAAO Registry, and STS/ACC TVT Registry. Over 2,000 facilities worldwide participate in one or more of the ACC's registries, forming a comprehensive cardiovascular care providers network.

The STS/ACC TVT Registry, created through a collaboration between the Society of Thoracic Surgeons (STS) and the ACC, has been approved by CMS for the CED for TAVR and TMVR since 2012. The TVT Registry is an example of a CDR managed by specialty societies and has been used to satisfy Medicare CED requirements and FDA's post-market surveillance requirements for novel cardiac valve therapies. Data from this registry has also been used in regulatory submissions for label expansions and informing clinical practice guidelines.

The National Oncologic PET Registry (NOPR) is another shining example how registry data are used, not only to gain coverage for a new technology but also broaden a whole new field. NOPR is a nationwide prospective internet-based registry created in 2006 to address CMS's CED requirements to cover previously noncovered cancer types and indications for positron emission tomography (PET) performed with the radiopharmaceutical 18F-FDG (FDG-PET). NOPR is sponsored by the World Molecular Imaging Society (formerly the Academy of Molecular Imaging) and managed by the ACR through the American College of Radiology Imaging Network.

FDG-PET is a diagnostic imaging procedure that allows for the assessment of regional glucose metabolism in normal and diseased organs and tissues. Its use in cancer imaging is based on the principle that most malignant neoplasms show increased use of glucose (and increased uptake of 18F- FDG) in comparison with normal tissues. FDG-PET had been applied in oncology primarily as a staging and restaging tool and showed great potential to improve patient management for detecting therapy response earlier. Between 1998 and 2005, CMS approved reimbursement of PET-FDG for specific indications in 9 malignancies. The 2005 CED established coverage for FDG-PET for all other cancers and indications when the provider is participating in, and patients are enrolled in NOPR.

The NOPR collected questionnaire data from referring physicians on intended patient management before and after an FDG-PET scan. The NOPR participating PET facilities collect a pre-PET questionnaire (documenting study indication, cancer type and anticipated stage, and planned management if PET were not available) and one of several post-PET questionnaires that assess the referring physician's planned management considering the FDG-PET findings.

Change in intended management is measured using three approaches. The first approach categorizes management intent before and after PET as being either treatment (surgery, chemotherapy, or radiation therapy alone or in combination) or nontreatment (watch, non-invasive imaging, tissue biopsy, and supportive care). The second approach splits the intent of the therapeutic management into curative or palliative intent. The third approach includes considering a change in therapeutic mode. For example, changing from surgery to chemotherapy would be a major change in mode even if the treatment goal were unchanged. Categories of change in management include changes in dose or duration of therapy, switching to another form of therapy, and stopping current therapy.

In one year, NOPR collected data from nearly 23,000 patients submitted by about 1,200 PET facilities. Prostatic, pancreatic, and ovarian cancers represented about 30% of cases. The numbers of scans performed for diagnosis of suspected cancer (or unknown primary cancer), initial cancer staging, restaging, and suspected cancer recurrence were about equal. Clinicians changed the intended care of more than one in three cancer patients as the result of FDG-PET scan findings. In patients with planned biopsy before PET, a biopsy was avoided in about 70%.

Based in part on data obtained from the NOPR, CMS expanded coverage for FDG-PET in patients with cancer on April 3, 2009, and expanded coverage for all oncologic indications for FDG-PET and ended data collection requirements under CED on June 11, 2013. Overall, nearly 288,000 scans were submitted to NOPR FDG-PET registry. On February 26, 2010, CMS announced CED for NaF-18 PET to identify bone metastasis. The NOPR obtained CMS approval to develop a registry for NaF-18 as an amendment to the then-existing NOPR for FDG-PET. The NaF-18 PET registry part of NOPR was activated in 2011. Estimated total accrual to the NaF-PET registry is 45,000 cases.

Although the value of CDRs is undeniable, submitting data to registries is associated with a real cost to healthcare providers. In 2019, the registry enrollment fee for STS/ACC TVT Registry ran $25,000 on top of the staff hours spent collecting and reporting all the data. The FDG-PET NOPR registry requires a $50 application fee and a $50 per-patient fee for processing data into the registry.

In Brigham and Women's hospital, the hospital participated in six cardiovascular registries in 2016, including the STS, STS/ACC TVT, the CathPCI, the Implantable Cardiac Defibrillator Registries and two state registries. They also contemplated joining three more registries, including two operated by ACC's NCDR. The hospital had six full-time staff in extracting, validating, and submitting data to registries with no external funding support. Many of the registries are collecting similar data but often with different definitions, which makes it difficult to report directly from the electronic medical record. The lack of standardization, compounded with redundancy of data collection, put a real burden on registry participating facilities.

VALUE-BASED PURCHASER

For most medical innovations, healthcare providers are the direct purchaser. They face important clinical and economic decisions related to drugs, devices, tests, and procedures, and are under increasing pressure to reduce the cost of the care while optimizing patient outcomes. New value-based payment models shift financial risk from health plans to providers, which changes how providers assess and adopt innovation. This is an especially challenging situation for medical devices. As most devices do not receive more reimbursement by payers, providers often need to absorb the costs within their operating budgets.

Orthopedic surgery, neurosurgery, interventional cardiology and radiology, and cardiothoracic surgery are the biggest users of medical devices and technology. Hospitals refer to an implantable medical device such as hip and knee implants, cardiac stents, cardiac pacemakers, cardiac valves, and spinal implants as physician preference items. While doctors often choose implant products, hospitals pay the bill. From 1991 until 2008, Medicare reimbursement for joint prostheses increased 27% while the average price of a total hip implant rose at least 132%. Physician preference items account for one-third of hospital supply costs and are rising.

Each hospital is different but the more expensive an item, the more layers of approval are required, from the board of trustees, C-suite, down to hospital administrative director and unit manager. Academic hospitals can be even more complicated with the dean of the medical school and the department chairs having variable influence in the purchase decisions of the hospital. Some hospitals or medical centers will have a chief operating officer and/or a chief administrative officer in addition to a chief executive officer. Many hospitals will have a chief technology officer who can also influence purchase decisions. Often, the clinical need for a new piece of equipment or a new line of supplies will be initially identified by the doctors who then express those needs to the medical director, who makes recommendations to the administrative directors or to the CEO.

Purchasing decisions are now often deliberated by hospital Value Analysis Committees (VACs), which evaluate evidence on efficacy, safety, cost, and feasibility of adoption, and align that with the healthcare delivery model that rewards hospitals delivering high-quality care safely, efficiently, and economically. Committees in this role can go by various other names, including value analysis teams, technology assessments committees, and clinical use evaluation.

A 2019 survey by Advisory Board revealed that most VACs have three main priorities: expanding oversight over health system-wide purchasing to reduce spend, enhancing data collection abilities, and engaging clinicians throughout and after the value analysis process to ensure clinician satisfaction. The goals and approaches within the VAC may vary at different institutions, such as for profit, not-for-profit, public hospitals, and academic institutions.

VACs can be diverse, comprised of members from different hospital departments bringing multiple perspectives. The most common participants of VACs include supply chain representatives, operating room managers, service line leaders, and clinical leaders. Supply chain representatives most often lead VACs. It is also common for a VAC to be co-managed by physicians and a supply chain representative, or even managed by a physician. Even when supply chain representatives lead a VAC, they don't hold sole decision-making power. Instead, supply chain, clinicians, and service line leaders all have a significant say in product and vendor selection. Products without a physician champion are less likely to be approved by VACs.

Vanderbilt's Medical Economic Outcome Committee (MEOC) is a facility-wide committee established in 2008 that includes ten physicians and six administrators. Two committees were created: one made up of faculty from the surgical subspecialties, and the other of faculty from radiology, cardiology, and cardiovascular subspecialists, and senior administrators. Both committees have similar structure and meet monthly.

MEOC's goals align with the findings of the Advisory Board's survey. The goals are clinical and financial and emphasize data-based decision-making. MEOC's clinical goals include "facilitating the adoption of safe and efficacious healthcare technologies to improve patient care, developing a capital assessment process that was transparent, as well as data and strategy driven, and finding new and innovative ways to impact healthcare delivery and costs." Financial goals include "evaluating the cost-effectiveness and financial impact of new healthcare technologies and physician preference items, empowering clinicians to standardize procedures, identifying reimbursement for new healthcare technologies before their introduction, improving the institution's capital budget, and utilizing benchmark data to compare financial outcomes."

The MEOC's review process is usually initiated by online submissions from physician champions interested in using a new product. The review process distinguishes between a trial request, which is short-term, and a permanent request. For a trial product, the physician champion provides information on cost-benefit and potential benefits, as well as a brief product description. A trial request must be FDA-approved, cost-neutral, and have no negative contractual impact on existing contracts.

For a permanent request, more in-depth information, including peer-reviewed articles, is required, and the physician champion must present to and answer questions from the MEOC committee. The committee also uses third-party product evaluations, for example from ECRI and the Advisory Board. The supply chain analytics team also provides information on potential usage and the effect on contribution margin and net margin, as well as existing contracts. The committee could grant full approval, reject the proposal, or approve with stipulations, such as short-term approval requiring data collection and reevaluation or cost neutrality.

Vanderbilt's practice is consistent with Advisory Board's survey findings, which indicate that VACs review many sources for data to build a complete picture of a product's clinical and financial impact, such as peer-reviewed journal articles, clinical guidelines, and internal health system data. Over 80% of survey respondents indicated that data on indications for use, financial impact, cost-effectiveness, price benchmarking, and quality outcomes were useful and readily available for VACs to leverage. However, more than 40% of survey respondents indicated that operational or efficiency outcome data, and patient experience data were not available.

VACs, however, vary in their levels of sophistication when performing value analysis. At a basic level, VACs evaluate cost and quality and compare a new technology with existing technology or standard of care. At the most sophisticated level, VAC review takes an integrated approach, "enabling an analysis of clinical outcomes, workflow efficiency, revenue cycle, supply chain impact, and risk sharing." Ideally, new technology should be tracked, and real impact measured against predictions. New value assessment models are emerging to perform proactive analysis, identify opportunities to standardize and reduce cost, and actively engage clinicians to obtain the best patient outcomes.

Survey findings also agree that a request from a physician champion is the most common way to start a VAC review process, even though supply chain may start a review process to reduce costs or replace an expiring/changing contract. It's also common to have a trial product process.

VACs have broad decision-making authority. Over three-fourths of VACs can make final decisions on new technology review, product selection, and trial allowance. More than two-thirds of VACs can authorize vendor selection, product pricing, and product quantity. VACs typically have monthly meetings, and some may allow participation of a product vendor.

It's common for organizations to have more than one VAC, each handling a specific subset of products or products used within a service line. VACs review nearly all medical and surgical products used in the hospital setting. Survey respondents indicated that all VACs evaluate commodities supplies, over 90% review surgical supplies, physician preference items, and drug-device combination items, and over 80% look at lab supplies. While hospitals often have a capital steering committee and pharmacy and therapeutics committee to review capital spending and pharmaceuticals, VACs may additionally evaluate these products in their impact on other product categories.

PART SIX

EVIDENCE

THE MOST EFFECTIVE TOOL TO COMMUNICATE WITH PAYERS AND PROVIDERS

The numbers of published systematic reviews, meta-analyses, and randomized clinical trials, considered the most robust and reliable forms of evidence, have substantially increased over the last two decades. Nearly 900 systematic review and meta-analysis studies and over 550 randomized clinical trial studies are published yearly.

There is inherent uncertainty with purchasing decisions of new medical innovations because at the time of FDA marketing approval, only limited information is available about their real-world performance. The basis for FDA approval does not currently involve comparing the new drug or device to any other available treatments. Furthermore, the new medical product does not need to be better and safer than other alternatives. Additionally, findings from FDA trials, whose study population tends to be small and highly selective, are often not broadly generalizable to the real-world patient population with diverse demographic and disease profiles. As a result, FDA approval, by itself, provides limited information about how well a new medical product will actually function in the population covered by an insurer or treated by a healthcare provider.

Evidence is an anchor in payers and providers' purchasing decisions, with the increasing focus on the principles of evidence-based medicine. Evidence that a medical innovation is safe, efficacious, and effective is primary requirement for requesting a new code, gaining payer coverage, and convincing healthcare provider to purchase, use and/or order a new product/service. Even though both payers and providers base their purchasing decisions on evidence of value, their value metrics differ, with payers focusing on clinical utility and provider emphasizing the value metrics they are measured against. And the burden of proof primarily lies on the developer or manufacturer of a product or service.

This chapter will dissect one Medicare national coverage determination and two local coverage determinations to evaluate evidential requirements for Medicare coverage. While cost is generally not considered in Medicare coverage determinations, it does matter to private payers. The discussion of economic impact will focus on two types of commonly used economic impact analyses. Lastly, this chapter will discuss commonly used datasets and analyses to support payment considerations such as NTAP and APC assignment.

DISSECT EVIDENTIAL REQUIREMENTS OF A NATIONAL COVERAGE DETERMINATION

A major step of CMS's NCD process is systematic reviews of evidence to assess whether evidence is of sufficient quality to support determination that an item or service is reasonable and necessary. The appraisal is about the findings – whether an item or service improves health outcomes – as much as it's about how the findings are drawn – whether the quality and body of evidence give confidence to the findings. For the NCD for NGS for advanced cancer, CMS reviewed over 250 studies, including over 200 submitted by Foundation Medicine who asked for the NCD as a part of FDA-CMS parallel review for its NGS companion diagnostic test, F1CDx™. This NCD, however, is not limited to Foundation Medicine's tests. CMS included three more NGS tests for advanced cancers approved or cleared by FDA in the review. An additional 25 studies were added to the review based on references submitted through public comment.

The general question all national coverage analyses aim to answer is "Is the evidence sufficient to conclude that the application of the item or service under study will improve health outcomes for Medicare patients?" For this NCD specifically, CMS focused on the question "Is the evidence sufficient to conclude that next generation sequencing when used as a diagnostic test for patients with advanced cancer meaningfully improves health outcomes?" The question defines the population – patients with advanced cancer – and intervention – NGS test – for the systematic review. CMS's approach in framing the systematic review question follows the PICO (Population, Intervention, Comparator, Outcomes) model, which is also widely used by state Medicaid programs and private plans.

CMS uses the hierarchical framework of Fryback and Thornbury (1991) to structure evidence and evaluate outcomes of diagnostic tests. Under this framework,

- Level 2 addresses diagnostic accuracy, sensitivity, and specificity of the test;
- Level 3 focuses on whether the information produces a change in the physician's diagnostic thinking;
- Level 4 concerns the effect on the patient management plan; and

- Level 5 measures the effect of the diagnostic information on patient outcomes.

There is a clear preference for Level 5 evidence as CMS viewed them as more "persuasive" compared to other Levels. Level 4 measures have satisfied CMS's evidential requirements for NCD review, like the case of FDG-PET.

For this NCD, CMS used the ACCE Model Process for Evaluating Genetic Tests developed by CDC. ACCE takes its name from the four main criteria for evaluating a genetic test – analytical validity, clinical validity, clinical utility, and related ethical/legal/social issues. Analytical validity evaluates the ability of a test to detect the mutation and/or variant accurately and reliably, while clinical validity assesses whether a test can accurately and reliably detect the disease of interest in the defined population, both of which are typically assessed by FDA during the approval or clearance processes. CMS focuses on assessing clinical utility – a domain evaluating whether the test result is actionable, from producing changes in the treating physician's diagnostic thinking, adjusting a patient's management plan, to improving outcomes for patients with advanced cancer.

The medical literature on NGS for advanced cancer at the time of the NCD review, had not consistently considered the impact of testing on physician decision-making and patient health outcomes, such as mortality, morbidity, or reduction of invasive testing. However, CMS stated that evidence of improved health outcomes is more persuasive. In the NCD decision memo, CMS summarized evidence on outcome measures of overall survival, progression-free survival, partial response, complete response, stable disease, time to tumor progression, overall response rate, or time to treatment failure.

The assessment of clinical evidence starts from grading the quality of individual studies. A key question to evaluate is scientific validity – whether there is a causal relationship between an intervention and health outcomes. For example, some have observed that smokers are more likely to have lung cancers. But does smoking cause lung cancer? To establish the causal relationship, studies must rule out biases, for example the possibility that smokers are more likely to live in urban areas with poor air quality.

Various study design techniques have been developed to reduce bias, including randomization, concurrent control groups, prospective (rather than retrospective) studies to follow individual overtime, and larger sample size. Non-randomized studies must especially evaluate potential biases, such as patient attributes may influence intervention participation or dropout, and how to reduce them in study design. The grading of each study factors in all the study design elements, but generally, randomized controlled studies have higher strength or quality grading than observational studies.

In this NCD decision memo, articles are arranged in the order of systematic reviews, meta-analysis, randomized controlled trials, prospective observational studies, retrospective observational studies, case series, and other studies. CMS highlighted a meta-analysis of 57 randomized and 55 non-randomized trials representing 38,104 patients to compare efficacy outcomes between approved treatments for providing "a strong level of evidence."

While observational studies represent a lower level of evidence, CMS praised five observational studies reported improvements in progression-free survival for providing "consistent supportive evidence across a broad number of patients with cancer." Several publications based on the clinical trials Foundation Medicine conducted to show improvements in health outcomes such as overall survival was credited for providing "important evidence to establish clinical utility for some diagnostic laboratory tests."

The next stage in the evidence review process is to evaluate the generalizability of each study to the Medicare population. One important question CMS considers during the NCD process is whether the evidence relates to the Medicare beneficiary population. In evaluating the generalizability of evidence to the Medicare population, particular attention is paid to the demographic characteristics and comorbidities of study participants, and the practitioner training and experience.

For this NCD review, for example, CMS included only studies that included adult subjects. Based on the evidence, CMS concluded that "patient characteristics most likely to benefit from molecular diagnostic tests are patients having recurrent, metastatic, or advanced stage IV cancer." Recognizing that not every cancer has a clinically consistent staging description, CMS expanded the patient population in the final NCD as having recurrent, relapsed, refractory, metastatic, or advanced stages III or IV cancer.

The practitioner part in this case is that clinical validity and clinical utility of individual diagnostic tests are specific to the condition and the test itself, due to the test methods, sample materials, and levels of experience among test developers and administrators. Clinical significance cannot be established without first confirming clinical validity and clinical utility. So, the final NCD requires that NGS tests be covered only if they have FDA approval or clearance as a companion in vitro diagnostic with an approved or cleared indication for cancer.

The final stage of the evidence review process is to draw overarching conclusions based on the direction and magnitude of the intervention's potential risks and benefits. Generally, if the risks outweigh the benefits, the intervention is not considered reasonable and necessary. CMS rarely considers cost in its NCD review but instead focusing on health outcomes with a greater emphasis on endpoint outcomes, such as quality of life, functional status, duration of disability, morbidity, and mortality, than intermediate or surrogate outcomes. The consistency of study findings is an important consideration when assessing an intervention's risks and benefits profile.

Based on the evidence reviewed, CMS believed that "FDA-approved and FDA-cleared laboratory in vitro diagnostic tests using NGS as a companion diagnostic are sufficient for patients with recurrent, relapsed, refractory, metastatic, or advanced stage III, or stage IV cancer to expect meaningful improvement in their health outcomes." At first, CMS proposed CED, but based on public comments, CMS removed the CED requirement in the final NCD. CMS strongly encourages continued studies and publications, especially on the endpoints such as overall survival, progression-free survival, objective response, and patient-reported outcomes relevant to the quality of life for Medicare beneficiaries.

EXAMINE MEDICARE CONTRACTORS' EVIDENCE ANALYSIS FOR TWO LOCAL COVERAGE DETERMINATIONS

How Medicare contractors make coverage decisions often appears as a black box from an outsider's perspective.

CMS's 2018 update to the LCD process outlined the evidentiary content requirements that MACs should incorporate into proposed and final LCDs. Published LCDs by different MACs show similar structure and approaches. A proposed or final LCD now includes a description of the item or service under review, the target Medicare population, and a summary of scientific evidence and intended use.

However, the evaluation process for the evidence remains somewhat elusive. With this question in mind, I contacted Dr. Gabriel A. Bien-Willner MD, PhD, FCAP, who serves as the Chief Medical Officer of Palmetto GBA (referred to as Palmetto) and a Medical Director of the MolDX program. Dr Willner's career path is intriguing, spanning from academic research in molecular diagnosis to the industry, and now to policymaking representing the payer. This is not the first time that I have sought Dr Willner's insights on evidential requirements. Our previous encounter took place during a panel discussion in 2020 at the Precision Medicine World Conference, where we both were on a panel discussing reimbursement challenges.

According to Dr Willner, one noticeable change in the updated LCD development process is the increased emphasis on evidence-based coverage policy. When conducting a review, MACs rely on evidence generally acceptable within the medical community, such as published original research in peer-reviewed medical journals, systematic reviews and meta-analyses, evidence-based consensus statements and clinical guidelines. Proprietary information, submitted by a requestor, which is not accessible to the public, is not considered. All articles and sources that contributed to the LCD are listed in the Bibliography.

Dr Willner further explained that MACs use the same evaluation framework used in NCD. For example, in the MolDX program, they also use the CDC's ACCE Model for test evaluation. Another widely used tool is PICO, which is also helpful for laboratories and MedTech companies when designing clinical studies, organizing literature searches, and describing the intended use of a medical product. However, there is no magic number of publications that would guarantee persuasion of a Medicare contractor that a new technology or service deserves coverage. Each product is evaluated individually based on the quality and strength of the evidence.

While no one has a crystal ball to predict coverage determinations with certainty, examining the LCD narratives provides some insight into the thought process behind MACs' evidence evaluation. Take, for example, the case of HeartFlow FFRCT. Five MACs have issued LCDs for specific patients with coronary artery disease, and these LCDs follow a similar format and reached largely the same coverage determinations. Because all the LCDs cite the same major trial findings, related clinical guidelines, and consistent research findings, including those from systematic reviews and meta-analyses, it is not surprising that MACs would reach similar determinations. There are minor differences among LCDs regarding excluded conditions, which often align with exclusion criteria used in major studies and/or clinical guidelines.

Palmetto, for example, organized the evidence on FFRCT by addressing three key questions: Is there evidence to support using FFRCT to guide determination for invasive coronary angiography? Are there evidence-based demonstrations of positive health outcomes? And have positive health outcomes been shown in the Medicare population. More detailed information on Palmetto's LCD can be found in the summary table.

However, there are critiques provided by Wisconsin Physicians Service Insurance Corporation (referred to as WPS) in its LCD, expressing reservations about some of these studies. As for the PLATFORM trial study, While WPS, like Palmetto, views the findings as promising, its LCD highlights significant study limitations. These include non-random patient allocation leading to a younger and healthier patient profile in the FFRCT arm and limited generalizability due to a small sample size. As for the ADVANCE registry, which enrolled over 5,000 patients with angina symptoms from 38 centers across three continents, WPS cautions that the lack of control over confounding factors may introduce multiple biases.

Unlike the LCD for FFRCT, which includes over 40 references such as systematic reviews, meta-analysis, various types of studies based on over 10 trials, and some large-scale studies that enrolled thousands of participants, the LCD for Oncotype DX breast cancer for ductal carcinoma in situ (DCIS) has fewer than 20 references. Oncotype DX is an RNA-based MDT that predicts the risks of breast cancer recurrence for individuals diagnosed with DCIS based on the activity level of certain genes affecting the behavior of the cancer.

DCIS is one of the most commonly diagnosed breast cancers, accounting for about 20% of newly diagnosed breast cancers in the US. Recurrences occur in roughly 25% to 30% of women in 10 years after surgical removal of cancer. Additional radiation therapy has been reported to reduce the risk of recurrence by about 50%. However, since most of the cases do not recur following surgery, radiation therapy would not be beneficial to most patients. Oncotype DX helps identify patients at high risk of cancer recurrence who would benefit from radiation therapy.

However, conducting a trial to examine the test's performance in reducing 10-year cancer recurrence would have taken more than 10 years. The studies submitted for LCD review are smartly designed. The two validation studies used specimens collected in an earlier trial where 5- and 10-year outcomes post-surgical cancer removal were available, or a population-cohort of women diagnosed with DCIS longitudinally followed. The clinical performance of the test was validated in two prospective multicenter studies that evaluated the impact of the test result on physician's recommendations for radiation therapy treatment.

While Palmetto acknowledged that the clinical evidence for the test is limited, they recognized the unique clinical benefit it offers and granted coverage for the test. Additionally, the coverage determination also required continued data submission as a condition for Medicare coverage.

Now, put yourself in the shoes of the writer of an LCD tasked with describing the covered item/service, the specific situations under which it will be covered, and the evidence on which these coverage decisions are based. The exercise is valuable in developing an LCD request, as it requires including the language that a requester wants in an LCD. The more details you include in your draft LCD, the clearer your understanding of the evidential requirements for an LCD will become. While specific details may vary, it is essential to address key questions when presenting evidence, such as:

- Who will benefit from the item or service, and who will not? The exclusion criteria are as important as the inclusion criteria, as the calculation of benefit vs harm may flip in different patient populations.

- What are the intended uses of the item or service? Which diseases or injuries can the item/service diagnose, treat, or monitor? Considering the availability of the item/service, what clinical actions can be taken to improve patient outcomes?

- What is the impact on health outcomes? Changes in physician decision-making are results directly from diagnostic tests, and improvements in a patient's medical condition are examples of better health outcomes. Avoiding the use of a toxic therapy that is unlikely to benefit a patient is another example. There is a wide range of outcomes to explore, including faster recovery, lower mortality, improved quality of life, and reduced consumption of high-cost services such as inpatient admissions or ER visits.

- How can the medical community trust the findings? It is a balance act between reducing bias and increasing generalizability. Double-blinded randomized clinical trials (RCTs) are often considered the gold standard because they are less prone to bias. However, the highly controlled environment of an RCT makes it less generalizable to real-world patient populations, and they are often lengthy and costly. On the other end of the spectrum, real-world evidence, most often observational studies retrospective in nature, provides insight into routine clinical settings and is more generalizable. However, they are often rated low in terms of evidence strength due to a lack of internal validity and potential bias. Both RCTs and real-world evidence have been cited and credited in supporting coverage determinations. The question is not about which study design is better, but rather how to combine the strengths and weaknesses of different study designs to present a compelling case for the efficacy and effectiveness of an intervention. For the Medicare program coverage determinations, generalizability also means demonstrated evidence for the Medicare population or age groups.

SUMMARY OF TWO LCDS ISSUED BY PALMETTO

LCD	Non-invasive FFR for stable ischemic heart disease	MolDX: Oncotype DX breast Cancer for DCIS
Population	Patients with known or suspected coronary artery disease	Women diagnosed with DCIS
Intervention	FFRCT uses computer-assisted processing of coronary CTA images to estimate changes in blood pressure inside coronary arteries with partial blockages, to determine how severely the blockages	The DCIS Score is a ribonucleic acid (RNA) based assay measuring the expression of 5 proliferation genes, progesterone receptor, GSTM1 and 5 reference genes with results reported as a

	impede blood flow to the heart.	numerical score along with interpretive information. The score is intended to predict a 10-year risk of cancer recurrence and guide the use of radiation therapy.
Outcomes	- Two prospective and two retrospective cohort studies provide evidence that FFRCT can guide the decision whether a patient needs an invasive coronary angiography. - A single-center, observational study on 2- year outcomes of over 3,500 patients provides the data to show positive health outcomes, including a composite of all-cause death, myocardial infarction, hospitalization for unstable angina, and unplanned coronary revascularization. - A study evaluating 254 Medicare-eligible patients in a sub-analysis for the NXT	- Two prospectively designed validation studies found DCIS Score result is a significant predictor of recurrence risk. - A prospective multicenter study of 115 patients shows that integration of the DCIS Score into clinical management decisions resulted in 31.3% change in radiation therapy recommendations. - A prospective multicenter study of 127 patients shows that integration of the DCIS Score changed 22% of recommendations by radiation oncologists and 30.7% of recommendations by surgeons.

	study shows positive health outcomes in Medicare population. - Additional literature recommended by the American College of Cardiology.	- A retrospective single-center health economic study involving 38 patients and a cost-effectiveness modeling study assessing potential impact on healthcare cost.
Level of evidence	Good (I-IIb, with risks of bias)	Quality – Moderate Strength – Limited Weight - Limited
Coverage decision	Coverage with inclusion and exclusion criteria	Coverage with data submission requirement

ASSESS A NEW INTERVENTION'S ECONOMIC IMPACT

CMS does not request or consider cost explicitly when making coverage determinations because they are not authorized by Congress to do so. Medicaid and private payers, on the other end, do not have such limitations and consider costs in coverage determination. In the executive summary, the AMCP format asks a manufacturer to briefly summarize the value proposition of its product, which is a value argument to justify expected expenditures for its product in anticipated effects on the clinical evidence, health outcomes, and the economic consequences for the healthcare system.

The executive summary section also includes a synopsis of economic benefits of the proposed product, in terms of cost per unit, potential clinical and economic benefits, and shortcomings of other therapies. The key data points, such as per member per month or incremental cost-effectiveness ratio, come from the chapter that reports economic value and modeling – primarily cost-effectiveness analysis and budget impact model.

A review of coverage policies for medical interventions issued by the 20 largest commercial payers shows that 14 payers review cost-effectiveness analyses (CEA) for at least some of the time, with frequency ranging from 8% to 43%, compared to reviewing clinical studies 87% of the coverage policies, with frequency ranging from 25% to 100%. Fewer payers reported reviewing budget impact analysis (BIA).

CEA measures the relative costs and benefits of one or more interventions. CEA uses a metric called incremental cost-effectiveness ratio (ICER). The generic formula for ICER is simple, just dividing the relative increase of cost associated with a new intervention compared to a reference by the relative increase of effectiveness. The ICER can be interpreted as the "price" for an additional unit of health gained through an intervention. While cost is measured in units of currency, clinical benefits are often expressed in nonmonetary terms such as quality-adjusted life years (QALYs).

A lower ICER ratio implies that an intervention can produce an incremental health gain, like QALYs gained, at a lower cost. While no single threshold exists for deciding whether an ICER is acceptable, ICER ratios of <$50,000 per QALY gained are generally considered attractive, and the willingness to pay threshold in the US usually ranges from $100,000 to $150,000 per QALY gained.

Using QALYs has faced criticisms. Patients with worse health, such as patients with disabilities, have a lower overall health utility weight. Any extension of their lives "would not generate as many QALYs as a similar extension of life for otherwise healthy people." The National Council on Disability has strongly denounced the use of QALYs. In response, the Institute for Clinical and Economic Review (ICER) has proposed an alternative – the equal value of life years gained metric, to supplement QALYs. In the calculation of equal value of life years, any life-year gained is treated the same, regardless an individual's health status. The limitation of this approach is that it undervalues interventions that substantially improve the quality of life when the number of years gained are the same compared to other interventions.

There are several main CEA modeling approaches. A systematic review of modelling approaches in economic evaluations of health interventions for drug and alcohol problems shows the majority (52%) of CEA studies examined used cohort Markov modeling. Decision trees were used in 29% of the CEA studies, followed by system dynamics (8%) and individual-based model (5%). When evaluating cost-effectiveness of testing and diagnosis of prostate cancer, more than one third (36%) of CEA studies used a combined decision tree and cohort Markov model, 36% used cohort Markov models, followed by 18% using decision tree model, and 9% using time discreet-event microsimulation models. Regarding model selection, simple scenarios over a short period may best be modelled using a decision tree. Otherwise, cohort Markov models may be adequate. When a later event dependent on a prior experience, micro-simulation Markov models and discreet event simulation may be appropriate.

A decision tree is a flowchart-like tree structure in which decisions and chance events are linked in the order in which they would occur. One example is the decision tree model developed by Navarro et al. to assess outcomes and costs of a general practitioner-delivered intervention for alcohol misuse. The model compared cost-effective outcomes for nine scenarios, including an increase in screening, brief intervention, a combination of screening and brief intervention, and current practice. While the CEA assesses the cost-effectiveness of different alternative interventions at an aggregate level, it does not factor in the role of individual attributes such as age, use and treatment history among the participants to determine the outcomes. The cost-effective assessment was built on the assumption that the effect is the same for all participants.

A Markov model assumes that a patient is in transition from one health state to another. It's a useful model when a decision problem involves risk continuous over time. A Markov model may be evaluated by matrix algebra, as a cohort simulation, or as a Monte Carlo simulation. One example of the application of cohort Markov model was an evaluation of cost-effectiveness of long-term outpatient buprenorphine-naloxone treatment for opioid dependence in primary care.

The cohort was allocated across four health states, including "In Treatment Off Drugs," "In Treatment On Drugs," "Out of Treatment Off Drugs," and "Out of Treatment On Drugs." The participants were then transitioned across states based on fixed transition probabilities. While the model sets a clear structure for economic evaluation of treatment, it also shares common limitations in cohort Markov models. Neither transition probabilities nor costs and benefits were adjusted for personal attributes, opioid use history and treatment history. The model is not reflective of the heterogeneity of the heroin treatment population.

System dynamics model accounts for the dynamic interaction between interventions or individuals in the cohort. These models are often used for modeling interventions for infectious diseases such as HIV/AIDs and COVID-19. For example, system dynamics models have been used in assessing effectiveness of COVID-19 vaccination and social mobilization policies on pandemic containment and the economy in the United States. Despite the complexity of such models, one limitation of the system dynamics model is that it ignores individual attributes and history (e.g., recovered, or reinfected individuals), thus effectively limiting the heterogeneity of the cohort. However, the system dynamics model has an advantage in modeling the interaction among entities, which is crucial to produce valid outcomes in the treatment and prevention of infectious diseases.

A discrete event simulation (DES) model simulates individual patient experience over time, tracking and summarizing events and their consequences. DES model offers more flexibility to investigate alternative scenarios. In a study by Glover et al., a DES model was used to assess cost effectiveness of abdominal aortic aneurysm screening with different screening intervals and protocols. The DES model was built on an original Markov model, but instead of simply considering "screening" or "no screening," the DES model addressed more nuanced screening policy questions, such as different surveillance intervals and different aortic diameter thresholds for referral for elective surgery.

Another economic model requested by AMCP dossier is a BIA, which estimates fiscal consequences of adopting a new health technology or intervention. The budget impact is often the net effect of budgetary increase to cover a new intervention, which varies based on the size of target population, frequency, duration and uptake of a new intervention, and potential risks of misdiagnosis or mistreatment, and any potential offsets by substituting current standard of care or improving health outcomes.

The ISPOR task force report II (2014) recommends that the design of a BIA for a new healthcare intervention should consider relevant features of the healthcare system, possible access restrictions, the expected uptake of the new intervention, and the use and effects of the current and new interventions. Published clinical trial estimates, comparator studies, and parameter estimates derived from a plan's own patient population, are recommended data sources. Other data sources include published data, well-recognized local or national statistical information, and expert opinion in special circumstances. The Task Force also recommends sensitivity analysis and model validation to incorporate decisionmakers' perspective. It's also a recommended practice to offer options so that different cost categories can be included or excluded from the analysis.

Unlike Australia and many European countries where a BIA is required alongside the CEA when submitting evidence to support national or local formulary approval or reimbursement, neither BIA nor CEA is necessary for Medicare's NCD/LCD review. However, the Congressional Budget Office (CBO) is required to produce a budgetary impact analysis for proposals to expand Medicare benefit categories, such as multi-cancer detection tests or at-home COVID-19 tests. It's often called a CBO score, which estimates the costs of proposed legislation compared to baseline projections of revenues and spending estimates under current law.

Like a regular BIA, the CBO's scoring contains steps to estimate target population and effects of new intervention on annual healthcare spending. However, what's unique about the CBO score is its focus on budgetary effects, which are usually smaller than the effects on healthcare spending because federal funds only finance a part of changes in healthcare spending and there are nonfederal funds, such as patient premiums and copayments, to fund the rest. In addition, most of CBO's cost estimates span 10 years, much longer than the time horizon of regular BIAs, which is commonly between one and five years.

COMMUNICATE VALUE AND ROI WITH PROVIDERS

Like payers, providers seek to answer the questions "What is the value and how much does it cost?" when making purchase decisions. To payers, value is reflected in the improvement of clinical outcome and measured by metrics like ICER and QALY. The value metrics used by value analysis committees (VACs) often reflect the value-based care reimbursement environment providers are facing.

According to a HealthLeaders Media Executive Compensation Survey, nearly three-quarters of healthcare systems include clinical quality measurements in incentive payments for hospital executives. Hospital CEOs listed operating margin (67%), patient satisfaction (60%), clinical quality (54%), and financial efficiency (44%) as the four top factors for their incentive payments. Such arrangements will likely trickle down to VACs with accountability for quality, patient satisfaction, and cost, and down to the selected vendors.

Medicare leads the way in value-based care, which includes pay-for-performance programs and alternative payment models. Here is a brief description of key programs:

- The Hospital Value-Based Purchasing Program (HVBP) includes 4 domains and 20 quality measures: clinical outcomes domain (six mortality measures), person and community engagement domain (eight Hospital Consumer Assessment of Healthcare Providers and Systems measures), safety domain (five infection measures), efficiency and cost reduction domain (one efficiency measure). Under HVBP, hospital inpatient payments are adjusted up or down based on a total performance score and the maximum payment reduction is 2% of total inpatient payment.

- The Hospital-Acquired Condition Reduction Program (HACRP) reduces 1% of overall Medicare fee for service (FFS) payments to hospitals whose overall performance on six hospital infection and safety measures is in the lowest quartile among all participating hospitals.

- The Hospital Readmissions Reduction Program (HRRP) penalizes hospitals if their readmission rates (six readmission measures) exceed risk-adjusted expected readmission rates. The HRRP penalty is capped at 3% of total Medicare inpatient payment.

- The Bundled Payments for Care Improvement (BPCI) initiative is also known as episode-based payment. BPCI participants must assume financial and performance risk for clinically defined episodes of care that go beyond a single care setting and can last up to 90 days after an inpatient procedure.

- The Medicare Shared Savings Program (MSSP) is a total cost of care model where groups of hospitals, doctors, and other providers form accountable care organizations (ACOs) that bear the responsibility for the total costs and quality of care for their patient population.

When asked to rate the importance of the five Medicare programs in value-analysis decisions, most surveyed VAC members consider HRRP and HVBP to be "extremely" or "very important" factors in their value-analysis decisions. The other three programs are rated as extremely/very important by 45% to 50% of respondents, which is likely because these programs only affect a minority of hospitals, either due to how penalties are assessed, or because participation is voluntary.

In addition, alternative payment models are designed for patients with certain conditions or receive certain treatments, such as Comprehensive Care for Joint Replacement Model, Kidney Care Choices model, and Radiation Oncology model (delayed). Many private payers run their own quality initiatives and new payment models that are more or less similar in terms of program structure and measures used.

With this context in mind, it is easy to understand why quality metrics, such as infection rate, readmission rate, mortality rate, and patient satisfaction, interest VACs. Hospitals committed to alternative payment models are more likely to focus on technologies with an impact on total costs of care, such as MSSP savings and episode benchmarks.

New technology suppliers can add value while serving their own cause by investing in well-designed research studies that tie product performance to quality and cost of care metrics. To communicate effectively with providers, suppliers need to articulate how their clinical impacts (e.g., lower infection rate) may translate into, for example, reduced readmission rate or better patient satisfaction. Absent a value story about why the product is better than current practice backed with evidence, decisions move toward price and discount.

Another translation needed in the communication with VACs is to turn value stories into the calculations of return on investment (ROI) and the impact on the hospital's bottom line. ROI is often expressed as a percentage and calculated by dividing an investment's net profit (or loss) by its cost or outlay. The calculation normally includes revenue and cost projections and allows comparison with replacements, similar products, or current standard of care. Volume projection is a key element in ROI assessment and can incorporate a hospital's historical experience and/or forecast data. Economic models that show cost savings, cost-effectiveness, and/or cost offsets resulting from using new medical technology are useful tools a technology supplier can develop and offer to support VACs' ROI analysis.

Reimbursement and projected revenue growth are key driver of financial returns. Details about reimbursement, including coding, coverage, and payment, are instrumental in revenue projection. In estimating potential returns from alternative payment models, hospitals engaged in these new payment arrangements often have strong internal analytics team and/or external analytical partners to analyze additional patient care data provided by CMS and identify operational strategies. Any data points that a new technology supplier can provide on per episode or annual total cost of care savings will make the process easier for the VACs.

In terms of modeling the financial returns from quality improvement, hospitals and health systems may have internal capabilities or can access external tools that can be used. Relevant data, quality measure design and quality program methodologies needed for modeling are publicly available through data.cms.gov, QualityNet.cms.gov and Medicare.gov, including hospital and quality measure level performance and benchmark data.

While it's possible to build tools that show the financial returns from quality improvement associated with a new technology, there are complexities associated with different quality program design. Modeling the impact on HRRP is relatively straightforward because the HRRP penalties can be assessed on individual measures. Potential returns associated with HACRP program could be zero or the maximum amount of HACRP penalty and nothing in-between due to the all-or-nothing design of the HACRP program. Hospitals whose HACRP performance is already close to the HACRP penalty threshold are more likely to reap big rewards from quality improvement investment. The HVBP program is the most challenging one to model because the performance of

20 individual measures is first aggregated to four domain level scores and then to one HVBP score with weighting mechanism and other adjustments complicating the calculation.

Gains from quality improvement in a specific quality measure can be shown in hospital rankings as these measures are also used in Hospital Quality Star Rating and other types of hospital rankings, which impact a hospital's reputation. In addition, the tools/models should let hospitals utilize their own internal data, for example collected through electronic medical records and other internal sources evaluating surgical site infections, transfusions, readmissions, costs, and patient satisfaction.

The costs associated with deploying a new technology can be extensive, far more than a single upfront transaction. These include acquisition, maintenance, and operation costs (e.g., disposal accessories). There are other cost variables may be relevant, including installation, training, service and repairs, storage, leasing or fee-for-use, and depreciation. To gain a full picture of the value of a new technology, these costs need to be captured and compared to those associated with the standard of care or similar technologies. Technology suppliers should highlight any potential cost saving opportunities, such as reduced length of stay or decreased operation or procedure time. These reductions in service use can add to a hospital's net profit, especially for inpatient stays and many outpatient procedures where hospitals typically receive a flat fee.

DATA AND ANALYSIS TO SUPPORT PAYMENT CONSIDERATION

Most payment considerations include a data analysis part, either required as part of the request submission, such as in the case of NTAP application, or built into CMS's decision-making process, such as in APC assignment. Payment policies are often implemented with methodologies, analytical steps, and datasets that range from grouping logic and rate setting to geographic and provider-level adjustments.

Generally, CMS communicates its approach and provides the public an opportunity to comment when an issue is introduced the first time or revised. Once adopted, CMS generally follows its own approach in making payment decisions. In the annual proposed and final payment rules, each section includes an overview of CMS's methods and historical changes with references to previous rules where more elaborate discussions are available.

Claims data, derived from bills submitted by doctors, hospitals, and other providers to payers for reimbursement for their services, is one of the primary datasets used in Medicare's payment considerations. Claims data have information about covered services used by enrollees in the

Medicare program, including admission and discharge dates, diagnoses, procedures, and service providers. Demographic data, such as age, date of birth, race, place of residence, and date of death, are also included in these administrative datasets and are considered largely reliable and valid.

It is estimated that over 98% of adults aged 65 and over are enrolled in Medicare, making Medicare claims data one of the richest sources of utilization information in the country. Over 45 million beneficiaries are enrolled in the Medicare program today, allowing for detailed sub-group analysis. The data also allow access to claims information across multiple providers for a beneficiary while providing a consistent reporting format. Medicare data can be linked to other datasets, such as the US Census, cancer registries, and surveys, which expands the richness of the dataset. Innovators and entrepreneurs can access Medicare claims after going through data use agreement (DUA) application and review process.

A major limitation of claims data is that it has limited clinical information. Physiological measurements, such as blood pressure, pulse, and cardiac ejection fraction, are absent from the claims data. In addition, results of common tests, such as PSA, angiography, and pathological tests, are not available. Exact timing of events can be difficult to discern. Specifically, the time from admission to an event or timestamps for dates of service cannot be found in the data.

While sequence of various service can be seen from claims data, it's impossible to draw causal connection between encounters.

Claims data are the primary source for the cost criterion analysis required as part of the NTAP application. To qualify for NTAP, the expected average charges for cases involving the new technology must exceed a threshold set for each MS-DRG. CMS provides a step-by-step example in Excel format to walk through the analytical steps. The spreadsheet asks for reporting of case counts and average charges in each DRG. Each DRG's share in total case counts is used to prorate a DRG's charges, which are summed together to derive total average charges.

Taking the NTAP application for Hemolung Respiratory Assist System (RAS) – an extracorporeal system removes CO_2 for patients with a variety of respiratory diseases – as an example, the analysis starts by identifying patients eligible for the Hemolung RAS. The applicant identified 68,317 cases from the FY 2019 MedPAR Limited Data Set (LDS) – a de-identified Medicare inpatient claims data specifically designed to analyze the inpatient PPS rules – using two ICD-10-PCS codes related to ventilator support. All the cases identified fell into two MS-DRGs.

The next step involves removing charges associated with past technology and adding charges associated with the Hemolung RAS. The applicant removed 100% of the charges associated with inhalation, as they can be replaced by the Hemolung RAS treatment and charges associated with a 1-day length of stay (LOS) in the ICU based on an estimated LOS reduction associated with the new technology. The applicant then standardized the charges and applied a 4-year inflation factor to bring the charges to this year (2022) using the inflation factor released in the FY 2022 inpatient PPS final rule. The charge for the new technology is calculated by dividing the cost of Hemolung RAS by the national average cost-to-charge ratio for inhalation therapy, the revenue center that Hmolung RAS will be billed under. The final inflated average case-weighted standardized charge per case exceeded the average case-weighted threshold, which means Hemolung RAS meets the NTAP cost criterion.

CMS releases public use files that include summaries of a subset of claims data variables, such as service use and payment, at various levels, including individual providers, types of services, and geographic areas. These datasets provide key utilization information and trends without DUA requirement or knowledge to analyze claims data.

The series of datasets on doctors and other practitioners have information on use, payments, and submitted charges organized by National Provider Identifier (NPI), HCPCS code, and geography provided to Medicare Part B beneficiaries. The Medicare Inpatient Hospitals by Provider and Service dataset provides information on the use, payment, and hospital charges for over 3,000 U.S. hospitals that received inpatient PPS payments. The data are organized by hospital and MS-DRG. The Medicare Outpatient Hospitals by Geography and Service dataset provides similar hospital level information but on outpatient services.

To help the public understand and validate the payment rules, CMS also releases data tables along with the proposed and final rules. For example, there are data tables listing MS-DRG weights, APC weights, and CPT RVUs, which allow calculations of payment rates. Many of the data tables, though, need subject matter knowledge to navigate. Various types of healthcare providers also submit annual Medicare cost reports, another key data source used in rate-setting process. The corresponding public use datasets include provider information such as facility characteristics, utilization data (not limited to Medicare), cost and charges, and Medicare settlement data.

These published data files can validate payment rules and simulate alternatives. One example is the assignment of a CPT to an APC, which determines outpatient PPS rate for a new service or procedure. A basic principle of APC grouping logic is that CPT codes assigned to an APC are clinically similar and similar in terms of the resources use, which is assessed using geometric mean costs of a CPT code that includes costs of services packaged into the code. The geometric mean costs of CPT codes are used to compute APC geometric costs where the CPT codes are mapped into.

Along with the rule, CMS releases APC and CPT cost statistics tables, which allow comparison of APC geometric means and the geometric means of all the CPT codes mapped into an APC. This helps answer, for example, whether the geometric mean cost of a CPT is close to the top or bottom of all the codes in an APC and whether a CPT may be eligible to the next level APC with a higher payment rate. It also allows validation of whether assigning a CPT code to a different APC will violate the 2-times rule that requires the cost for the highest cost service within an APC cannot be over 2 times the cost for the lowest cost service in the APC. These data allow simulation of the geometric mean cost of the APCs based on old and new APC assignments – remove a CPT code from one APC and add to another APC – and assess the impact of the CPT code reassignment on geometric mean costs/payment rates of old and new hosting APCs.

PART SEVEN

STRATEGY TO NAVIGATE THE HEALTHCARE REIMBURSEMENT MAZE

Reimbursement is a maze of many options. It's a labyrinth with more than one entrance, whether it be through coding, or coverage, or payment directly, and each section has its own small universe of defined paths and adjoining sideways linked to others. Although the exit point is clear, some paths may be circular and convoluted, taking longer to reach the destination. Time spent on finding the right path increases the risk that a new venture may run out of steam before reaching the exit. Time is of the essence in a market access strategy – a plan of actions to ensure a new technology can reach the target patient population at the right price, sooner rather than later. So, the process of reimbursement planning involves identifying, calculating, and comparing probabilities and risks of different market access pathways in a multidimensional possibility maze.

Having an idea of potential reimbursement dead-end issues before committing to a course that may be difficult to reverse will save a lot of time and money. Questions such as whether the new technology falls into at least one defined Medicare benefit category or categories, whether the new technology will be packaged into other services or separately reimbursed, and whether the result from a diagnostic test will be actionable, for example, with treatment options, are some issues that should be evaluated upfront. If financing is a critical consideration, knowing whether there is a path to reimbursement for a new technology is one of the expected questions from potential investors.

Until recently, reimbursement planning has typically happened at the end of the FDA regulatory process or haphazardly to address questions raised by investors. Clinical trials are designed primarily to meet the FDA's safety and effectiveness requirements for regulatory approval. The same data elements collected and analyzed for regulators are often used for coverage and reimbursement decisions.

Even though Medicare and private payers share a keen interest in both the safety and effectiveness of medical products and services, the coverage determination is based on whether the service or item is considered reasonable and necessary for the diagnosis or treatment of an illness or injury. Failing to meet evidentiary requirements to demonstrate clinical value set by payers increases the risk of insurance denial, which can significantly delay market access of a new technology. While there is some awareness about the importance of payer's coverage determination and rate-setting, little attention has been paid to provider's unique value environment and assessment in evidentiary development and pricing strategies, which may leave a new technology stalled in marketplace.

The reimbursement planning process brings in the perspective of payers and providers with a goal of market success instead of just market approval. It enables more coordinated development of evidence, pricing, and marketing strategy when started alongside the regulatory process. Early planning can contribute to design considerations that shape the technology into a marketable product and create value for payers, providers, and patients. It also helps prevent missteps that can cause delays and significant restrictions in access, such as overlooking crucial requirements, mistargeting patient populations, pricing a product over payers' cost-effectiveness coverage threshold, or failing to gain market access with ill-prepared value propositions for providers. Additionally, adding clinical, economic considerations and provider value endpoints to the regulatory approval studies for a new technology may save time, money, and effort.

REIMBURSEMENT ASSESSMENT

As the cliché goes, you can't know where you are going until you know where you are. Reimbursement planning starts with assessing the reimbursement landscape to understand where a new technology fits in the existing reimbursement structure. It's a survey of the current coverage, coding, and payment landscape for a new technology or similar technology. As importantly, it helps identify reimbursement challenges and opportunities as you move forward. While individual assessments will vary depending on the technology, common questions to address include:

1. Who is the target population of your technology and who will pay for the services provided to your target populations?

2. What is the benefit category or categories of your new technology?

3. What's the care setting(s) where the technology is used, who are the primary healthcare providers use your technology, and what payment system(s) will reimburse for their services?

4. Would the new technology receive separate payment, or would it be packaged into other services?

5. Can you bill directly to the payer or provider for each service or item provided?

6. How does the new technology compare to existing covered technologies? One way of categorizing technology improvement is by using the labels "continuous improvement," "incremental innovation," "radical innovation," and "disruptive innovation," with the latter categories are more likely to require new codes to accurately describe the service or item.

7. Does a code for a similar product already exist? Does your product fit under the existing code? Which coding system applies to your technology?

8. If an existing code is applicable, what's the payment rate? If a new code application is needed, how will the cost of the new technology be reflected in the payment rate? How does reimbursement compare to pricing?

9. What is the linkage between coding, payment, and coverage for the product? Should you ask for a coverage determination?

10. What are your value propositions for payers and providers? Does the technology improve health outcomes, and is it cost-effective? Does the technology improve quality of care, patient satisfaction, and/or operational efficiency?

The assessment informs payment opportunities and market valuation. The information is also the foundation for building a market access plan. A well-designed plan should help you gain clarity on what market access initiatives need to be completed and when. Key elements of a market access plan include evidence development, coding initiatives, payment and pricing strategy, and coverage strategy, even though the exact parts and priority may vary depending on the technology.

EVIDENCE DEVELOPMENT STRATEGY

Regarding new medical innovation, value is in the eye of the beholder. To the FDA, it means ensuring a medical product is safe and effective. To payers, it means improving the health and well-being of patients and being cost-effective. To providers, value can come in different shapes and forms, including speedy recovery, improved mortality, lower infection rates, reduced rehospitalization, shorter length of stay and operation time, improved patient satisfaction, safer for clinicians, fewer medical errors, more durable, cheaper to maintain, easier to learn and maneuver, increased revenue, improved margins, and so on. Due to the dynamic roles that payers and providers play in market access, the innovative medical technology's value must be tailored and shown to different stakeholders.

Successful value creation and communication requires a meticulous plan for evidence development that proactively address expected objections from the marketplace. Evidence-generation plans should encompass a range of study goals and designs, such as traditional randomized trials, comparative effectiveness research, studies focusing on patient outcomes and patient-reported outcomes, long-term safety and effectiveness assessment in real-world populations, burden of disease studies, cost-effectiveness evaluations, and budget-impact analyses from hospital and payer perspectives.

Medicare is the largest payer for healthcare in the US, and its coverage and payment policy are the most noticeable and influential in the marketplace. As CMS cannot consider cost in making coverage determination, clinical outcomes are the focus of evidential requirements. For diagnostic tests, CMS's hierarchical framework offers an evidential tier based on effect on the patient management plan besides effect on patient outcomes, which may allow faster data collection, especially when outcomes are shown through long-term follow-up data collection like the case of Oncotype DX breast cancer for DCIS. Study design matters and it's an essential part in CMS and its contractors' appraisal of evidence in supporting coverage determinations. Besides well-designed trials, CMS also seeks real-world evidence to show that findings from clinical trials are generalizable in clinical practice. Particularly, they are interested in positive outcomes shown in Medicare population.

Besides clinical effectiveness, private payers also consider evidence of the cost-effectiveness of a new technology. The inputs of a cost-effectiveness analysis often include the net cost of a new technology and changes in health outcomes, which rely on findings from clinical trials and other types of studies. Coordination is key to make sure that outcomes are designed and measured properly in trials to feed in cost-effectiveness analysis. The cost of a new technology often means payment rate, and depending on the payment settings and technology, it may not reflect product pricing directly. This cost input needs to be coordinated with pricing, payment, and coverage strategy, especially when differential payment strategy might be pursued with different payers.

Integrating providers' viewpoint into evidential development can improve the chance a medical innovation will achieve faster adoption once launched and better meet patient needs. Effort should be made early on to capture a kernel of truth about the customer – target providers, who they are, what they care about, and how they view the returns on their purchasing decision. In the data collection process, careful consideration should be made about collecting outcomes that matter to hospitals or other providers from quality improvement and cost-efficiency standpoints, such as reduced hospital-acquired infection, blood loss, hospital length of stay, procedure time, and rehospitalizations, in addition to improved clinical outcomes. Providers are also specially interested in the real-world performance of technologies, such as safety and long-term performance. For technologies like those on the market, the expectation is that the new technology is faster, cheaper, and/or more efficient, which can ideally be demonstrated with data.

CODING STRATEGY

If there is no existing code that can adequately describe a new medical technology and facilitate proper billing of the diagnosis, procedure, service, or item provided to a patient, an application for a new code may be needed. There is no shortage of codes. The first step is to identify the correct code needed and who is responsible for maintaining the coding system. CMS is responsible for maintaining the HCPCS level II codes used to bill for services paid under various payment systems, including the outpatient PPS, PFS, Durable Medical Equipment, Prosthetics, Orthotics and Supplies (DMEPOS), and Ambulatory Surgical Center (ASC) payment system, and ICD-10-PCS codes used primarily to bill for procedures provided during hospital inpatient stays. The AMA develops and manages CPT or HCPCS level I codes.

Each coding system has its own application and review timeframes and requirements, and generally has an annual approval cycle. It's essential to plan and ensure accuracy and completeness of coding applications as missteps can cause long delay counted by year instead of by month. For a CPT application, it's advisable to consult associated specialty societies and gain their support before submission. Most often coding applications are submitted by specialty societies with technology developers playing a supporting role.

Coordinating coding applications with coverage and payment strategy can help streamline the reimbursement process. Coding and payment changes are commonly made annually, while in some instances coding and payment changes may occur quarterly. Medicare's local and national coverage decisions are made under specific timeframes to accommodate public notice and comment requirements. Here are examples of how the timeframes of coding, payment, and coverage can be potentially integrated:

- Although the application for outpatient pass-through status requests CPT and/or HCPCS level II codes, applicants can request a new code along with the application for pass-through status. An application for outpatient New Technology APC does not need a code. If a service meets the criteria for New Technology APC, CMS will consider creating a level II HCPCS code to facilitate payment for New Technology APC.

- Applicants for inpatient NTAP payment are instructed to submit a request for a new ICD-10-PCS code separately, which means the coding application needs to be planned according to the NTAP application timeline. Another consideration is CMS lets applicants submit NTAP applications several months before the technology's receipt of FDA approval, as long as FDA approval is granted before CMS decides for the inpatient PPS final rule.

- If all criteria are met, it's possible for a new Category I CPT code application to be submitted and cleared the CPT editorial panel in as little as 3 months. However, the code application process can often take much longer and be uncertain. The criteria for code approval include volume/frequency requirements such as being "performed by many physicians or other qualified healthcare professionals across the United States" and being "appropriate for the intended clinical use," in addition to having well-documented clinical efficacy. Once a code is approved by the CPT panel, it typically takes at least another year to obtain a national payment rate for the code, assuming no objections or delays. First, medical specialty societies need to conduct a survey on the cost inputs of the service and present the findings to the RUC. The RUC then discusses and votes on a valuation of the code, and finally, CMS proposes and finalizes a national payment rate for the code.

Category III CPT codes are comparatively easier and faster to obtain. However, unlike Category I CPT codes, Category III CPT codes are not automatically reviewed by the RUC for payment valuation. One way to seek payment for a temporary code is by requesting an LCD. NCD and LCD are the policies, as explained by CMS, whereas codes reflect the operationalization of a policy. This means that the policy can remain the same while coding is updated. CMS may decide to provide a national payment rate for a temporary code through an annual rulemaking process.

PAYMENT AND PRICING STRATEGY

The relationship between payment rates and product pricing is complicated. Sometimes, payment rates determine pricing. For example, under the clinical lab fee schedule, the initial payment rate for a new lab test is established by either cross-walking to a comparable existing test or gap-filling using various information available before the weighted median of private insurer rates becomes available – a fee schedule method introduced by the PAMA of 2014. On the other end of the spectrum, pharmaceutical companies still have the autonomy to price a Part B drug themselves, and Medicare's payment rate is based on the average sales price of a drug. The arrangement may undergo some modifications under the Inflation Reduction Act of 2022.

The relationship between payment and pricing has another layer of intricacy for medical devices. Usually, the cost of a medical device equipment is prorated and allocated to the direct cost of practice expense and reflected in the PE RVU under the PFS. Under the outpatient PPS, the cost can be reflected in the charges hospital bill for a procedure and/or the bill an independent diagnostic test facility invoices a hospital, which affect the geometric mean cost of a code and then APC assignment and APC payment rate. In these scenarios, the costs of medical devices influence the rate-setting for a service or procedure. However, it's not always possible to measure the exact contribution of the cost/pricing of a medical device in the payment rate of a service or procedure.

The new wave of Software as a Service (SaaS) or Software as Medical Device (SaMD) often includes capital equipment and digital or AI-assisted diagnostic tools. Along with the new technology setup and value propositions, pricing models are also more diversified. Besides the traditional upfront purchase, fee for use, and leasing models, device manufacturers now offer subscription fee models that might include capital equipment. All these advancements make a complicated relationship even more intricate to untangle.

Payment and pricing strategy can play a huge role in market access's success – or failure. Innovators must consider whether the expected product value will be acceptable to payers and hospital purchasers. In the US, private payers' willingness to pay threshold usually fall between \$100,000 to \$150,000 per QALY gained. The payment rate, frequency, and duration of a new intervention are the direct cost inputs of a cost-effectiveness analysis, for which payers might bear if significant gains in health outcomes justify them.

For providers, direct returns from purchasing a new medical technology come from reimbursement from payers and patients, while the price for a medical device, drugs, services, or other items charged by manufacturers are considered costs or investments. Other returns, such as improving quality performance and operational efficiency, increase providers' ROI for their purchasing decision and can make a new technology standout in providers' internal value-based purchasing process. Other factors, such as the price of comparator products and discounts and the potential for offering innovative services, may also influence a provider's value assessment. Developing comprehensive, methodologically sound, and adaptable tools and tailoring value/ROI analyses to hospital-specific parameters will improve the communication about clinical and economical product value and make the value communication more applicable and concrete to a specific provider.

COVERAGE STRATEGY

While the fragmentation of the US insurance market can be overwhelming to navigate, it also provides ample space for strategic mapping and plan Bs. There are different ways to slice and dice the payer market to map out the best way forward. One characteristic of the US health insurance market is that it's divided into geographic regions. Taking the BCBS as an example, which was formed in 1982 from the merger of the two Blues, it's a federation of 34 independent and locally operated BCBS companies. Health insurance markets are often highly concentrated with one insurer accounting for over 50% of a local market. Public programs are no exception with Medicaid programs operated at the state level and Medicare's path of local coverage determination administered by local administrative contractors in defined jurisdictions.

Another aspect to explore is the different demographics and burden of disease of covered lives by different payers. For example, because of Medicare's extended coverage for ESRD, over four out of five ESRD patients are covered by Medicare for their medical care, which makes Medicare the predominant payer for these patients. The elderly (65 and above) account for more than half of all new cancer cases in the US. For developers of cancer-related products, Medicare is the obvious target, including health insurance companies with a large share of Medicare MA enrollment (e.g., United Health Care and Humana), unless, for example, the therapeutic area is pediatric cancers. Here, Medicaid might be a more suitable target as Medicaid & CHIP cover more than one-third of Children under 19.

When building a coverage strategy, there are a few questions will help identify target payers and priorities of a coverage strategy:

1. Will the new technology benefit the Medicare population (mostly seniors aged 65 and above)? If yes, should you seek explicit Medicare coverage determination (LCD or NCD) to get the service or item reimbursed? If yes, should it be an LCD or NCD? Should you request LCDs one jurisdiction at a time or all at once? For LCDs, which Medicare contractor should you send your request? Even if you don't plan to request a coverage determination, it's beneficial to prepare for such a possibility as CMS or its contractors or other stakeholders can request a coverage determination.

2. Will the new technology benefit the Medicaid population (a large percentage are children, pregnant women, low-income adults, and dually eligible elderly)? If yes, which states should you target?

3. When approaching private plans, should you start with large national plans or regional plans to test the water first? For example, should you approach one or two regional BCBS plans first or submit a request for technology assessment to BCBSA's Evidence Street, a health technology assessment platform used by many regional Blues and other payers? A positive technology assessment from the latter will help expand the breadth of market access faster. On the flip side, a negative assessment might be a major roadblock with broad impact.

The goal of market access planning is to create a more holistic, integrated approach to identify, build, and communicate value with payers and providers that facilitates fast market deployment. The prioritization of the markets in which to launch and different routes to get there needs to balance risks and benefits. All the parts of market access — coding, coverage, and payment decisions — are interconnected, with progress in one area relying on progress in another area. And each has their own timeframes. To reduce unnecessary wait time and improve effectiveness of efforts, different timelines need to be coordinated. The ecosystem is dynamic. So, the market access plan can't be static. It's essential to continuously monitor changes and development and make necessary readjustments to make sure that the market access plan remains aligned with the dynamic ecosystem.

During my conversation with Dr. Singh, we discussed whether the assessments and metrics employed in evaluating a startup company could guarantee success. Dr. Singh's response was clear: they cannot. He added the insightful perspective that "nothing ventured, nothing gained." This insight also holds true for market access strategy and planning.

APPRECIATION

I am immensely grateful for the many people who invested their time and effort into the success of the book. I am fortunate to have crossed paths with such valuable individuals who have become invaluable in my life.

Foremost, I would like to express my gratitude to Paul Gerrard for suggesting the idea for this book and to Ajit Singh for the encouragement that set me on this rewarding journey of writing this book.

I am eternally grateful to the readers who generously offered their time to review early drafts of the book and provide valuable advice. Special thanks to Matt Baker, Michael Arce, Kathryn Phillips, and Christine Chang for their insightful feedback on various aspects, from identifying the potential audience to formatting and cover design.

I am deeply indebted to the individuals who contributed their expertise and insights, adding a wealth of policy and technical knowledge to this book. My sincere appreciation goes to Gabriel Bien-Willner, Gayle Lee, Jeff Stensland, Marc Hartstein, Lixia Yao, Jay Ahlman, and Sherry Smith. Thank you for indulging my endless questions.

I would like to extend a note of immense gratitude to Mary Beth White for being my unwavering cheerleader and advocate throughout this journey. My thanks also go to

Margaret Garikes for her exceptional help and persistence in coordinating feedback, Irene Wang for connecting me with cover designers and other professionals and Hope He for capturing my best self in the author photos.

I would like to give special recognition to two individuals whose contributions have taken the book to the next level. First, I want to express my gratitude to Sam for being a thoughtful editor and for sharing valuable insights about writing and publishing. Secondly, I want to extend my appreciation to Longze for his artistic contribution that has enhanced the overall presentation of the book and translated my vision into a functional and visually captivating book cover design.

Finally, I want to acknowledge ChatGPT, whose unwavering patience as a reviewer and editor has been invaluable. Your availability and eagerness to help, regardless of the time of day or the number of revisions, have been truly remarkable.

To all of you mentioned here and countless others who have supported me along the way, thank you for your invaluable contributions to this book. Your support and guidance have been instrumental, and I am deeply grateful for your presence in my life.

GLOSSARY

AAO	American Academy of Ophthalmology
ACA	Affordable Care Act
ACC	American College of Cardiology
ACCE	Analytic Validity (AV), Clinical Validity (CV), Clinical Utility (CU) and Ethical, Legal, and Social Implications
ACO	Accountable Care Organization
ACR	American College of Radiology
ADLT	Advanced Diagnostic Laboratory Test
AHA	American Hospital Association
AHRQ	Agency for Healthcare Research and Quality
AI	Artificial Intelligence
AMA	American Medical Association
AMCP	Academy of Managed Care Pharmacy
AMP	Association for Molecular Pathology
APC	Ambulatory Payment Classifications
APM	Alternative Payment Models
ASC	Ambulatory Surgical Center
ASCO	American Society of Clinical Oncology
ASP	Average Sales Price
BBA	Balanced Budget Act
BCBS	BlueCross and BlueShield
BCBSA	BlueCross and BlueShield Association

GLOSSARY

BIA	Budget Impact Analysis
BPCI	Bundled Payments for Care Improvement
CAC	Contractor Advisory Committee
CAG	Coverage and Analysis Group
CAP	College of American Pathologists
CBO	Congressional Budget Office
CC	Complications and Comorbidities
CCSQ	Center for Clinical Standards and Quality
CCTA	Coronary CT Angiography
CDC	Centers for Disease Control and Prevention
CDLT	Clinical Diagnostic Laboratory Test
CDR	Clinical Data Registry
CEA	Cost-Effectiveness Analyses
CED	Coverage with Evidence Development
CER	Comparative Effectiveness Review
cfDNA	Circulating free DNA
CGM	Continuous glucose monitoring
CHIP	Children's Health Insurance Program
CLFS	Clinical Lab Fee Schedule
CLIA	Clinical Laboratory Improvement Amendments
CMD	Contractor Medical Director
CMMI	Center for Medicare & Medicaid Innovation
CMS	Center for Medicare & Medicaid Services
CMSS	Council of Medical Specialty Societies
CPEP	Clinical Practice Expert Panels
CPG	Clinical Practice Guidelines

CPT	Current Procedure Terminology
CRS	Congressional Research Service
CT	Computed Tomography
CTA	Computed Tomographic Angiogram
DERP	Drug Effectiveness Review Project
DES	Discrete Event Simulation
DEX	Diagnostics Exchange
DME	Durable Medical Equipment
DMEPOS	Durable Medical Equipment, Prosthetics, Orthotics and Supplies
DMPAG	Digital Medicine Payment Advisory Group
DOH	Department of Health
DR	Diabetic Retinopathy
DRG	Diagnosis-Related Group
DUA	Data Use Agreement
EHR	Electronic Health Record
EPC	Evidence-Based Practice Center
EPSDT	Early and Periodic Screening, Diagnostic and Treatment
ER	Emergency Room
ERG.	Electroretinogram
ESRD	End-Stage Renal Disease
FDA	Food and Drug Administration
FDCA	Food, Drug, and Cosmetic Act
FDG-PET	Positron Emission Tomography with F-18 FluoroDeoxyGlucose

FFR	Fractional Flow Reserve
FFRCT	Fractional Flow Reserve – Computed Tomography
FFS	Fee for Service
GAO	General Accountability Office
GDP	Gross Domestic Product
GPCI	Geographic Practice Cost Indices
GRADE	Grading of Recommendations Assessment, Development and Evaluation
HACRP	Hospital-Acquired Condition Reduction Program
HCFA	Health Care Financing Administration
HCPAC	Health Care Professionals Advisory Committee
HCPCS	Healthcare Common Procedures Coding System
HERC	Health Evidence Review Commission
HHS	US Department of Health and Human Services
HIPAA	Health Insurance Portability and Accountability Act
HMO	Health Maintenance Organization
HRRP	Hospital Readmissions Reduction Program
HVBP	Hospital Value-Based Purchasing Program
ICD	International Classification of Diseases
ICD-10-CM	ICD-10 Clinical Modifications
ICD-10-PCS	ICD-10 Procedure Coding System
ICER	Incremental Cost-Effectiveness Ratio

ICER	Institute for Clinical and Economic Review
ICU	Intensive Care Unit
IDE	Investigational Device Exemption
IDTF	Independent Diagnostic Testing Facility
IOM	Institute of Medicine
IRA	Inflation Reduction Act
LCD	Local Coverage Determination
LDS	Limited Data Set
LOS	Length of Stay
LVO	Large Vessel Occlusion
MA	Medicare Advantage
MAAA	Advanced Diagnostic Laboratory Test
MAB	Monoclonal Antibody
MAC	Medicare Administrative Contractor
MACRA	Medicare Access and CHIP Reauthorization Act
MCC	Major Complications and Comorbidities
MCD	Medicare Coverage Database
MCED	Multi-Cancer Early Detection
MCO	Managed Care Organization
MDC	Major Diagnostic Categories
MDT	Molecular Diagnostic Test
MED	Medicaid Evidence-Based Decisions
MEDCAC	Medicare Evidence Development and Coverage Advisory Committee
MedPAC	Medicare Payment Advisory Commission

GLOSSARY

MIPPA	Medicare Improvements for Patients and Provider Act
MIPS	Merit-based Incentive Payment System
MMA	Medicare Prescription Drug, Improvement, and Modernization Act
MolDX	Molecular Diagnostic Services
MRI	Magnetic Resonance Imaging
MS-DRG	Medicare Severity Diagnosis Related Group
MSSP	Medicare Shared Savings Program
NAMCP	National Association of Managed Care Physicians
NCD	National Coverage Determination
NCDR	National Cardiovascular Device Registry
NIH	National Institutes of Health
NOPR	National Oncologic PET Registry
NPI	National Provider Identifier
NTAP	New Technology Addon Payment
OHSU	Oregon Health Sciences University
OIG	Office of Inspector General
OTA	Office of Technology Assessment
OTC	Over-the-counter
PAMA	Protecting Access to Medicare Act
PC	Professional Component
PDL	Preferred Drug List
PE	Practice Expense
PEAC	Practice Expense Advisory Committee

PERG	Electroretinogram Pattern
PET	Positron Emission Tomography
PFS	Physician Fee Schedule
PHE	Public Health Emergency
PICO	Population, Intervention, Comparator, and Outcome
PLA-TAG	Proprietary Laboratory Analyses Technical Advisory Group
PLA.	Proprietary Laboratory Analyses
PPIS	Physician Practice Information Survey
PPS	Prospective Payment System
PRO	Peer Review Organizations
QALY	Quality-Adjusted Life Year
RAC	Recovery Audit Contractor
RAS	Respiratory Assist System
RCT	Randomized Clinical Trial
REMS	Risk Evaluation and Mitigation Strategies
RTC	Response to Comment
RUC	Relative Value Update Committee
RVU	Relative Value Unit
SaaS	Software as a Service
SaMD	Software as Medical Device
SGR	Sustainable Growth Rate
SNF	Skilled Nursing Facility
STS	Society of Thoracic Surgeons
TA	Technology Assessment

GLOSSARY

TAVR	Transcatheter Aortic Valve Replacement
TC	Technical Component
TPT	Transitional Pass-Through
USPSTF	U.S. Preventive Services Task Force
VAC	Value Analysis Committee

NOTES

PREFACE

1. Feng, Xing Lin, Melisa Martinez-Alvarez, Jun Zhong, et al. Extending access to essential services against constraints: the three-tier health service delivery system in rural health (1949-1980). Int J Equity Health. 2017;16;49.
2. Wang, Nuo, Christian Gericke, and Huixin Sun. Comparison of health care financing schemes before and after market reforms in China's urban areas. Frontiers of Economics in China, 4 (2) (2009), pp. 173-191
3. Wagstaff, Adam, Magnus Lindelow, Shiyong Wang, and Shuo Zhang. Reforming China's rural health system. The World Bank, Washington DC (2009)
4. Bradsher, Keith. How health insurance works in China, and how it's changing. The New York Times. Feb. 23, 2023. https://www.nytimes.com/2023/02/23/business/china-health-insurance-explained.html

INTRODUCTION

5. Helmuth, Laura. Why are you not dead yet? Slate. September 5, 2017.
6. An estimated 75-80% of the costs of biopharmaceuticals are borne by payers, according to Kaiser Family Foundation calculations (2008) using National Health Expenditure historical data from the Centers for Medicare and Medicaid

Services (https://www.cms.gov/Research-Statistics-Data-and-Systems/Statistics-Trends-and-Reports/NationalHealthExpendData/index.html?redirect=/NationalHealthExpendData); unfortunately, there is relatively little data available pertaining to insurance cost share for medical devices.

7. Centers for Medicare and Medicaid Services . Pub 100-04 Medicare Claims Processing: Transmittal 2378. Change Request 7682: January 2012 update of the ambulatory surgery center payment system. December 29, 2011.

8. Centers for Medicare and Medicaid Services . Pub 100-04 Medicare Claims Processing: Transmittal 2234. Change Request 7443: July 2011 update of the hospital outpatient prospective payment system. May 27, 2011.

9. Puri, Pranav, Denis Cortese, and Sujith Baliga. A time series analysis of trends in Medicare utilization and reimbursement for cancer immunotherapy drugs: 2012-2017. medRxiv preprint doi: https://doi.org/10.1101/2020.06.27.20141721

MARKET ACCESS GATEKEEPERS

10. The US hospital count is from American Hospital Association's U.S. hospital statistics. The number of physicians is from the physician specialty data report released by the Association of American Medical Colleges. The nursing home count is from CDC's National Center for Health Statistics.

11. Minor, David. Kimball, Justin Ford (1872-1956). Handbook of Texas Online. Texas State Historical Association.

https://www.tshaonline.org/handbook/entries/kimball-justin-ford

12. Blue Cross and Blue Shield Association. Blue Cross and Blue Shield history fact sheet. https://digitalcommons.unf.edu/cgi/viewcontent.cgi?article=3089&context=flablue_text. Private health insurance originates with Blue Cross and Blue Shield. https://www.encyclopedia.com/science/medical-magazines/private-health-insurance-originates-blue-cross-and-blue-shield

13. Tarazi, Wafa, Peter Welch, Nguyen Nguyen, et al. Medicare beneficiary enrollment trends and demographic characteristics. Issue Brief No. HP-2022-08. Assistant Secretary for Planning and Evaluation. U.S. Department of Health and Human Services. https://aspe.hhs.gov/reports/medicare-enrollment

14. Corallo, Bradley and Sophia Moreno. Analysis of national trends in Medicaid and CHIP enrollment during the COVID-19 pandemic. Kaiser Family Foundation. Issue Brief, April 4, 2023. https://www.kff.org/coronavirus-covid-19/issue-brief/analysis-of-recent-national-trends-in-medicaid-and-chip-enrollment/

15. Young, James Harvey. The Long Struggle for the Law. https://www.fda.gov/media/110318/download

16. Janssen, Wallace F. The Story of the Laws Behind the Labels. From FDA Consumer magazine (June 1981). https://www.fda.gov/media/116890/download

17. Food and Drug Administration. A History of the FDA and Drug Regulation in the United States.

https://www.fda.gov/files/drugs/published/A-History-of-the-FDA-and-Drug-Regulation-in-the-United-States.pdf

18. Ottes, Ronald T. and Fred L. Lofsvold. Oral History Interview with William W. Goodrich, Office of the General Counsel, 1939–1971.October 15, 1986. Rockville, Md.: U.S. Food and Drug Administration. https://www.fda.gov/media/87084/download

19. Epstein, Jessica. Drugs that shaped the FDA: From Elixir Sulfanilamide to Thalidomide. Bull. Hist. Chem., 2018, 43(2): 102-110. Elixir Fatal to 14 in West Is Seized Here. Washington Post, Oct. 20, 1937, p 1. Venereal Disease Cure Kills 8 of 10 Patients in Oklahoma. Washington Post, Oct. 19, 1937, p 3. Near End of Chase for Deadly Elixir. New York Times, Oct. 25, 1937, p 21.

20. Ballentine, Carol. Sulfanilamide disaster. FDA From Consumer magazine. June 1981. https://www.fda.gov/files/about%20fda/published/The-Sulfanilamide-Disaster.pdf

MEDICAL CODING – THE CODE TO REIMBURSEMENT

21. World Health Organization. History of the development of the ICD. https://cdn.who.int/media/docs/default-source/classification/icd/historyoficd.pdf?sfvrsn=b9e617af_3

22. Centers for Medicare and Medicaid Services. Independent diagnostic testing facility (IDTF). The Medicare Learning Network (MLN) booklet, MLN909060. October 2022. https://www.cms.gov/outreach-and-education/medicare-

learning-network-mln/mlnproducts/downloads/icn909060-idtf-fact-sheet.pdf

23. Food and Drug Administration. FDA news release: FDA permits marketing of artificial intelligence-based device to detect certain diabetes-related eye problems. April 11, 2018. https://www.fda.gov/news-events/press-announcements/fda-permits-marketing-artificial-intelligence-based-device-detect-certain-diabetes-related-eye

24. American Medical Association. Category I/III CPT code change application literature requirements. https://www.ama-assn.org/practice-management/cpt/cpt-code-change-applications

25. National Government Services, Inc. LCD – implantable continuous glucose monitors (I-CGM). L38623.

26. CGS Administrators, LLC. LCD – electroretinography (ERG). L38992.

27. American Medical Association. Criteria for CPT Category I and Category III codes. https://www.ama-assn.org/practice-management/cpt/criteria-cpt-category-i-and-category-iii-codes

28. American Medical Association. CPT Category III codes: the first ten years. https://www.ama-assn.org/sites/ama-assn.org/files/corp/media-browser/public/cpt/cat-3-codes-first-10-yrs_1.pdf

29. American Medical Association. CPT PLA codes. https://www.ama-assn.org/practice-management/cpt/cpt-pla-codes

30. Centers for Medicare and Medicaid Services. Healthcare Common Procedure Coding System (HCPCS) level II coding

procedures.
https://www.cms.gov/Medicare/Coding/MedHCPCSGenI
nfo/Downloads/2018-11-30-HCPCS-Level2-Coding-
Procedure.pdf

31. Centers for Medicare and Medicaid Services. Fact sheet: final policy, payment, and quality provisions in the Medicare Physician Fee Schedule for calendar year 2018. November 2, 2017. https://www.cms.gov/newsroom/fact-sheets/final-policy-payment-and-quality-provisions-medicare-physician-fee-schedule-calendar-year-2018

32. Centers for Medicare and Medicaid Services. HCPCS level II coding for 505(b)(2)-approved drugs or biologicals – frequently asked questions. https://www.cms.gov/files/document/frequently-asked-questions-single-source-drugs-and-biologicals.pdf

33. Centers for Medicare and Medicaid Services. Centers for Medicare & Medicaid Services' (CMS') Healthcare Common Procedure Coding System (HCPCS) level II final coding, benefit category and payment determinations. Second biannual (B2), 2022 HCPCS coding cycle. https://www.cms.gov/files/document/2022-hcpcs-application-summary-biannual-2-2022-non-drug-and-non-biological-items-and-services.pdf

34. Butler, Rhonda R., Robert L. Mullin, Thelma M. Grant, et al. ICD-10-PCS reference manual. Centers for Medicare & Medicaid Services, contract No. 90-1138, 91-22300, 500-95-0005, and HHSM-500-2004-00011C to 3M Health Information Systems.

https://www.cms.gov/medicare/coding/icd10/downloads/pcs_refman.pdf

35. Centers for Medicare and Medicaid Services. Using the ICD-10-PCS new technology section codes. https://www.cms.gov/files/document/using-icd-10-pcs-new-technology-section-codes.pdf

PAYMENT SYSTEMS AND MEDICAL INNOVATIONS

36. Medicare Payment Advisory Commission. Payment basics: Hospital acute inpatient services payment system. October 2022. https://www.medpac.gov/wp-content/uploads/2021/11/MedPAC_Payment_Basics_22_hospital_FINAL_SEC.pdf

37. Medicare Payment Advisory Commission. Payment basics: Outpatient hospital services payment system. October 2022. https://www.medpac.gov/wp-content/uploads/2022/10/MedPAC_Payment_Basics_22_OPD_FINAL_SEC_v3.pdf

38. Medicare Payment Advisory Commission. Payment basics: Physician and other health professional payment system. October 2022. https://www.medpac.gov/wp-content/uploads/2021/11/MedPAC_Payment_Basics_22_Physician_FINAL_SEC.pdf

39. West, Howard. Five years of Medicare – a statistical review. Social Security Bulletin, December 1971. https://www.ssa.gov/policy/docs/ssb/v34n12/v34n12p17.pdf

40. Ball, Robert M. Social Security Amendments of 1972: summary and legislative history. Social Security Bulletin, March 1973. https://www.ssa.gov/policy/docs/ssb/v36n3/v36n3p3.pdf

41. Centers for Medicare and Medicaid Services. Design and development of the Diagnosis-Related Group. https://www.cms.gov/icd10m/version37-fullcode-cms/fullcode_cms/Design_and_development_of_the_Diagnosis_Related_Group_(DRGs).pdf

42. Berkowitz, Edward. Medicare and Medicaid: The past as prologue. Health Care Financ Rev. 2005 Winter; 27(2): 11-23. https://www.ncbi.nlm.nih.gov/pmc/articles/PMC4194925/. Savage T. Introduction to Medicare Part C. Chicago Sun Times. 1998 Apr 30.

43. Jackson, Dallas M. Health care coverage in the 90s. Los Angeles Times, March 5, 1993. https://www.latimes.com/archives/la-xpm-1993-03-05-fi-332-story.html

44. Catlin, Aaron C. and Cathy A. Cowan. History of spending in the United States, 1960-2013. November 19, 2015. https://www.cms.gov/Research-Statistics-Data-and-Systems/Statistics-Trends-and-Reports/NationalHealthExpendData/Downloads/HistoricalNHEPaper.pdf

45. Centers for Medicare and Medicaid Services. News and Media Group. CMS Newsroom Fact Sheet: Medicare "pay for performance" initiatives. January 31, 2005. https://www.cms.gov/newsroom/fact-sheets/medicare-pay-performance-p4p-initiatives

46. Reed, Louis S. and Ruth S. Hanft. National health expenditures, 1950-64. Social Security Bulletin, January 1966. https://www.ssa.gov/policy/docs/ssb/v29n1/v29n1p3.pdf

47. Medicare FY 2020 Inpatient PPS DRG rates effective 10/1/19. The payment rate is computed using tables 1A, 1D and 5 released along with the FY 2020 Inpatient PPS final rule (CMS-1716-F) and correction notice (CMS-1716-CN2).

48. Medicare FY 2023 Inpatient PPS DRG rates effective 10/1/22. The payment rate is computed using tables 1A, 1D and 5 released along with the FY 2023 Inpatient PPS final rule (CMS-1771-F)

49. Centers for Medicare and Medicaid Services. Innovation center strategy refresh. October 2021. https://innovation.cms.gov/strategic-direction-whitepaper

50. King, Robert. ACO participation reaches new low as advocates press Biden for major changes. Fierce Healthcare. January 21, 2021. https://www.fiercehealthcare.com/payer/aco-participation-reaches-new-low-as-advocates-press-biden-for-major-changes

51. Dalton, Kathleen. A study of charge compression in calculating DRG relative weights. The project was funded by CMS under Contract No. 500-00-0024. January 2007. RTI International. https://www.cms.gov/Research-Statistics-Data-and-Systems/Statistics-Trends-and-Reports/Reports/downloads/Dalton.pdf

52. Centers for Medicare and Medicaid Services. Medicare Program: Hospital Inpatient Prospective Payment System for Acute Care Hospitals and the Long-term Care Hospital

Prospective Payment System and Proposed Policy Changes and Fiscal Year 2020 Proposed Rule (CMS-1716-P). May 3, 2019. 84 FR 19182.

53. Centers for Medicare and Medicaid Services. Medicare program: Hospital Outpatient Prospective Payment and Ambulatory Surgical Center Payment Systems and quality reporting programs; organ acquisition; rural emergency hospitals: payment policies, conditions of participation, provider enrollment, physician self-referral; new service category for hospital outpatient department prior authorization process; overall hospital quality star rating; COVID–19. November 23, 2022. 87 FR 71755.

54. Centers for Medicare and Medicaid Services. Medicare Program. Hospital inpatient prospective payment systems for acute care hospitals and the long-term care hospital prospective payment system and final policy changes and fiscal year 2021 rates; quality reporting and Medicare and Medicaid promoting Interoperability programs requirements for eligible hospitals and critical access hospitals (CMS-1735-F). September 18, 2020. 85 FR 58625-58636.

55. Centers for Medicare and Medicaid Services. Medicare program; Hospital Inpatient Prospective Payment systems for acute care hospitals and the Long-Term Care Hospital Prospective Payment System and policy changes and fiscal year 2023 rates; quality programs and Medicare promoting interoperability program requirements for eligible hospitals and critical access hospitals; costs incurred for qualified and non-qualified deferred compensation plans; and changes to

hospital and critical access hospital conditions of participation (CMS-1771-F). August 10, 2022. 87 FR 48902.

56. Centers for Medicare and Medicaid Services. Overview of the New Technology Add-on Payment. https://www.cms.gov/Medicare/Medicare-Fee-for-Service-Payment/AcuteInpatientPPS/newtech

57. Medicare Payment Advisory Commission. Comment letter on Hospital Inpatient Prospective Payment System FY 2021 proposed rule. Accessed March 2023: https://www.medpac.gov/wp-content/uploads/import_data/scrape_files/docs/default-source/comment-letters/07072020_fy2021_ipps_medpac_comment_v2_sec.pdf

58. Association of American Medical Colleges. Comment letter on Hospital Inpatient Prospective Payment System FY 2020 proposed rule. https://www.aamc.org/media/13936/download?attachment

59. Medicare FY 2023 wage index effective 10/1/22. The wage index is from FY 2023 final rule and correcting amendment impact file released along with the FY 2023 Inpatient PPS final rule corrections (CMS-1771-F2)

60. The resident to bed ratio and IME payment adjustment are from FY 2023 final rule and correcting amendment impact file released along with the FY 2023 Inpatient PPS final rule corrections (CMS-1771-F2)

61. Approved Cellular and Gene Therapy Products. (2022, December 16). U.S. Food And Drug Administration. https://www.fda.gov/vaccines-blood-biologics/cellular-gene-

therapy-products/approved-cellular-and-gene-therapy-products.

62. Evaluate Pharma. (2022). Genetic Medicine: The Next Generation. https://www.evaluate.com/thought-leadership/vantage/genetic-medicine-next-generation

63. O'Connor, Kristi. Novant Health utilizes new technology to detect strokes quicker. WBTV. October 21, 2019. Accessed March 2023: https://www.wbtv.com/2019/10/22/novant-health-utilizes-new-technology-detect-strokes-quicker/

64. Hassan, Ameer E., Victor M. Ringheanu, Laurie Preston and Wondwossen G. Tekle. Artificial intelligence-parallel stroke workflow tool improves reperfusion rates and door-in to puncture interval. Vascular and Interventional Neurology. 2022; 2:e000224. September 7, 2022.

65. Wynn, Barbara O. Medicare payment for hospital outpatient services: a historical review of policy options. RAND working paper prepared for MedPAC. May 2005. https://www.rand.org/pubs/working_papers/WR267.html

66. Rovinsky, Michael, Sean Looby, and Laura Zacchigna. The shift to outpatient TKA – what's the big deal? June 26, 2018. Healthcare Financial Management Association. https://www.hfma.org/finance-and-business-strategy/healthcare-business-trends/61100/

67. Centers for Medicare and Medicaid Services. Process and information required for a New Technology Ambulatory Payment Classification (APC) assignment under the Hospital Outpatient Prospective Payment System (OPPS). https://www.cms.gov/Medicare/Medicare-fee-for-service-

payment/HospitalOutpatientPPS/Downloads/newtechapc.pdf

68. Office of Inspector General. Data brief: Trend toward more expensive inpatient hospital stays in Medicare emerged before COVID-19 and warrants further scrutiny. February 2021, OEI-02-18-00380. https://oig.hhs.gov/oei/reports/OEI-02-18-00380.pdf

69. Centers for Medicare and Medicaid Services. Part B Average Sales Price (ASP) data reporting guidance: clarification on Medicaid Drug Rebate Program "Multiple Best Prices" reporting option. https://www.cms.gov/files/document/part-b-asp-data-reporting-guidance-clarification-medicaid-drug-rebate-program-multiple-best-prices.pdf

70. Centers for Medicare and Medicaid Services. Process and information required to determine eligibility of drugs, biologicals, and radiopharmaceuticals for transitional pass-through status under the hospital Outpatient Prospective Payment System (OPPS). https://www.cms.gov/medicare/medicare-fee-for-service-payment/hospitaloutpatientpps/downloads/drugapplication.pdf

71. iRhythm billing and reimbursement. https://www.irhythmtech.com/providers/billing-and-reimbursement

72. Hammerand, Jim. iRhythm stays silent on federal grand jury subpoenas. Medical Design and Outsourcing. May 16, 2022. https://www.medicaldesignandoutsourcing.com/irhythm-stays-silent-on-federal-grand-jury-subpoenas/

73. iRhythm's Medicare pricing saga defined its 2021. Medtech Dive. December, 2021. https://www.medtechdive.com/news/irhythm-medicare-pricing-2021-blackford/611830/

74. Kelly, Susan. iRhythm stock leaps 33% after CMS pitches new reimbursement codes. Medtech Dive. August 5, 2020. https://www.healthcaredive.com/news/irhythm-stock-leaps-33-after-cms-pitches-new-reimbursement-codes/582966/

75. American Medical Association. RVS update process. 2023. https://www.ama-assn.org/system/files/ruc-update-booklet.pdf

76. Zipp, Ricky. iRhythm stock jumps nearly 28% after Novitas doubles Medicare rates for cardiac monitoring. Medtech Dive. January 11, 2022. https://www.medtechdive.com/news/irhythm-stock-jumps-novitas-doubles-medicare-rates/616969/

77. FDA Press Announcements. FDA permits marketing of artificial intelligence-based device to detect certain diabetes-related eye problems. April 12, 2018. https://www.fda.gov/news-events/press-announcements/fda-permits-marketing-artificial-intelligence-based-device-detect-certain-diabetes-related-eye

PAYER'S COVERAGE DECISION MAKING

78. Pendo, Elizabeth A. Images of health insurance in popular file: the dissolving critique. 2004. Saint Louis University School of Law Scholarship Commons.

79. Time. The best inventions of 2022: earlier detection Grail Galleri cancer test. https://time.com/collection/best-inventions-2022/6225228/grail-galleri-cancer-test/

80. Deloitte and AdvaMed. New strategies for MedTech startups: attracting investment from across the innovation ecosystem. https://www2.deloitte.com/content/dam/Deloitte/us/Documents/life-sciences-health-care/new-strategies-for-medtech-startups.pdf

81. S.1873 - Medicare Multi-Cancer Early Detection Screening Coverage Act of 2021. https://www.congress.gov/bill/117th-congress/senate-bill/1873?s=1&r=3#:~:text=Introduced%20in%20Senate%20(05%2F27%2F2021)&text=This%20bill%20provides%20for%20Medicare,cancer%20across%20many%20cancer%20types.

82. Congressional Research Service. Medicare coverage of clinical preventive services. March 18, 2010. https://crsreports.congress.gov/product/pdf/R/R40978/6

83. USPSTF. Grade definitions. https://www.uspreventiveservicestaskforce.org/uspstf/about-uspstf/methods-and-processes/grade-definitions

84. HHS Press Office. Biden-Harris Administration Requires Insurance Companies and Group Health Plans to Cover the Cost of At-Home COVID-19 Tests, Increasing Access to Free Tests. January 10, 2022. https://www.hhs.gov/about/news/2022/01/10/biden-harris-administration-requires-insurance-companies-group-health-plans-to-cover-cost-at-home-covid-19-tests-increasing-access-free-tests.html

85. Centers for Medicare and Medicaid Services. Medicare coverage of over-the-counter COVID-19 tests: frequently asked questions. April 4, 2022. https://www.cms.gov/files/document/4422-frequently-asked-questions-medicare-coverage-otc-covid-tests.pdf

86. Centers for Medicare and Medicaid Services. CMS manual system. Pub.100-16 Medicare managed care. Chapter 4, benefits and beneficiary protections. August 23, 2013. https://www.cms.gov/Regulations-and-Guidance/Guidance/Transmittals/Downloads/R115MCM.pdf

87. Gold, Marsha. Medicare Advantage Benefit Design: What Does It Provide, What Doesn't It Provide, and Should Standards Apply? Washington DC. AARP Public Policy Institute. March 2009. http://assets.aarp.org/rgcenter/health/2009_03_medicare.pdf.

88. UnitedHealthCare. Formal request for national coverage determination for chimeric antigen receptor T-cell therapies. https://www.cms.gov/Medicare/Coverage/DeterminationProcess/downloads/id291.pdf

89. Centers for Medicare and Medicaid Services. Medicare Program; Criteria and Procedures for Making Medical Services Coverage Decisions That Relate to Health Care Technology. 54 FR 4302, 4302–4318 (Jan. 30, 1989).

90. Centers for Medicare and Medicaid Services. Medicare Program; Revised Process for Making National Coverage Determinations. FR 68(187). September 26, 2003. CMS-3062-N.

91. Centers for Medicare and Medicaid Services. Medicare program integrity manual. Chapter 13 – local coverage determination. 13.5 LCD content.

92. Centers for Medicare and Medicaid Services. Medicare program integrity manual. Chapter 1.4 – Contractor Medical Director

93. Centers for Medicare and Medicaid Services. Charter: Medicare Evidence Development & Coverage Advisory Committee. https://www.cms.gov/Regulations-and-Guidance/Guidance/FACA/Downloads/MEDCACcharter.pdf

94. Centers for Medicare and Medicaid Services. Factors CMS considers in commissioning external technology assessment. April 11, 2006. https://www.cms.gov/medicare-coverage-database/view/medicare-coverage-document.aspx?MCDId=7

95. Podemska-Mikluch, Marta. FDA-CMS parallel review: a failed attempt at spurring innovation. Journal of Entrepreneurship and Public Policy.2019; 8(4): 433-441.Pavlovic, Yarmela and Beth Halpern. Parallel Review Evolves: FDA Expands from Pilot to Considering Private Payers. DeviceTalk. October 23, 2015

96. Water, Paul N. Van de. Medicare changes can complement health reform. July 30, 2008. Center on Budget and Policy Priorities. https://www.cbpp.org/sites/default/files/archive/7-31-08health.pdf

97. Key Milestones in Medicare and Medicaid History, Selected Years: 1965-2003. Health Care Financ Rev. 2005

Winter;27(2):1-3. https://www.ncbi.nlm.nih.gov/pmc/articles/PMC4194922/

98. Centers for Medicare and Medicaid Services. Items & services not covered under Medicare. MLN906765 June 2022. Accessed March 2023: https://www.cms.gov/outreach-and-education/medicare-learning-network-mln/mlnproducts/downloads/items-and-services-not-covered-under-medicare-booklet-icn906765.pdf

99. Presentation by Lee Fleisher, MD, CMS Chief Medical Officer and Director for the Center for Clinical Standards and Quality. https://healthpolicy.duke.edu/sites/default/files/2022-04/TCET%20Webinar_Slides%203.28.22.pdf

100. Centers for Medicare and Medicaid Services. Decision memo for the clinical trial policy. July 9, 2007. CAG-00071R.

101. Centers for Medicare and Medicaid Services. Guidance for the public, industry, and CMS staff: coverage with evidence development. CMS. November 20, 2014. https://www.cms.gov/medicare-coverage-database/view/medicare-coverage-document.aspx?MCDId=27

102. Centers for Medicare and Medicaid Services. Coverage with evidence development proposed guidance document. June 22. 2023

103. Zeitler, Emily P, Lauren G Gilstrap, Megan Coylewright, et al. Coverage with evidence development: where are we now? Am J Manag Care. 2022: 28(8):382-389.

104. Phend, Crystal. TAVR at 20: how much longer will Medicare mandate a registry? Medpage Today. December 8, 2022.

https://www.medpagetoday.com/special-reports/exclusives/102144

105. Sundt, Thoralf M and Hani Jneid. Guideline update on indications for Transcatheter Aortic Valve Implantation based on the 2020 American College of Cardiology/American Heart Association Guidelines for management of valvular heart disease. JAMA Cardiol. 2021;6(9):1088-1089.

106. Sukul, Devraj, Joseph Allen and Dharam J Kumbhani. Volume considerations for transcatheter aortic valve replacement in Medicare's National Coverage Determination. Cardiovascular Qualify and Outcomes. 2019;12:e005216.

107. Whitaker, Scott, Jack Richmond, and Bruce Williams. It's time to reform the process for determining what Medicare covers. STAT. June 27, 2018. https://www.statnews.com/2018/06/27/medicare-local-coverage-reform/

108. Centers for Medicare and Medicaid Services. MLN Matters Article: Local coverage determinations. MM10901. Released on February 12, 2019 and revised on February 14, 2019. https://www.cms.gov/Outreach-and-Education/Medicare-Learning-Network-MLN/MLNMattersArticles/downloads/MM10901.pdf

109. Centers for Medicare and Medicaid Services. Local Coverage Determination (LCD) process modernization Qs & As. https://www.cms.gov/Medicare/Coverage/DeterminationProcess/downloads/LCD_QsAs.pdf

110. Centers for Medicare and Medicaid Services. Fact sheet: Summary of significant changes to the Medicare Program

Integrity Manual Chapter 13 – Local Coverage Determinations. October 3, 2018.

111. Palmetto GBA. Article – Billing and coding: MolDX: Molecular Diagnostic Tests (MDT). A56853.

112. American Medical Association House of Delegates meets in person; ACR successfully advances new policies. The Rheumatologist. June 17, 2022. https://www.the-rheumatologist.org/article/american-medical-association-house-of-delegates-meets-in-person-acr-successfully-advances-ama-policies/

113. Palmetto GBA. Molecular diagnostic program (MolDX) – coverage, coding, and pricing standards and requirements. M00106. Version 26.0, December 2019.

114. DiPrete, Bob and Darren Coffman. A brief history of health services prioritization in Oregon. https://www.oregon.gov/oha/HPA/DSI-HERC/Documents/Brief-History-Health-Services-Prioritization-Oregon.pdf

115. New York Department of Health. Evidence-based review process for coverage determination: dossier methods guidance.

116. Center for Evidence-based Policy. 2021 annual report: the science of good policy. https://centerforevidencebasedpolicy.org/wp-content/uploads/2022/03/CEbP-2021_AnnualReport_draft8.pdf

117. Ray, Turna. BCBS 'Evidence Street' group enabling engagement with MDx players. Genomeweb. February 9, 2017. https://www.genomeweb.com/molecular-

diagnostics/bcbs-evidence-street-group-enabling-engagement-mdx-players#.ZCOLwi-B1qs

118.AMCP. A format for submission of clinical and economic evidence in support of formulary consideration. April 2016. https://www.amcp.org/sites/default/files/2019-03/AMCP-Format-V4.pdf A Yan and A Loos. ICER's growing influence on payer decision making: the impact of ICER assessments on market dynamics and patient access. AmerisourceBergen Xcenda. HTA Quarterly. Winter 2020. https://www.xcenda.com/insights/htaq-winter-2020-icer-payer-decision-making

THE MULTIFACETED ROLES OF HEALTHCARE PROVIDER

119.Batchelor, Jonathan S. PET registry primed for takeoff. March 27, 2006. AuntMinnie.com

120.American Medical Association. RVS update process. 2023. https://www.ama-assn.org/system/files/ruc-update-booklet.pdf

121.American Medical Association Specialty Society Relative Value Update Committee (RUC). Final vote release – CPT 2022. https://www.ama-assn.org/system/files/ruc-voting-2022.pdf

122.National Government Services, Inc. LCD- implantable continuous glucose monitors (I-CGM). L38623.

123.Centers for Medicare and Medicaid Services. Medicare Evidence Development & Coverage Advisory Committee Roster. https://www.cms.gov/files/document/medcac-roster-updated-92022.pdf

NOTES

124. Centers for Medicare and Medicaid Services. NCA – next generation sequencing (NGS) for Medicare beneficiaries with advanced cancer (CAG-00450N) – decision memo.

125. Wisconsin Physicians Service Insurance Corporation. Non-invasive fractional flow reserve (FFR) for ischemic heart disease. L38839. 6/30/2022. March 16, 2018.

126. Council of Medical Specialty Societies. Code for interactions with companies. April 2015. https://cmss.org/wp-content/uploads/2016/02/CMSS-Code-for-Interactions-with-Companies-Approved-Revised-Version-4.13.15-with-Annotations.pdf

127. National Quality Registry Network. An inventory of national clinical registries. November 2015. https://www.nmdi.org/media/file/nqrn-national-clinical-registry-inventory%202015.pdf

128. Allen, James. How do hospitals make new equipment purchases? Hospital Medical Director. November 11, 2022. https://hospitalmedicaldirector.com/how-do-hospitals-make-new-equipment-purchases/

129. Kotler Marketing Group. The current state of hospital value analysis: implications for suppliers. https://www.kotlermarketing.com/resources/ValueAnalysis_abstract_July217.pdf

130. Obremskey, William T, Teresa Dail, and A Alex Jahangir. Value-based purchasing of medical devices. Clin Orthop Relat Res. 2012 Apr; 470(4): 1054-1064.

131. Hula, Nicholas, Jessie Goldman, and Lindsay Conway. Value Analysis Committee – Frequently asked questions. Advisory Board. 2019. https://advisory-prod.azureedge.net/-

/media/project/advisoryboard/shared/research/cic/events /webconferences/2019/orientation_to_value_analysis_com mittees_faq.pdf

EVIDENCE – THE MOST EFFECTIVE TOOL TO COMMUNICATE WITH PAYERS AND PROVIDERS

132. The annual numbers of publications are estimated using publication counts provided by Niforatos et al in their research letter titled Assessment of publication trends of systematic reviews and randomized clinical trials, 1995 to 2017 published in JAMA Internal Medicine on July 29, 2019. JAMA Intern Med. 2019;179(11):1593-1594.

133. Centers for Medicare and Medicaid Services. NCA – Next Generation Sequencing (NGS) for Medicare beneficiaries with advanced cancer (CAG-00450N) – Decision memo. Appendix A. March 16, 2018.

134. Palmetto GBA. LCD – Non-invasive fractional flow reserve (FFR) for stable ischemic heart disease (L38278).

135. Wisconsin Physicians Service Insurance Corporation. LCD – Non-invasive fractional flow reserve (FFR) for ischemic heart disease (L38839).

136. AMCP. A format for submission of clinical and economic evidence in support of formulary consideration. April 2016. https://www.amcp.org/sites/default/files/2019-03/AMCP-Format-V4.pdf

137. National Council on Disability. Quality-Adjusted Life Years and the Devaluation of Life With Disability. November 6, 2019.

https://ncd.gov/sites/default/files/NCD_Quality_Adjusted _Life_Report_508.pdf

138. Neumann, Peter J, Joshua T Cohen, Milton C Weinstein. Updating cost-effectiveness—the curious resilience of the $50,000-per-QALY threshold. N Engl J Med. 2014;371(9):796-797.

139. Navarro, Hector Jose, Anthony Shakeshaft, Christopher M Doran, and Dennis J Petrie. The potential cost-effectiveness of general practitioner delivered brief intervention for alcohol misuse: evidence from rural Australia. Addict Behav. 2011;36:1191–8.

140. Orlewska, Ewa, Laszlo Gulacsi. Budget-impact analyses: a critical review of published studies. Pharmacoeconomics. 2009;27:807–827.

141. Congressional Budget Office. CBO explains scorekeeping guidelines. January 2021.

142. Fierce Healthcare. Hospital CEO incentives focus on clinical quality, patient satisfaction. December 10, 2012. https://www.fiercehealthcare.com/healthcare/hospital-ceo-incentives-focus-clinical-quality-patient-satisfaction

143. Kotler Marketing Group and MedtechAnalysis. The current state of hospital value analysis implications for suppliers.

144. Research Data Assistance Center (ResDAC). Strengths and limitations of CMS administrative data in research. https://resdac.org/articles/strengths-and-limitations-cms-administrative-data-research

STRATEGY TO NAVIGATE THE HEALTHCARE
REIMBURSEMENT MAZE

145. Centers for Medicare & Medicaid Services. Local Coverage Determination (LCD) process modernization Qs & As. https://www.cms.gov/Medicare/Coverage/DeterminationProcess/Downloads/LCD_QsAs.pdf

146. Austin, D. Andrew and Thomas L. Hungerford. CRS report for Congress: The market structure of the health insurance industry. Congressional Research Service. May 25, 2010.

147. United State Renal Data System. The United States Renal Data System 2022 Annual Data Report. https://usrds-adr.niddk.nih.gov/2022 National Institute of Diabetes and Digestive and Kidney Diseases; 2022

148. American Cancer Society. Cancer facts & figures 2022. Estimated number of new cases for the four major cancers by sex and age group, 2022. https://www.cancer.org/content/dam/cancer-org/research/cancer-facts-and-statistics/annual-cancer-facts-and-figures/2022/2022-case-estimates-by-age.pdf

149. Mykyta, Laryssa, Katherine Keisler-Starkey and Lisa Bunch. Uninsured rate of U.S. children fell to 5.0% in 2021: more children were covered by Medicaid and CHIP in 2021. U.S. September 13, 2022. Census Bureau. https://www.census.gov/library/stories/2022/09/uninsured-rate-of-children-declines.html

BIBLIOGRAPHY

Ackerly, D Clay, Ana M Valverde, Lawrence W Diener, et al. Fueling innovation in medical devices (and beyond): Venture capital in health care. Hlth Aff. 2009;28(1): w68-w75.

Adams, David J. The valley of death in anticancer drug development: a re-assessment. Trends Pharmacol Sci. 2012 Apr;33(4):173-180.

Allen, Bibb Jr, Anita Pennington and Kathryn J Keysor. The current status of local Medicare payment policy: how specialty societies can influence local coverage determinations. Journal of the American College of Radiology. June 2008, 5(6): P727-736.

Anderson, Lori, Gabriel Bien-Willner, and Patricia Goede. The burden of proof – what laboratories need to know about evidence development before launching a new test. Journ Prec Med. June 2020, 6(2): 51-55. https://www.thejournalofprecisionmedicine.com/the-journal-of-precision-medicine/the-burden-of-proof-what-laboratories-need-to-know-about-evidence-development-before-launching-a-new-test/

Auerswald, Philip E and Lewis M. Branscomb. Valleys of death and Darwinian seas: financing the invention to innovation transition in the United States. J. Technol. Tran. 2003; 28:227-239.

Bachrach, Deborah, Naomi Newman, and Keith Nevitt. In or out: an examination of Medicaid's coverage determination policies. Manatt Health Solutions and The California HealthCare Foundation. August 2015. https://www.chcf.org/wp-content/uploads/2017/12/PDF-InOutMedicaidDetermination.pdf

Ball, Robert M. What Medicare's Architects Had In Mind. Health Affairs. 1995 Winter;14(4):62–72.

Barr, Donald A (March 12, 2010). Questioning the Premedical Paradigm: Enhancing Diversity in the Medical Profession a Century after the Flexner Report. Baltimore: Johns Hopkins University Press. ISBN 9780801898402.

Basu, Anirban, Josh J Carlson, David Veenstra. Health years in total: a new health objective function for cost-effectiveness analysis. Value Health. 2020;23(1):96-103.

Baumgartner, Helmut, Volkmar Falk, Jeroen J Bax, et al. ESC Scientific Document Group. 2017 ESC/EACTS Guidelines for the management of valvular heart disease. Eur Heart J. 2017; 38:2739–2791.

Bhatt, Deepak L, Joseph P Drozda, David M Shahian, et al. ACC/AHA/STS Statement on the Future of Registries and the Performance Measurement Enterprise: A Report of the American College of Cardiology/American Heart Association Task Force on Performance Measures and The Society of Thoracic Surgeons. J Am Coll Cardiol. 2015 Nov, 66 (20) 2230–2245.

Bockstedt, Lindsay A. The effect of Medicare's New Technology Add-on Payment. A dissertation submitted to the faculty of the graduate school of the University of Minnesota for the degree of Doctor of Philosophy. June, 2010. Accessed March 2023: https://conservancy.umn.edu/bitstream/handle/11299/937 50/Bockstedt_umn_0130E_11164.pdf?sequ

Boyce, Niall. Bills of mortality: tracking disease in early modern London. Lancet. 2020, April 11-17;395(10231): 1186-1187. https://www.ncbi.nlm.nih.gov/pmc/articles/PMC7154511/

Bruen, Brian, Elizabeth Docteur, Ruth Lopert, et al (February 2016). The impact of reimbursement policies and practices on healthcare technology innovation: final report. This project was supported by the U.S. Department of Health and

Human Services, Office of the Assistant Secretary for Planning and Evaluation (Contract No. HHSP23320095635 Order No. WCHHSP23337014T).

Burgette, Lane F, Jodi L Liu, Benjamin M Miller, et al. Practice Expense Methodology and Data Collection Research and Analysis. RAND Corporation, April 11, 2018. https://www.rand.org/pubs/research_reports/RR2166.html .

Carroll, John D. Different health care systems with a common message: experience has a major impact on transcatheter aortic valve replacement outcomes. JACC Cardiovasc Interv. 2018; 11:1680–1682.

Carter, Grace M and J. David Rumpel. Cost estimates for cost outlier cases under Medicare's prospective payment system. Prepared for the Health Care Financing Administration, US Department of Health and Human Services. 1994. RAND/UCLA/Harvard Center for Health Care Financing Policy Research.

Carter, Grace M, Peter D Jacobson, Gerald F Kominski, and Mark J Perry. Use of Diagnosis-Related Groups by non-Medicare payers. Health Care Financ Rev. 1994 Winter; 16(2): 127-158.

Cartwright, Frederick F. The development of modern surgery. London: Arthur Barker, 1967.

Centers for Medicare and Medicaid Services. Medicare and Medicaid Programs: Hospital Outpatient Prospective Payment; Ambulatory Surgical Center Payment; Hospital Value-Based Purchasing Program; Physician Self-Referral; and Patient Notification Requirements in Provider Agreements; Final Rule. CMS-1525-FC. 76 FR, No. 230. November 30, 2011.

Centers for Medicare and Medicaid Services. Improving data and methods related to indirect practice expense in the Medicare Physician Fee Schedule: read-ahead materials for the virtual town hall. 2021. https://www.cms.gov/Medicare/Health-Plans/HealthPlansGenInfo/Downloads/testfile.pdf

Centers for Medicare and Medicaid Services. Innovators' guide to navigating Medicare. Version 3. 2015.

Centers for Medicare and Medicaid Services. Medicare and Medicaid Programs; CY 2023 Payment Policies under the Physician Fee Schedule and Other Changes to Part B Payment and Coverage Policies; Medicare Shared Savings Program Requirements; Implementing Requirements for Manufacturers of Certain Single-dose Container or Single-use Package Drugs to Provide Refunds with Respect to Discarded Amounts; and COVID-19 Interim Final Rules. November 18, 2022. 87 FR 69404.

Centers for Medicare and Medicaid Services. Medicare claims processing manual, Chapter 1, Section 50.2.2, Frequency of billing for providers submitting institutional claims with outpatient services.

Centers for Medicare and Medicaid Services. Medicare Program; CY 2021 Payment Policies Under the Physician Fee Schedule and Other Changes to Part B Payment Policies; Medicare Shared Savings Program Requirements; Medicaid Promoting Interoperability Program Requirements for Eligible Professionals; Quality Payment Program; Coverage of Opioid Use Disorder Services Furnished by Opioid Treatment Programs; Medicare Enrollment of Opioid Treatment Programs; Electronic Prescribing for Controlled Substances for a Covered Part D Drug Under a Prescription Drug Plan or an MA–PD Plan; Payment for Office/Outpatient Evaluation and Management Services; Hospital IQR Program; Establish New Code Categories; and Medicare Diabetes Prevention Program (MDPP) Expanded Model Emergency Policy. August 17, 2020. FR 85(159).

Centers for Medicare and Medicaid Services. Medicare program; CY 2021 payment policies under the Physician Fee Schedule

and other changes to Part B payment policies; Medicare
Shared Savings Program requirements; Medicaid Promoting
Interoperability Program requirements for eligible
professionals; quality payment program; coverage of opioid
use disorder services furnished by Opioid Treatment
Programs; Medicare enrollment of Opioid Treatment
Programs; electronic prescribing for controlled substances
for a covered Part D drug; payment for office/ outpatient
evaluation and management services; hospital IQR program;
establish new code categories; Medicare Diabetes Prevention
Program (MDPP) expanded model emergency policy; coding
and payment for virtual check-in services interim final rule
policy; coding and payment for Personal Protective
Equipment (PPE) interim final rule policy; regulatory
revisions in response to the Public Health Emergency (PHE)
for COVID–19; and finalization of certain provisions from
the March 31st, May 8th and September 2nd interim final
rules in response to the PHE for COVID–19. December 28,
2020. FR 85(248).

Centers for Medicare and Medicaid Services. Medicare program;
CY 2022 payment policies under the Physician Fee Schedule
and other changes to Part B payment policies; Medicare
Shared Savings Program requirements; provider enrollment
regulation updates; and provider and supplier prepayment
and post-payment medical review requirements. November
19, 2021. FR 86(221).

Centers for Medicare and Medicaid Services. Medicare Program;
Hospital Inpatient Prospective Payment Systems for Acute
Care Hospitals and the Long-Term Care Hospital
Prospective Payment System and Proposed Policy Changes
and Fiscal Year 2020 Rates; Proposed Quality Reporting
Requirements for Specific Providers; Medicare and Medicaid
Promoting Interoperability Programs Proposed

Requirements for Eligible Hospitals and Critical Access Hospitals, CMS-1716-P. May 3, 2019. 84 FR 19158.

Centers for Medicare and Medicaid Services. Medicare Program: Hospital Outpatient Prospective Payment and Ambulatory Surgical Center Payment Systems and Quality Reporting Programs; new categories for hospital outpatient department prior authorization process; Clinical Laboratory Fee Schedule: laboratory date of service policy; overall hospital quality star rating methodology; physician-owned hospitals; notice of closure of two teaching hospitals and opportunity to apply for available slots, Radiation Oncology Model; and reporting requirements for hospitals and Critical Access Hospitals (CAHs) to report covid–19 therapeutic inventory and usage and to report acute respiratory illness during the Public Health Emergency (PHE) for coronavirus disease 2019 (COVID–19). December 29, 2020. FR 85(249).

Centers for Medicare and Medicaid Services. Medicare program: Hospital Outpatient Prospective Payment and Ambulatory Surgical Center Payment Systems and quality reporting programs; organ acquisition; rural emergency hospitals: payment policies, conditions of participation, provider enrollment, physician self-referral; new service category for hospital outpatient department prior authorization process; overall hospital quality star rating; COVID–19. November 23, 2022. FR 87(225).

Chambers, James D, Katherine E May, and Peter J Neumann. Medicare covers the majority of FDA-approved devices and Part B drugs, but restrictions and discrepancies remain. Health Aff. 2013 Jun;32(6):1109-15.

Chambers, James D, Matthew D Chenoweth, Peter J Neumann. Mapping US commercial payers' coverage policies for medical interventions. Am J Manag Care. September 2016, 22(9).

BIBLIOGRAPHY

Chen, Jiayi, Shuo-Yan Chou, Tiffany Hui-Kuang Yu, et al. System dynamics analysis on the effectiveness of vaccination and social mobilization policies for COVID-19 in the United States. PLoS ONE. August 2022, 17(8):e0268443.

Chou, Tsung-Han, Jonathon Toft-Nielsen, and Vittorio Porciatti. High-throughput binocular pattern electroretinograms in the mouse. Methods Mol Biol. 2018;1695: 63-68.

Classen, David C, Leonard A Mermel. Specialty society clinical practice guidelines: time for evolution or revolution? JAMA. 2015; 314(9): 871–8722.

Clemens, Jeffrey and Joshua D Gottlieb. In the shadow of a giant: Medicare's influence on private physician payments. Journal of Political Economy. 2017. Vol 125, No. 1.

Cohen, Robin A, Diane M Makuc, Amy B Bernstein, et al. Health insurance coverage trends, 1959-2007: estimates from the national health interview survey. National Health Statistics Reports. No. 17. July 1, 2019. Centers for Disease Control and Prevention. National Center for Health Statistics.

Congressional Budget Office. Medicare baseline projects. May 2022. https://www.cbo.gov/system/files/2022-05/51302-2022-05-medicare.pdf

Congressional Research Service. Drug shortages: causes, FDA authority, and policy options. December 27, 2018.

Congressional Research Service. Medicare coverage of clinical preventive services. March 18, 2010. https://crsreports.congress.gov/product/pdf/R/R40978/6

Coulam, Robert F and Gary L Gaumer. Medicare's prospective payment system: a critical appraisal. Health Care Financ Rev. 1992 Mar; 1991 (Suppl): 45-77.

Craft, Edward M. Health care prices, 1950-1967: discussion of trends and their significance. JAMA. 1968;205(4):231-234.

Crimmins, Eileen M. Lifespan and healthspan: past, present, and promise. Gerontologist, 2015, Vol. 55, No. 6, 901–911 doi:10.1093/geront/gnv130

Cunningham, Robert III and Robert M. Cunningham Jr. The Blues: History of the Blue Cross and Blue Shield System. 1997

Davitt, Joan K and Sunha Choi. Tracing the history of Medicare home health care: the impact of policy on benefit use. Contemporary Social Policy. March, 2008. Vol 35(1): 247-276.

Didyuk, Olesya, Nicolas Econom, Angelica Guardia, et al. Continuous glucose monitoring devices: past, present, and future focus on the history and evolution of technological innovation. Journal of Diabetes Science and Technology. 2021, 15(3): 676-683.

Donohue, Julie. A history of drug advertising: the evolving roles of consumers and consumer protection. Milbank Q. 2006 Dec; 84(4): 659-699.

Duffy, Thomas P. The Flexner report – 100 years later. Yale J Biol Med. 2011 Sep; 84(3): 269-276.

Eccles, Martin P, Jeremy M Grimshaw, Paul Shekelle, et al. Developing clinical practice guidelines: target audiences, identifying topics for guidelines, guideline group composition and functioning and conflicts of interest. Implementation science. 2012, 7, No. 60.

Editorial. Expensive treatments for genetic disorders are arriving. But who should foot the bill? Nature. December 4, 2019.

Epstein, Jessica. Drugs that shaped the FDA: from Elixir Sulfanilamide to Thalidomide. Bull. Hist. Chem., Vol 43, No. 2 (2018): 102-110.

Faulhner, Eric, Michael Werner, and Robert Falb. Roadmap for navigating cell and gene therapy value demonstration and reimbursement in US managed care: reimbursement roadmap monograph 2019. National Association of

Managed Care Physicians and Alliance for Regenerative Medicine.

Faxon, David P and Anne Burgess. Cardiovascular registries – too much of good thing? Circulation: Cardiovascular Interventions. 2016;9;e003866.

Fee, Elizabeth. 1987. Disease and Discovery: A History of the Johns Hopkins School of Hygiene and Public Health 1916–1939. Johns Hopkins University Press, Baltimore.

Field, Marilyn J, Robert L Lawrence, and Lee Zwanziger. Extending Medicare Coverage for Preventive and Other Services. Institute of Medicine, Committee on Medicare Coverage Extensions, Division of Health Care Services, (2000) National Academy Press, Washington, D.C., p. 16.

Fisher, Charles R. Trends in Medicare enrollee use of physician and supplier services, 1983-86. Health Care Financ Rev. 1988 Fall; 10(1): 1-15.

Fonseca, Vivian A, George Grunberger, Henry Anhalt, et al. Continuous glucose monitoring: a consensus conference of the American Association of Clinical Endocrinologists and American College of Endocrinology. Endocr Pract. 2016;22:1008-21.

Fontenot, Keith, Caitlin Brandt, and Mark B McClellan. A primer on Medicare physician payment reform and the SGR. USC-Brookings Schaeffer on Health Policy. February 2, 2015. https://www.brookings.edu/blog/usc-brookings-schaeffer-on-health-policy/2015/02/02/a-primer-on-medicare-physician-payment-reform-and-the-sgr/

Fox, Jacqueline. The hidden role of cost: Medicare decisions, transparency and public trust. U. Cin. L. Rev. 2011, 79(1): Artl 1.

Frank, Clyde, Claire Sink, LeAnn Mynatt, et al. Surviving the valley of death: a comparative analysis. J. Technol. Tran. 1996; 21:61-69.

Frank, Richard A, Robert Jarrin, Jordan Pritzker, et al. Developing current procedural terminology codes that describe the work performed by machines. Npj Digital Medicine. 2022; 5:177. https://www.nature.com/articles/s41746-022-00723-5

Fronstin, Paul and Stephen A Woodbury. 2020. How many Americans have lost jobs with employer health coverage during the pandemic? Washington, DC: The Commonwealth Fund. https://research.upjohn.org/cgi/viewcontent.cgi?article=10 96&context=externalpapers

Fryback, Dennis G, John R Thornbury. The efficacy of diagnostic imaging. Med Decis Making. 1991;11(2):88-94.

Gabel, Jon. Ten Ways HMOs Have Changed during the 1990s. Hlth Aff. 1997;16(3):134–45.

Gifford, Kathleen, Anne Winter, Linda Wiant, et al. How state Medicaid programs are managing prescription drug costs. Results from a state Medicaid pharmacy survey for state fiscal years 2019 and 2020. Henry J Kaiser Family Foundation and Health Management Associates. April 2020. https://files.kff.org/attachment/How-State-Medicaid-Programs-are-Managing-Prescription-Drug-Costs.pdf

Gluck, Michael, Virgnina Reno, (eds.). Reflections on Implementing Medicare. (Washington, DC: National Academy of Social Insurance, January 2001).

Government Accountability Office. Medicare physician fee schedule: practice expense payments to oncologists indicate need for overall refinements. October 2001. GAO-02-53. https://www.gao.gov/assets/gao-02-53.pdf

Government Accountability Office. Medicare: divided authority for policies on coverage of procedures and devices results in inequities. May 12, 2003. GAO-03-175.

Government Accountability Office. Technology assessment design handbook: handbook for key steps and considerations in the design of technology assessments. GAO-21-347G. February 2021.

Graham, Robin, Michelle Mancher, Dianne Miller Wolman, et al (eds). Clinical practice guidelines we can trust. Institute of Medicine. Washington, DC: The National Academies Press, 2011.

Grover, Frederick L, Sreekanth Vemulapalli, John D Carroll, et al. 2016 annual report of the Society of Thoracic Surgeons/American College of Cardiology Transcatheter Valve Therapy Registry. J Am Coll Cardiol. 2017 Mar 14; 69(10):1215–1230.

Hassan, Ameer E. New Technology Add-on Payment (NTAP) for Viz LVO: a win for stroke care. Journal of NeuroInterventional Surgery. 2021;13:406-408.

Hillner, Bruce E, Barry A Siegel, Dawei Liu, et al. Impact of Positron Emission tomography/Computed Tomography and Positron Emission Tomography (PET) alone on expected management of patients with cancer: initial results from the National Oncologic PET Registry. Journal of Clinical Oncology. May 2008, 26(13): 2155-2161

Hillner, Bruce E, Dawei Liu, R Edward Coleman, et al. The National Oncologic PET Registry (NOPR): design and analysis plan. Journal of Nuclear Medicine. November 2007,48(11): 1901-1908

Hilts, Philip J. Protecting America's Health: The FDA, Business and One Hundred Years of Regulation. The University of North Carolina Press, 2004.

Hirsch, JA, G Nicola, G McGinty, et al. ICD-10: history and context. Am J Neuroradiol. 2016 Apr; 37(4): 596-599. https://www.ncbi.nlm.nih.gov/pmc/articles/PMC7960170/

Hoang, Van Phuong, Marian Shanahan, Nagesh Shukla, et al. A systematic review of modelling approaches in economic evaluations of health interventions for drug and alcohol problems. BMC Health Serv Res. 2016. 16, 127.

Hogue, Susan L, Andrew P Brogan, Stephanie R Earnshaw, et al. Academy of managed care pharmacy dossiers: use in health care decision making. Value in Health. 2014, 17. A18. https://www.valueinhealthjournal.com/article/S1098-3015(14)00165-X/fulltext

Institute for Clinical and Economic Review. The QALY: rewarding the care that most improves patients' lives. December 2018. https://icer.org/wp-content/uploads/2020/11/QALY_evLYG_FINAL.pdf

Institute of Medicine (US) Committee for the Study of the Future of Public Health. The Future of Public Health. Chapter 3, A History of the Public Health System. Washington (DC): National Academies Press (US); 1988.

Jampel, Henry D, Kuldev Singh, Shan C Lin, et al. Assessment of visual function in glaucoma: a report by the American Academy of Ophthalmology. Ophthalmology. 2011 May;118(5):986-1002.

Kaiser Family Foundation. Use of comparative effectiveness reviews in Medicaid drug reviews – state reported policies as of July 1, 2019. https://www.kff.org/other/state-indicator/use-of-comparative-effectiveness-reviews-in-medicaid-drug-reviews/?currentTimeframe=0&sortModel=%7B%22colId%22:%22Location%22,%22sort%22:%22asc%22%7D

Karnon, J and, J Brown. Selecting a decision model for economic evaluation: a case study and review. Health Care Manag Sci 1998; 1: 133-40

Kawamoto, Kensaku, Cary J Martin, Kip Williams, et al. Value Driven Outcomes (VDO): a pragmatic, modular, and extensible software framework for understanding and improving health care costs and outcomes. J Am Med Inform Assoc. 2015 Jan; 22(1):223-235.

Keeney, Edna, Howard Thom, Emma Turner, et al. Systematic review of cost-effectiveness models in prostate cancer:

exploring new developments in testing and diagnosis. Value in Health. January 2022, 25(1):133-146.

Kelloff, Gary J, John M Hoffman, Bruce Johnson, et al. Progress and promise of FDG-PET imaging for cancer patient management and oncologic drug development. Clin Cancer Res. 2005;11:2785–2808.

Kendellen, Rosalind M. The Food and Drug Administration Retreats from Patient Package Inserts for Prescription Drugs. Food Drug and Cosmetic Law Journal. 1985;40:172–87.

Kim, David D, and Anirban Basu. How does cost-effectiveness analysis inform health care decisions? AMA J Ethics. 2021,23(8):E639-647.

Kola, Ismail, and John Landis. Can the pharmaceutical industry reduce attrition rates? Nat Rev Drug Discov. 2004;3:711–715.

Kvedar, Joseph C, Mirja Mittermaier, and Jordan Pritzker. The industry impact of the American Medical Association's Digital Medicine Payment Advisory Group (DMPAG). NPJ Digit Med. 2022;5:193.

Leech, Paul Nicholas, Elixir of Sulfanilamide-Massengill. Chemical, pharmacologic, pathologic and necropsy reports; preliminary toxicity reports on Diethylene Glycol and Sulfanilamide J. Am. Med. Assoc., 1937, 109, 1531-1539.

Lehoux, P, FA Miller, and G Daudelin. How does venture capital operate in medical innovation? BMJ Innov. 2016;2:111-117.

Lesser, Cara S, Paul B Ginsburg, and Kelly J Devers. The end of an era: what became of the "managed care revolution" in 2001? Health Serv Res. 2003 Feb; 38(1 pt 2): 337-355.

Lew, Nancy De. Medicare: 35 years of service. Health Care Financ Rev. 2000 Fall; 22(1): 75-103.

Makkar, Raj R, Vinod H Thourani, Michael J. Mack, et al, for the PARTNER 2 Investigators. Five-year outcomes of transcatheter or surgical aortic-valve replacement. N Engl J Med. 2020; 382:799–809.

Manning, Kenneth. Prepaid family medical care. Proceedings of the Annual Meeting (Western Farm Economics Association). Vol. 19 (June 26-27-28, 1946): 167-171

Manz, Christopher R, Justin E Bekelman, and Jalpa A, Doshi. The changing characteristics of technologies covered by Medicare's New Technology Add-on Payment Program. JAMA Network Open. 2020;3(8):e2012569.

Marquis, M Susan, Jeannette A Rogowski, and Jose J Escarce. The managed care backlash: did consumers vote with their feet? Inquiry 41: 376–390 (Winter 2004/2005). Excellus Health Plan, Inc.

McDonagh, Marian S, Sujata Thakurta, and Kim Peterson. A study of the value of requesting information from drug manufacturers for systematic reviews; 9 years of experience from the drug effectiveness review project. Syst Rev, October 22, 2018, 7: 172(2018).

Mcguire, Thomas G, Joseph P Newhouse, and Anna D Sinaiko. An economic history of Medicare Part C. Milbank Q. 2011 Jun; 89(2):289-332.

Medicare Payment Advisory Commission. June 2015 report to the Congress: Medicare and the health care delivery system. Chapter 7: hospital short-stay policy issues.

Medicare Payment Advisory Commission. June 2018 report to the Congress: Medicare and the health care delivery system. Chapter 3: Rebalancing Medicare's physician fee schedule toward ambulatory evaluation and management services.

Medicare Payment Advisory Commission. June 2021 Report to Congress: Medicare and the health care delivery system. Chapter 2: streamlining CMS's portfolio of alternative payment models.

BIBLIOGRAPHY

Medicare Payment Advisory Commission. June 2021 Report to the Congress. Chapter 6: Medicare and the health care delivery system.

Medicare Payment Advisory Commission. March 2003 report to Congress: Medicare payment policy. Appendix B. An introduction to how Medicare makes coverage decisions.

Medicare Payment Advisory Commission. March 2021 report to the Congress: Medicare payment policy. Chapter 3, hospital inpatient and outpatient services.

Millenson, Michael L. Medicare, fair pay, and the AMA: the forgotten history. Hlth Affr Forefront. September 10, 2015.

Morrisey, Michael A. Health Insurance, Second Edition. Health Administration Press. 2013.

Moseley, George B III. The U.S. Health Care Non-System, 1908-2008. Virtual Mentor. 2008; 10(5): 324-331.

Mulligan, Karen, Darius Lakdawalla, Dana Goldman, et al. Health technology assessment for the U.S. healthcare system. A white paper from the USC Schaeffer Center for Health Policy & economics – the Aspen Institute Advisory Panel on Health Technology Assessment in the U.S. February 2020. Accessed March 2023: https://healthpolicy.usc.edu/wp-content/uploads/2020/02/Health_Technology_Assessment_for_the_U.S..pdf

National Academies of Sciences, Engineering, and Medicine. 2012. Essential Health Benefits: Balancing Coverage and Cost. Washington, DC: The National Academies Press

National Academy for State Health Policy. State definitions of medical necessity under the Medicaid EPSDT benefit. State Tracker, 04-23-21. https://nashp.org/state-definitions-of-medical-necessity-under-the-medicaid-epsdt-benefit/

Nichols, Christopher McKnight, and Nancy C. Unger A Companion to the Gilded Age and Progressive Era. Wiley Blackwell. 2017

Office of Inspector General. Coding of physician services. May 1994. OEI-03-91-00920. https://oig.hhs.gov/oei/reports/oei-03-91-00920.pdf

Office of Inspector General. Expansion of the diagnosis related group payment window (A-01-02-00503). Aug 20, 2003. Accessed March 2023: https://oig.hhs.gov/oas/reports/region1/10200503.pdf

Office of Inspector General. Local coverage determinations create inconsistency in Medicare coverage. January 2014. OEI-01-11-00500.

Office of Inspector General. Memorandum: improper Medicare payments to hospitals for nonphysician outpatient services under the prospective payment system (A-01-95-00508). May 23, 1996.

Office of Technology Assessment. Benefit Design: Clinical Preventive Services. OTA-H-580, Washington, DC, September 1993. Available at https://ota.fas.org/reports/9309.pdf.

Perl, Juliana R, Kunj R Sheth, Kevin G Shea, and James Wall. Hospital value committees: the role of surgeon in new technology adoption. Surgical Innovation. 2021, 28(4):401-402.

Phillips, Kathryn A, Patricia A Deverka, Gillian W Hooker, and Michael P Douglas. Genetic test availability and spending: where are we now? where are we going? Health Aff. 2018 May;37(5):710-716.

Phillips, Kathryn A. CMS coverage with evidence development – challenges and opportunities for improvement. JAMA Health Forum. 2022;3(9):e223061.

Popma, Jeffrey J, Michael J Reardon, Kamal Khabbaz et al. Early clinical outcomes after transcatheter aortic valve replacement using a novel self-expanding bioprosthesis in patients with severe aortic stenosis who are suboptimal for surgery: results of the evolut R U.S. study. JACC Cardiovasc Interv. 2017; 10:268–275.

Pulte, Dianne, Janick Weberpals, Lina Jansen, and Hermann Brenner. Changes in population-level survival for advanced solid malignancies with new treatment options in the second decade of the 21st century. Cancer 125:2656-2665, 2019

Rivers, Bill, Bruce Jenson, and Jane Koenigsman. U.S. health insurance industry analysis report: 2021 annual reports. National Association of Insurance Commissioners. https://content.naic.org/sites/default/files/2021-Annual-Health-Insurance-Industry-Analysis-Report.pdf

Robinson, JC. Value-based purchasing for medical devices. Health Aff (Millwood) 2008;27:1523–1531.

Sargent, JF Jr. The Office of Technology Assessment: History, Authorities, Issues, and Options. Congressional Research Service. April 29, 2020.

Schackman, Bruce R, Jared A Leff, Daniel Polsky, et al. Cost-effectiveness of long-term outpatient buprenorphine-naloxone treatment for opioid dependence in primary care. J Gen Intern Med. 2012;27(6):669–76.

Senger, Cassia, Renata Moreto, Sung E S Watanabe, et al. Electrophysiology in Glaucoma. J Glaucoma. 2020;29(2):147-153.

Seth, Rahul, Hans Messersmith, Varinder Kaur, et al. Systemic therapy for melanoma: ASCO guideline. Journal of Clinical Oncology. November 20, 2020; 38(33): 3947-3970.

Sharon, Solomon D, Emily Chew, Elia J Duh, et al. Diabetic retinopathy: a position statement by the American Diabetes Association [published corrections appear in Diabetes Care. 2017;40(6):809, and Diabetes Care. 2017;40(9):1285]. Diabetes Care. 2017;40(3):412-418

Sireci, Anthony N, Jay L Patel, Loren Joseph, et al. Molecular pathology economics 101: an overview of molecular diagnostics coding, coverage, and reimbursement. A report of the association for molecular pathology. J Mol Diagn. August 2020;22(8):975-993.

Smith, Sheryl Winston and Andrew Sfekas. How much do physician-entrepreneurs contribute to new medical devices? Med. Care. 2013 May, 51(5), 461-467.

Sonnenberg, Frank A, J Robert Beck. Markov models in medical decision making: a practical guide. Med Decis Making. 1993 Oct-Dec;13(4):322-338.

Starr, Paul. The social transformation of American medicine: the rise of a sovereign profession and the making of a vast industry. 1982. ISBN 0-465-07935-0

Steiner, CA, NR Powe, GF Anderson, A Das. The review process used by US health care plans to evaluate new medical technology for coverage. J Gen Intern Med. 1996 May; 11(5): 294-302.

Sullivan, Sean D, Josephine A Mauskopf, Federico Augustovski, et al. Budget impact analysis-principles of good practice: report of the ISPOR 2012 Budget Impact Analysis Good Practice II Task Force. Value Health. 2014;17(1):5-14.

Temin, Peter. Taking Your Medicine: Drug Regulation in the United States. Cambridge, Mass.: Harvard University Press; 1980.

The Boards of Trustees, Federal Hospital Insurance and Federal Supplementary Medical Insurance Trust Funds. 2022 annual report of the Boards of Trustees of the federal hospital insurance and federal supplementary medical insurance trust funds. Washington, DC. June 2, 2022. https://www.cms.gov/files/document/2022-medicare-trustees-report.pdf

Thomasson, Melissa (September 2003). The importance of group coverage: How tax policy shaped US health insurance. American Economic Review. 93 (4): 1371–1384.

Tompkins, Christopher P, Stuart H Altman, and Efrat Eilat. The precarious pricing system for hospital services. Hlth Aff. 2006;25(1):45–46.

Toner, Mehmet and Ronald G Tompkins. Invention, innovation, entrepreneurship in academic medical centers. Surgery. 2008 February;143(2):168-171.

Treweek, Shaun, Andrew D Oxman, Philip Alderson, et al. Developing and evaluating communication strategies to support informed decisions and practice based on evidence (DECIDE): protocol and preliminary results. Implement Sci. 2013;8:Article 6.

Tunis, Sean, Peter Neumann, James Chamber, Nola Jenkins. Medicare coverage of emerging technologies: challenges and opportunities. Tufts Center for the Evaluation of Value and Risk in Health. https://tuftsmedicalcenter.app.box.com/s/xs9muttgz0qivvel 9aqaiwzo2xgw2hn1

Ubel, Peter A, Richard A Hirth, Michael E Chernew, A Mark Fendrick. What is the price of life and why doesn't it increase at the rate of inflation? Arch Intern Med. 2003;163:1637–1641.

Vanness, David J, James Lomas, Hannah Ahn. A health opportunity cost threshold for cost-effectiveness analysis in the United States. Ann Intern Med. 2021;174(1):25-32.

Watts, Clark. Erosion of physician autonomy and public respect for the profession. Surg Neurol. 2009 Mar, 71(3): 269-273.

Werner, Rachel M, Ezekiel J Emanuel, Hoangmai H Pham, Amol S Navthe. The future of value-based payment: a road map to 2030. White paper. https://ldi.upenn.edu/our-work/research-updates/the-future-of-value-based-payment-a-road-map-to-2030/

Winslow, Charles Edward Amory. The evolution and significance of the modern public health campaign. Yale University Press, 1923.

Wong, Chi Heem, Dexin Li, Nina Wang, et al. (2021). Estimating the financial impact of gene therapy in the U.S.. National Bureau of Economic Research. Working paper 28628. https://doi.org/10.3386/w28628

Yao, Nengliang and Sekwon Jang. Adoption of ipilimumab in the United States: a Medicare study. Expert Rev Pharmacoecon Outcomes Res. 2016 Aug;16(4):439-40.

Young, James Harvey. The Toadstool Millionaires: A Social History of Patent Medicines in America before Federal Regulation. Princeton, N.J.: Princeton University Press; 1961.

Zeitler, Emily P, Sana M Al-Khatib, David Slotwiner, et al. Proceedings from Heart Rhythm Society's emerging technologies forum. Heart Rhythm. 2016 Febrary;13(2):e39-e49.

www.ingramcontent.com/pod-product-compliance
Lightning Source LLC
Chambersburg PA
CBHW031522150726
47990CB00001B/39